Commur Emergency Preparedness

Practical Strategies for the
Public and Private Sectors

Communicating Emergency Preparedness

Practical Strategies for the Public and Private Sectors

Second Edition

Damon P. Coppola • Erin K. Maloney

CRC Press
Taylor & Francis Group
Boca Raton London New York

CRC Press is an imprint of the
Taylor & Francis Group, an **informa** business

CRC Press
Taylor & Francis Group
6000 Broken Sound Parkway NW, Suite 300
Boca Raton, FL 33487-2742

© 2017 by Taylor & Francis Group, LLC
CRC Press is an imprint of Taylor & Francis Group, an Informa business

No claim to original U.S. Government works

Printed on acid-free paper

International Standard Book Number-13: 978-1-138-72106-7 (Hardback)
978-1-498-76236-6 (Paperback)

Visit the Taylor & Francis Web site at
http://www.taylorandfrancis.com

and the CRC Press Web site at
http://www.crcpress.com

This book is dedicated to Shannon, Kelly, Will, Annabelle, and Miles, who remind us that risk messages are best measured by the lives they've protected.

Contents

Acknowledgments

Damon Coppola would like to express his profound gratitude to his wife, Mary Gardner Coppola, for her guidance and patience; to Jane Bullock and George Haddow for their friendship and support and for continuing to give freely of their expertise and experience; and to the following friends, mentors, and colleagues without whom this book would not have been possible: Jack Harrald, Greg Shaw, J. René van Dorp, Joe Barbera, Ryan Miller, Louise Comfort, Barbara Johnson, Sanjaya Bhatia, Gerry Potutan, Gulzar Kayyim, Irmak Renda-Tanali, Ehren Ngo, Ollie Davidson, Jack Suwanlert, and Rich Marinucci.

Erin Maloney would like to thank her husband, Sean McConnell, for his amazing support and encouragement, and her sister-in-law, Molly McConnell, for the countless hours she spent playing with the girls so that Erin Maloney could write.

The authors would also like to thank Jennifer Abbott, Natalja Mortensen, and Eve Strillacci at Taylor & Francis Group for the assistance they provided in the development of this book.

Authors

Damon P. Coppola, MEM, ARM, is the founder of the Singapore-based Shoreline Risk Management, partner at Bullock & Haddow LLC, and adjunct assistant professor at the Loma Linda University School of Public Health. Mr. Coppola is an accomplished emergency management systems engineer who has bridged the gap between practice and academia. In his professional career, he has consulted as an analyst and technical assistant to clients in the public, nonprofit, and private sectors. Mr. Coppola is a recognized emergency management training and education specialist, having developed and co-developed programs and courses for the FEMA Emergency Management Institute Higher Education Program and the DHS National Training and Education Division. Mr. Coppola has authored and co-authored more than a dozen academic and professional emergency management textbooks in use at over 200 colleges and universities worldwide.

Erin K. Maloney, PhD, is a research director at the Tobacco Center of Regulatory Science (TCORS) in the Annenberg School for Communication at the University of Pennsylvania, and an adjunct instructor for George Washington University's Master of Public Health Online program and West Chester University's Department of Communication Studies. She specializes in health communication, social influence, and quantitative research methods. Dr. Maloney's research explores message effects in mediated and face-to-face contexts and seeks best practices for message design in public health communication campaigns. Her work has been presented at dozens of national and international academic conferences and published in prestigious academic journals across disciplines, including *Human Communication Research, Journal of Applied Social Psychology, Journal of Clinical Oncology*, and *Nicotine & Tobacco Research*. She has consulted on a wide variety of public health and environmental campaigns at the grassroots level and contributed to the development of the nationally attended communication skills training programs for clinicians at the Memorial Sloan-Kettering Cancer Center. Dr. Maloney is currently funded by the U.S. Food and Drug Administration to conduct research that has implications for tobacco control.

Introduction

There are two indisputable truths that together drive the need for this book.

The first is that major disasters, whether natural, technological, or terrorism-based, are increasing in both their number and their intensity. Hurricanes have devastated cities and political administrations alike; floods have washed away businesses and strained whole economies; new and exotic diseases have remained one step ahead; while terrorists and psychopaths have inflicted debilitating fear into millions of lives more than the thousands, their attacks have extinguished. And this list is not comprehensive. Today, the vast majority of the global population—perhaps every human—lives in perpetual risk from at least one major disaster threat. Through ongoing urbanization, a changing global climate, and widespread geopolitical instability, the problems merely grow. There is no exaggeration in stating that disasters punctuate 21st century life.

The second truth, which comes in stark contrast to the first, is that the vast majority of people are woefully unprepared for the hazards that threaten them. After-action reporting following several recent events found that only a very small percentage of disaster-affected populations had acted to reduce their vulnerability. More than half of the disaster-impacted businesses never reopened or closed within a year. In many of these cases and others like them, national and international governments and nongovernmental organizations (NGOs) alike expended tremendous human and financial resources in an effort to promote disaster preparedness. Clearly, most of these efforts fell far short of their expected outcomes.

Together, these truths obligate the adaptation of a more effective practice. Individual, family, and business preparedness are vital to increasing overall community resilience, especially in light of the limitations typically experienced by the emergency services at the outset of large-scale events. Even in countries whose governments boast of the most highly advanced emergency management capacities, leaders have found it necessary to warn average citizens that a minimum of

48–72 hours of self-reliance in the aftermath of a major disaster should be anticipated.

Disaster preparedness is by no means a new concept; however, the recognition of its true lifesaving potential has elevated its prominence among professionals in the fields of emergency management, risk management, and business continuity planning. In response to a 2006 Council for Excellence in Government study, which reported that "most Americans haven't taken steps to prepare for a natural disaster, terrorist attack, or other emergency" (*USA Today*, 2006), Michael Chertoff, former Department of Homeland Security Secretary, echoed an even wider societal recognition of the dire need for increased public disaster preparedness efforts in stating, "Everybody should have [disaster preparedness] basics down. I think Katrina shook people up. A lot of messaging and a lot of education, particularly at the local level, is the key" (*Government Executive*, 2006). Furthermore, the University of Colorado Natural Hazards Center, a leader in the advancement of emergency management throughout the world, stated in a January 2007 edition of *Natural Hazards Observer* that: (1) there is a positive correlation between public awareness and positive disaster outcomes; (2) opportunities exist to better educate the public, coordinate messages, and initiate social change; (3) recent studies and surveys all indicate that there is an immediate need for better public education before disaster; and most importantly (4) there exists no comprehensive review of practices and resources and identification of components that make up an effective disaster public education program (*Natural Hazards Observer*, 2007).

Perhaps, most significantly, a June 2007 report released by the Emergency Preparedness Institute stated, "The current approach to encouraging preparedness is ineffective, and a new method of communicating the importance of developing business and personal preparedness plans is needed." While other industries, most notably the public health sector, have enjoyed great success in shaping public attitudes and actions about their risk reduction behavior, the emergency management sector has thus far been largely unsuccessful in its endeavors. Despite the high cost and high profile of the penultimate preparedness effort, the Department of Homeland Security's Ready.gov preparedness campaign has failed to make use of strongly supported public education methodologies that would have most certainly improved outcomes (*Washington Post*, 2006). Years after hurricane Katrina—arguably America's most widely reported disaster—and despite the existence of widespread preparedness messaging, the American Red Cross found that only 1 in 20 coastal residents had taken key preparedness actions (Citizen Corps, 2013). What is most troubling is that it isn't a lack of will standing in the way of preparedness but rather an industry-wide lack of knowledge about how people learn new behaviors, what influences them to act upon this knowledge, and the best way to create messages catering to those individual factors.

All communities are vulnerable to the effects of natural, technological, and intentional hazards. Every day, in every community, these hazard risks result in emergency events of varying size and intensity. Occasionally, they are of such great magnitude that they result in a major disaster. To minimize the consequences posed by known and unknown hazards, or to limit their likelihood of occurrence, communities perform mitigation and preparedness actions and activities. Individuals and businesses alike may be equipped with the skills and knowledge to further reduce their own vulnerability, and that of their families, employees, neighborhoods, and communities—if they are given the right kind of training, using appropriate communication methods and channels. Once prepared, these stakeholders become an integral part of the community's emergency management capacity. Properly trained individuals not only influence their own and their family's disaster risk but also use the skills they have learned to rescue their neighbors, relieve shelter staff, retrofit homes for earthquakes, save their businesses, and take countless more actions to extend the reach of their local emergency services.

As is true with the emergency manager and the first responders in a community, members of the general public and of the business community need information and training if they are to know what is best to do before, during, and after emergencies. The information provided must reflect their true risk and must be tailored to their needs, preferences, and abilities; transmitted in a way they can receive and understand; and tested for effectiveness. Any education provided will be received in conjunction or in competition with a wide range of other messages relating to hazards, each considered a "risk communication," regardless of its influence. In addition, while some of this coincident information will be accurate, effective, and useful, much of it is misleading, inaccurate, and ultimately harmful. Individuals are left to their own devices to cull through the daily onslaught of information received for that which will help them prepare.

Creating risk messages and conveying them to the intended audiences requires time, planning, and learning. Unfortunately, disaster preparedness education and training is not as easy as simply telling people what they should do. This process, which includes public awareness, education, and outreach, is an involved one relying on many years of practice and many different disciplines (including psychology, sociology, graphic design, marketing, communication, emergency management, and many others). Risk communication efforts are ongoing and long-term in nature, and must adhere to strategic plans to be effective. They should be coordinated with other providers in the community, and are most successful when they involve partners drawn from throughout the community and even beyond its borders.

This resource has been developed to provide practitioners in the United States and the rest of the world, at both the local and national levels, with the background and the tools they need to plan, design, and carry out their public disaster preparedness efforts. The book is intended as an academic resource as well as a practical how-to guide.

REFERENCES

Foster, Chad. 2007. On the Line. Natural Hazards Observer. January 3. http://bit.ly/2iflp5l.

Goldfarb, Zachary. 2006. Is DHS Site Really Ready? Science Intern Thinks Not. Washington Post. August 10. http://bit.ly/2imjgos.

Hall, Mimi. 2006. Most People Unprepared for Disaster. USA Today. December 18. http://bit.ly/2jCFsjz.

Harris, Shane. 2006. Chertoff Discusses Goals, Responds to Critics. Government Executive. December 20. http://bit.ly/2ji3vRb.

CHAPTER 1

Individual Preparedness
In Theory and in Practice

INTRODUCTION

Risk-related messages permeate all facets of modern life. Automobiles chime to remind us we must "Click It or Ticket"; cigarette boxes warn in no uncertain terms of the cancer threat contained within; lids on disposable coffee cups proclaim the obvious heat contained within; and pharmaceutical prescriptions are accompanied by pages of warnings and dangers that more than counterbalance the sentence or two that detail the intended benefits. The flood of risk information we receive can be so great that, in fact, we simply stop paying attention to most of it (Figure 1.1).

Every moment of our lives entails risk. And for every contributing hazard, there are actions we can take that will either increase or decrease our risk. For many—if not most—of these hazards, one might expect that common sense dictates the wisest risk reduction measures: holding a handrail while descending a staircase; wearing a seatbelt while driving or riding in an automobile; or avoiding cigarette smoke or quitting smoking. Regrettably, such simple and sensible actions are often neglected, and each year in the United States alone more than 1,600 people die by falling down the stairs; more than 10,000 people perish in motor vehicle accidents *while neglecting to wear a seatbelt* (accounting for approximately 40% of all daytime and 60% of nighttime accident deaths); and approximately 480,000 people succumb to smoking-related illnesses (one-fifth of all deaths that occur each year) (National Safety Council [NSC] 2007; National Highway Traffic Safety Administration [NHTSA] 2014; Centers for Disease Control and Prevention [CDC] 2015). As a species, humans are ineffective at assessing or even estimating their own risk and likewise seldom prepare for or even fear the right things. Fortunately, through the application of effective risk communication, it is possible to correct risk-related misperceptions, miscalculations, and misguided behaviors at both the individual and population levels.

FIGURE 1.1   Click It or Ticket Campaign. (This image was developed by the National Highway Traffic Safety Administration for use by the media, http://www.nhtsa.gov/buckleup/ciot-planner/planner07/index.htm.)

The majority of the risk-related messaging we encounter has been generated in the public health sector. In fact, the most common avoidable or reducible risks we face as individuals are those that fall within the public health domain. For decades, public health professionals have studied the most prevalent causes of mortality and morbidity, discovered appropriate methods for reducing them, and crafted effective messages and communication strategies to empower the public with this knowledge. Public health practitioners and health communication specialists have steadily improved their methodologies, resulting in increasingly greater population-wide risk reduction success. Through their efforts, people are living longer, healthier, and more productive lives.

Public health risks, however, constitute only one of the many categories of risk we face as individuals and societies. We also face financial risks related to our income, job security, physical health, and legal liabilities, among other factors; safety risks on account of crime, occupational hazards, our physical surroundings, and other factors; and risks from many other sources as well. There are also many larger-scale and occasionally catastrophic hazard risks that fall within the purview of the emergency management community.

Emergency managers and the various emergency services have been tasked with the heavy burden of preparing for, mitigating, responding to, and recovering from a full and growing list of natural, technological, and intentional hazards that each year affect millions of people worldwide and destroy property, infrastructure, and personal and national wealth worth billions of dollars. Like their counterparts in the public health sector, emergency managers are acutely concerned with population-wide risk. However, rather than addressing commonly occurring hazards that affect individual citizens on a more personal level—like heart disease and HIV infection—their foci are those disaster-triggering hazards that impact entire communities, cities, states, and even whole nations or regions.

Private-sector entities, inclusive of both for-profit businesses and nonprofit and voluntary organizations, are also concerned with the resilience of their own staff and, depending on the nature of their business, their customers, and supply-chain partners. The operations of a business or nonprofit organization will quickly become diminished or may even cease—even if the entity was not impacted directly—if its employees are unable to report to work. Private-sector entities are recognizing to an increasing degree that encouraging employees to address personal and household vulnerabilities (and even facilitating those efforts) greatly increases the chance of them avoiding interruptions and ultimately remaining in business if and when disasters occur.

Because the emergency management became professionalized much later than the public health sector, few emergency managers possess the requisite communication background or skills. For private and nonprofit risk management professionals, recognition of the need for individual preparedness in messaging and the availability of required communication skills beyond simple occupational safety and health are even less prevalent. And, in fact, outside of the public health profession in general, we find very few areas of specialty where the requisite knowledge and practical experience needed to develop and run impactful preparedness campaigns is common. And likewise we find few public- or private-sector offices that enjoy the leadership or financial support needed to adequately plan and fund campaigns or to gauge the effectiveness of those campaigns they manage to launch.

That being said, it would not be correct to accuse the emergency management community of being entirely inexperienced when it comes to individual and household preparedness messaging. In recent years, especially since the September 11, 2001 terrorist attacks, there have been a number of awareness and training programs that seek or sought to reduce population-wide risk from major hazards (and likewise to reduce the post-disaster response burden on emergency services agencies). Some of the most memorable campaigns predate the watershed 9/11 attacks. For instance, almost every American over the age of 40 possesses an instinctive understanding of what to do when instructed to "Duck and cover!" An even larger population is familiar with the command "Stop, drop, and roll." These two phrases, developed to address the risk of an air raid in the first case and one's clothes catching fire in the second, are

FIGURE 1.2   Civil defense era poster, Pennsylvania. (Library of Congress 2000.)

the products of two very widespread and successful disaster prepared-ness campaigns that were institutionalized throughout American public school systems in partnership with local emergency services (Figure 1.2).

Despite the wide success of these two examples, most public and private disaster preparedness efforts have failed to achieve similar levels of success. In fact, year after year, studies report that the vast majority of individuals and households have done surprisingly little or even noth-ing to prepare for disasters and hazards despite the increasing onslaught of information. The 21st century has thus far proven to be one marked by frequent and sometimes catastrophic hazards in the United States, including terrorist attacks, hurricanes, floods, tornadoes, blackouts, and much more. Even with extensive media coverage of these events, and the ongoing conduct of what may be one of the most widely touted disas-ter preparedness campaigns in decades (the Department of Homeland Security's Ready.gov Website and its related Disaster Preparedness Month), recent research indicates that most individuals and families are still woefully unprepared for the risks they know to be affecting them (see Sidebar 1.1).

SIDEBAR 1.1   RECENT DISASTER PREPAREDNESS SURVEY FINDINGS

Year	Sponsor	Findings
2014	Allstate Insurance	92% of Americans claimed to have been personally impacted by a disaster but less than 10% have practiced an evacuation plan and 30% claim they would disregard an evacuation order
2014	SUNYIT	Americans claimed to be knowledgeable about risk but only 1 in 3 had taken any efforts to plan for a disaster
2014	Energizer Holdings	Only 38% of Americans have an emergency kit at home
2013	American Red Cross	Only 1 in 20 coastal residents had taken seven key preparedness actions identified by the American Red Cross
2013	FEMA	Low levels of individual preparedness identified in a 2007 survey remained unchanged in 2013
2012	*National Geographic*	Less than 15% of the U.S. population is prepared for a major disaster event, with more than 25% having taken no action at all.
2012	Adelphi University	Nearly half of U.S. adults do not have the resources or plans in place in the event of a disaster.

Source: Citizen Corps Disaster Preparedness Surveys Database: Public, Businesses, and Schools, http://bit.ly/1QHtPiz.

The poor success rates of the wider emergency and risk management communities are frustrating, but they in no way suggest that the goal of a "culture of disaster preparedness" is unattainable. Organizations like the American Red Cross, in fact, have proven through the success of their cardiopulmonary resuscitation (CPR) and first aid training programs that ordinary citizens can and are willing to learn how to help themselves and others in emergencies. The Citizen Corps program has seen similar success with the Community Emergency Response Team (CERT) program. The knowledge and experience of these organizations that are directly attributable to their successes are not widely enjoyed in the greater emergency and risk management communities. Most notably, in the case of the American Red Cross, public preparedness efforts have bridged the gap between public health capabilities and emergency management concerns, and their practitioners have successfully incorporated the communication sector's lessons-learned into their individual and household disaster preparedness education efforts.

Risk communication in practice is difficult at best, requiring a detailed understanding of the population targeted, the methods (channels) most suitable for reaching them, and the types of messages most likely to be received and acted upon. There is no such thing as a one-size-fits-all risk communication message, and any attempt to do so is doomed to fail. By learning and applying the effective practices developed over many decades by the public health community and others, emergency managers and private-sector risk managers can enjoy similar levels of success.

This chapter introduces public (e.g., individual, household, or employee) disaster preparedness education and the concepts that guide its successful practice. To begin, a short overview of the experience gleaned in the public health sector, where risk communication efforts have advanced most significantly, is provided. This will help to familiarize readers with the relevant terms and concepts used by risk communication professionals, and the principles and theories that drive preparedness education and the behaviors desired. Finally, the foundational elements of preparedness education—its goals, limitations, and requirements—are presented and explained.

COMMUNICATION SCIENCE: A PRIMER

Communication science is a field of practice and research that has great potential to advance the preparedness efforts of businesses and communities alike. While all sectors and all professions utilize communication to some degree, the success of disaster preparedness efforts are wholly determined by the successful utilization of communication science principles. For instance, communication science explains how the mechanisms through which information is conveyed to individuals or groups will play an imminent role in the impact a message will have on the intended message recipients. Through the application of these lessons, which have been developed through decades if not centuries of research and practice and which have been presented in the chapters that follow, it is possible to influence positive behaviors and thus increase disaster resilience.

Research has defined the mechanisms according to which individuals process the information they receive through the following six distinct stages (McGuire 1968):

1. Exposure to the message
2. Attention to the message
3. Comprehension of the arguments and conclusions presented in the message

4. Yielding to the message
5. Accepting the message
6. Information integration (which allows for message retention)

Thus, once individuals pay attention to and understand a message to which they have been exposed, they will use past experience with regard to the issue to evaluate the new information. If after being compared with the old information the new information is accepted, it is integrated into one's knowledge structure. This integration is said to produce a change in one's belief system, leading individuals to change their attitude toward the topic. Attitudes are composed of three components: (1) cognitive (one's opinions or beliefs about the issue), (2) affective (one's feelings about the issue), and (3) behavioral (one's behaviors related to the issue). Because these components are so closely intertwined, influencing the cognitive and affective elements of an attitude may bring about behavior change.

The act of changing a person's attitude on an issue for the purpose of creating, reinforcing, or changing responses is called *persuasion*. Much of communication science and research seeks to uncover different techniques that can be used while delivering a message in order to make it more persuasive.

One of the most important factors to consider when attempting to construct messages that persuade an audience is the degree to which the members of the audience are *involved* with the topic being discussed. Involvement in this realm is defined as how much people feel that decisions about the issue will have direct implications on their lives and the things that are important to them; it is how much they care about decisions surrounding the issue. For example, some areas of the medical sector that may be considered high involvement issues are the legality of abortion and whether health insurance will cover the cost of prescribed medications. Issues that might be considered low involvement are the importance of washing one's hands properly in order to prevent the spread of disease or whether health insurance covers the cost of a medication that he or she do not use.

Those who are highly involved with the topic are much more likely to carefully scrutinize the message itself, so the degree to which a message persuades them is based mostly on the strength of the argument presented. For example, an individual with a great interest in emergency preparedness who is seeking information specifically on that topic will most likely pay close attention to information presented in preparedness promotions. And he or she will most likely grasp upon inconsistencies and will question any counter-intuitive facts that are presented. As such, campaign planners targeting audiences that include highly involved people must be certain that they have presented logical, sound arguments. If the communication program planner knows beforehand that his or her highly involved audience already holds unfavorable attitudes toward the behavior(s) being presented, then he or she must be especially careful not to present any extreme viewpoints that counter the beliefs of the audience. For example, imagine a community located downstream from a dam that is well-built and presents very little risk to the community even if it were to fail. Also, imagine that there has long persisted a perception among the community members that the dam could burst and inundate the town, destroying property and threatening the life of residents. Any communicator, whether from outside or within the community, risks low credibility if he or she fails to address these perceptions head-on. Pursuing approaches that are counter-attitudinal to an audience have been shown to backfire because the audience will focus on counter-arguing (i.e., criticizing every point made, finding something wrong with each points in their own minds, and ending up with a more extreme viewpoint against the message) rather than helping to move toward a preparedness goal.

Another important issue is how actively engaged the target audience already is with regard to the issues being communicated. People who are uninvolved with the topic being promoted have been shown to pay less attention to the message itself. They will not likely be able to pick out inconsistencies in the message or counter-intuitive claims and instead will be influenced by features of the message (such as perceptions of source credibility, message length, and the sheer number of arguments in favor of the issues presented within the message). Therefore, a person who is not highly involved with the issue of emergency preparedness and is not seeking information about the topic is likely to be more influenced by a promotion that contains a list of semi-compelling reasons to engage in the behavior being promoted than a promotion that offers a single highly logical and rational reason.

In the case of emergency preparedness messages, those tasked with crafting the campaign are more likely to find themselves contending with audiences who are uninvolved with the issue. There are advantages to this scenario in that recipients will not be likely to have strong attitudes that run counter to the promoted behavior given that they do not care very much about the issue. This can also be a drawback, however, in that no matter how logical and sensible it may be for people to engage in the behavior the communicator is promoting, it will take more than just rational arguments to convince them to assume the inconvenience of a new behavior. Chapter 4 discusses a number of different appeals and communication theories that have been successful in the past in persuading audiences and motivating behavior change. These appeals will be especially important for target audiences that are not involved with the topic of emergency or disaster preparedness. See Sidebar 1.2 for more information about the potential and limitations of communication campaigns.

SIDEBAR 1.2 THE POTENTIAL AND LIMITATIONS OF COMMUNICATION CAMPAIGNS

Communication campaigns are organized efforts that use communication to bring about a specified goal of informing, reinforcing, or persuading a defined group of people. While communication campaigns can be a very powerful tool of social influence, it is important to distinguish between the things that communication can and cannot do. In order to clarify these capabilities, the National Cancer Institute has offered the following explanation:

- Communication alone can:
  - Increase the intended audience's knowledge and awareness of an issue, problem, or solution
  - Influence perceptions, beliefs, and attitudes that may change social norms
  - Prompt action
  - Demonstrate or illustrate skills
  - Reinforce knowledge, attitudes, or behavior
  - Show the benefit of behavior change
  - Advocate a position on an issue or policy
  - Increase demand or support for social services
  - Refute myths and misconceptions
  - Strengthen organizational relationships
- Communication combined with other strategies can:
  - Cause sustained change in which an individual adopts and maintains a new behavior or an organization adopts and maintains a new policy direction
  - Overcome barriers or systemic problems, such as insufficient access to health care
- Communication cannot:
  - Compensate for inadequate opportunities or services
  - Produce sustained change in complex behaviors without the support of a larger program for change, including components addressing services, technology, and changes in regulations and policy
  - Be equally effective in addressing all issues or relaying all messages because the topic or suggested behavior change may be complex, because the intended audience may have preconceptions about the topic or message sender, or because the topic may be controversial

In addition to these limitations, it is crucial that practitioners recognize that successful communication campaigns are highly audience centered. Costs and benefits that are likely to produce an effect must be emphasized. Because of this, it is often preferable to focus on specific target audiences rather than trying to reach everyone. Communication planners must always keep in mind that any attempt at eliciting behavior change is ambitious, and it is not realistic to expect people to casually change lifelong habits even in the face of the most persuasive information. Communication campaigns are most effective when they seek to persuade a specific group of people to change a very specific attitude or behavior; no single campaign should ever ask "everyone" to do "everything" that needs to be done to solve a problem.

Source: National Cancer Institute, *Making Health Communication Programs Work*, Department of Health and Human Services, National Institutes of Health, 2004. http://bit.ly/1KZAQHb

SOCIAL MARKETING

Understanding how an audience's attitudes and opinions about an idea influence their reception to messages is an essential part of the persuasion process. Audiences themselves also hold attitudes and opinions about the messages, and about the methods by which they are communicated. People have routines and patterns of movement that dictate how they go about their day and why they do the things they do. Each of these influences communication effectiveness. Even perfectly constructed messages will have no impact of the intended audience is not exposed to them. To better understand how message designers can gain insight into their target audience's beliefs, attitudes, values, and behaviors so that positive results are achieved, we look to the practice of social marketing.

Social marketing is the practice of utilizing marketing concepts, whether on their own or in conjunction with other communication approaches, to influence positive behaviors among individuals or designated target populations. We know that practitioners must invest time into learning about the audience whose behavior they are trying to change, and marketing approaches offer a reliable, time-tested methodology. Those tasked with or interested in crafting preparedness campaign messages may already have a basic or perhaps even a comprehensive understanding of their audience's lives or routines—as might be the case with an employer and his or her employees, a government and their constituents, or a school administration and their students. But unless this knowledge is pertinent to the behavior changes that are sought, it will not likely be relevant to the needs of the campaign. As such, we look to the historical experience of commercial products marketing where there exists perhaps the most celebrated track record of research-driven audience persuasion. Businesses annually spend billions of dollars on products marketing because they are confident that these investments will influence message recipients to buy their products or use their services, which would ultimately result in profits. In the past three decades, the nonprofit and pro-social sectors have also demonstrated proficiency in the use of the same or similar marketing tools and techniques to more effectively pursue their own goals for social change. Marketing strategies have guided the design and implementation of campaigns and interventions of some of the most successful governmental agencies, including the CDC, the U.S. Environmental Protection Agency (EPA), the National Institutes of Health (NIH), the U.S. Coast Guard, and the National Traffic Safety Administration (NTSA), as they have for many nonprofit organizations, including the American Cancer Society, the American Red Cross, the American Heart Association, the American Lung Association, and the American Diabetes Association, to name just a few.

Like traditional products marketing, social marketing employs elements of the "marketing mix" to spread their message. In this manner, campaign design is guided by the traditional "four p's of marketing," which include:

1. *Product*: In social marketing, the "product" is directly related to the end goal of the marketing campaign. The product may be a tangible good (e.g., hurricane straps), a behavior (e.g., clearing wildfire fuel, stockpiling food and water), a service (e.g., a home safety inspection), or an idea (e.g., family preparedness).
2. *Price*: The price refers to any cost (money, time, energy, embarrassment, etc.) associated with the product being promoted. It is essential to a marketing campaign to establish the perception among members of the target audience that the benefits of the product outweigh the costs associated with it.
3. *Place*: There are a number of different "places" that need to be considered in the design of a social marketing campaign. First, it must be determined where people may go to consume the product being promoted (where smoke detectors will be distributed, where response training may be offered, etc.). Practitioners also must decide upon placement of promotions in order to maximize exposure among the target population. This requires that promoters become familiar with the population being targeted, common media used among the group, and the ways in which members of this population obtain trusted information.

4. *Promotion:* Perhaps even more dependent upon practitioners' understanding of the target audience's beliefs, attitudes, and behaviors is the promotion itself. The promotion stage is the effort to communicate the message to the target audience. This stage takes the three previous "p's" into account in order to reach the target audience effectively with a message that promotes a clear product, emphasizing the benefits over the barriers of adhering to suggestions made by the message source.

In her book *Hands-On Social Marketing: A Step-by-Step Guide*, Nedra Kline Weinreich notes that there are four additional "p's" of social marketing that should be considered in conjunction with those that guide the traditional marketing sector. These include:

1. *Publics:* Weinreich draws a distinction between "external publics," which often include primary audiences (those most in need of influence) and secondary audiences (those who can be persuaded to contribute to influencing the primary audience), policymakers, gatekeepers, and "internal publics," composed of those who are involved with program implementation. Both are crucial to successful campaigns.
2. *Partnerships:* Issues being promoted by social marketing are often highly complex. Successful campaigns often involve multiple organizations playing different roles in the multifaceted goals of the campaign effort.
3. *Policy:* Sometimes the most realistic method of bringing about sustained behavior change is to implement policy change. Social marketing campaigns can aid in generating the support needed for such changes.
4. *Purse Strings:* Social marketing programs are often funded by grants and donations from foundations or the government. Practitioners should consider all funding possibilities before planning their social marketing efforts in order to keep their program plans within a realistic budget.

Another research team, Walsh et al. (1993), studied different social marketing efforts and noted that while the processes used differ from case to case, virtually all share in common that they are:

1. Disciplined in setting objectives and using a variety of techniques to achieve them
2. Centered around a target audience
3. Continuously refined throughout the campaign to meet the needs and desires of the intended audience

As these commonalities suggest, there is a necessity for research and adjustment guided by the information and feedback the target audiences themselves provide through their insight and their actions

The U.S. Department of Health and Human Services (HHS), NIH, and the National Cancer Institute have developed and refined a social marketing strategy known as the Health Communication Program Cycle. This process has become something of a risk communication standard because of its comprehensive approach, elements of which have been highly effective in promoting both the preventive and reactive behaviors that typify disaster preparedness goals. Many of the elements developed for this process, and likewise many of the associated actions, are easily transferable to campaigns seeking individual, employee, or community disaster preparedness. The Health Communication Program Cycle divides the public health campaign process into four distinct stages:

Stage 1 involves planning and strategy development. It is essential that practitioners "do their homework" during this stage in order to better understand the problem and the role that communication can play in moving toward a solution. As noted earlier, there are no one-size-fits-all communication campaigns that inspire every targeted recipient to take every prescribed action. Therefore, while conducting their initial research, campaign planners are best served by identifying segments of their target audience who are in the greatest need of intervention. Based on this research, they are better able to set realistic and measurable objectives involving a more refined segment of their target audience. The team must set goals that can be measured objectively throughout and at the end of the campaign in order to track progress and assess the campaign's effectiveness.

Stage 2 involves developing and pretesting campaign concepts, messages, and materials. During this stage, planners apply the insight gained from their previously conducted problem (e.g., hazard risk vulnerability) and audience research in order to create initial campaign messages and materials. A variety of messages and materials may be developed and pilot tested with focus groups, through interviews, or using surveys, in order to gain more comprehensive feedback from members of the intended audience. This process of pilot testing is used to eliminate all options except those that are best received by the audience they are intended to influence.

Stage 3 involves the actual implementation of the program. In addition to reaching out to the target audience, program planners will track exposure and reactions to the campaign. These organized evaluations help to ensure that all materials are being distributed properly and to highlight aspects of the campaign that may need to be adjusted on an ongoing basis.

Stage 4 involves assessing the effectiveness of the campaign upon its completion and making refinements for possible future use. During this stage, campaign success is assessed by measuring how close program planners came to reaching each targeted goal. Many social scientists argue that campaigns without assessments are not worth conducting, as there are many documented examples of campaigns that produced either no effect or unintended negative effects that made the problem even worse. Campaign evaluation is discussed in greater depth in Chapter 5.

A SYSTEMS APPROACH TO DISASTER PREPAREDNESS CAMPAIGNS

All forms of risk communication depend upon an intimate understanding of the problems being addressed; the individuals and groups being communicated with; and the methods, partners, and resources available. The single most effective way to ensure that these factors are not only fully understood but also appropriately utilized is to follow a step-by-step systems approach.

This text presents a systems approach drawn from the successes of the public health sector where the study, conduct, and improvement of communication methods have been most intensive. The approach presented in this text has been developed to help planners to consider each and every important factor; to identify the likely obstacles; and to capitalize on the available resources, stakeholders, and partners that will together support the campaign. The approach is scalable to accommodate any project scope or size, and may be used in whole or in part as dictated by project needs.

Disaster preparedness campaigns are complex endeavors, regardless of their audience, their topic, or their reach. While it may be possible to hastily design, produce, and release individual risk information materials and messages, poorly aimed "hip shots" rarely achieve significant or measurable changes in public behavior given their lack of any foundational strategy. If program planners seek to facilitate actual improvements in the community, company, or organizational resilience, they must ensure their efforts are not ad hoc or disorganized and they must commit ample time to addressing each of the critical issues involved. To do otherwise is at best a waste of time and money but at worst detrimental to the reputation of the organization or entity as well as the safety of the target population.

Step 1: Early planning	Step 2: Develop campaign strategy	Step 3: Implementation and evaluation
• Define the problem • Perform research • Determine feasibility • Establish goals and objectives • Form the planning team/ coalition	• Project kickoff • The campaign strategy • Settings channels/methods • Selecting communicators • Design and develop message content • Design materials • Pilot test and adjust • Plan activities and events	• Campaign launch • Measuring message exposure • Process evaluation • Summative evaluation

FIGURE 1.3   Emergency management public education process diagram.

We organize the disaster preparedness campaign planning approach based on three separate phases: (1) early planning, (2) developing a campaign strategy, and (3) implementing and evaluating the campaign. The following (Figure 1.3) is a brief summary of our approach.

Phase 1: Early Planning

All projects must be built upon a solid, stable foundation of comprehensive planning. In this initial stage, program planners explicitly define the problem they are hoping to address, and perform an assessment to ensure that their estimations and impressions are as accurate as possible. At the same time, they define and analyze the target population, learning as much they can about their risk perceptions, abilities, wants, cultures, and other characteristics.

Once the problem has been defined and a target population has been selected, it is possible to conduct a thorough assessment of population risk. Based upon the outcome of that assessment, planners can begin to establish the goals and objectives of their campaign. They can also begin to form the larger planning team or coalition that will carry out the planning, management, and operations of the full campaign (and in the case of public education campaigns, that will identify, contact, and begin securing partners and stakeholders who will make the campaign possible through financial and technical assistance). Finally, they begin to identify the various obstacles that may be encountered in the course of implementation and strategize methods for overcoming those obstacles.

Phase 2: Developing a Campaign Strategy

The second phase entails developing a campaign strategy to guide actual operations after kickoff, and developing the materials and methods that will be used to communicate with the target population. Program planners perform market and data research to determine what information already exists that might either help or hinder their efforts, and determine the best ways to transmit their messages. Using these data together with a target population analysis and an assessment of available resources, the communicators select the channels, settings, and methods they will use in executing their campaign. Message content and materials are designed and developed, followed by pilot testing to ensure that the desired level of efficacy is attainable. Finally, activities and events are planned and the staff are trained—all in preparation for the campaign that is about to begin.

Phase 3: Implementing and Evaluating the Campaign

It is in the third and final phase that program planners begin implementing the various operational elements of their campaign strategy for the benefit of the target population. Program planners will regularly measure their levels of exposure and assess the success of their efforts. Using these measures, they evaluate and adjust their methods and materials to keep improving their ability to influence behavior. Program planners also assess their progress toward achieving or exceeding stated goals. Using this information, they will be able to evaluate what actions and methods they chose that worked, and what they did or encountered along the way that hindered their progress. Project outcome evaluation is important for many reasons, as is described in Chapter 5.

PURPOSE, GOALS, AND OBJECTIVES

All disaster preparedness communication or education efforts share a common purpose, namely:

> To reduce individual vulnerability to one or more identified hazard risks as much as possible among as many members of a defined target population as possible.

Vulnerability, as will be explained in detail in Chapter 2, is the propensity to incur harm—in this case from the negative consequences of an emergency or disaster. There are countless methods by which vulnerability may be reduced and, likewise, resilience bolstered. However, the specific actions by which this is actually achieved—and to what degree of success—are highly dependent on the ability of the preparedness campaign planning team to correctly identify the problem (i.e., the reason why vulnerability is high), assess the targeted population, identify the most appropriate methods to address the problem, and select the best mechanisms for communication.

The following three primary risk communication goals apply either in part or in whole to all risk communication efforts:

1. Raising awareness about the hazard risk(s)
2. Guiding behavior, including:
    a. Pre-disaster risk reduction behavior
    b. Pre-disaster preparedness behavior
    c. Post-disaster response behavior
    d. Post-disaster recovery behavior
3. Warning

While the most comprehensive campaigns might actually manage to accomplish all three of these goals, the majority pursue only the first two. Each of these goals is described in the following pages.

Goal 1: Raising Awareness about the Hazard Risk

The first goal of any risk communication effort is to notify individuals about their exposure to a hazard risk and to give them an accurate impression of how that risk affects them personally. Because most people already have a general awareness that a hazard risk exists, this goal is most typically more a matter of correcting inaccuracies and minimizing feelings of apathy about preparedness for the particular hazard or hazards. Adjusting these types of sentiments, which are most often the product of misguided assumptions regarding the need or ability to affect one's fate, is likewise accomplished by raising awareness about the particulars of the hazards and risks of concern. While the occurrence of an actual disaster is the most likely and effective means by which people become aware of a specific hazard risk, it is preferable for obvious reasons that target audiences be enlightened long before a disaster happens. In addition, the mere experience of surviving a disaster has not been shown to increase future preparedness behavior by any significant degree if a disaster preparedness effort does not follow the event (American Red Cross and The Weather Channel 2013).

The task of raising awareness about a hazard or risk involves much more than simply telling people what causes it. They must also be informed of how they are affected as individuals, what they are doing that places them at risk, and where and when disaster will likely strike. They must fully understand the risk as it applies to them personally and to the population as a whole in order to effectively absorb, process, and act upon all subsequent information they receive.

Raising awareness about hazard risk is a difficult task because communicators face significant competition for their audience's attention. Program planners must always be aware that members of their target population face numerous risks on an individual level—many of which present a much greater day-to-day threat and therefore occupy much of their limited attention. People must already worry about financial problems, crime, illness, problems at work and school, and many other immediate issues before they even begin to focus on the community-scale hazard risks that program planners are trying to inform them about. Leading risk communications expert M. Granger Morgan stated in a 2002 report on a study of how people receive disaster preparedness information that "the time that most people can devote to rare or unusual risks is usually very limited" (Morgan, Fischhoff, Bastrom, and Atman). In order to overcome these formidable social and psychological obstacles, preparedness education aimed at raising hazard risk awareness must be as accurate, trustworthy, and effective as possible.

Goal 2: Guiding Behavior

Once an audience is sufficiently and appropriately informed about a hazard, they are primed to receive and process information that will help them take appropriate action to reduce their vulnerability to one or more hazard risks. This information will guide them in taking one or more of the following categories of risk reduction action (each distinguished by when the action is taken and for what greater purpose):

1. Pre-disaster risk reduction behavior
2. Pre-disaster preparedness behavior
3. Post-disaster response behavior
4. Post-disaster recovery behavior

Preparedness messages that address *pre-disaster risk reduction behavior* seek to instruct a population that is already aware of the existence of a hazard risk about the range of available options that can help reduce their individual and collective vulnerabilities to that risk. For instance, people living in earthquake-prone areas might be informed about ways to secure furniture to walls or floors in order to avoid injuries associated with toppling. Once they learn how such actions can influence their risk, people are more likely to act in a manner that improves their likelihood of avoiding a future disaster.

Preparedness messages that address *pre-disaster preparedness behavior* attempt to inform recipients about actions they can take before a disaster that rather than reducing the likelihood of an event, empower them to better manage the consequences that present. Examples of such actions might include stockpiling emergency supplies; establishing individual, family, and community action plans; or identifying safe and well-located post-disaster shelters or assembly sites.

Messages about *post-disaster response behavior* seek to inform a knowledgeable audience about actions they might take in the midst of, and following, a hazard event. For instance, individuals must often learn how to recognize key hazard indicators and know what they should do when confronted by them which might include participating in a mass evacuation. This category of preparedness messaging also includes those efforts that seek to empower individuals to render first-response assistance to their families, friends, neighbors, and themselves, thereby relieving pressure on the community's assuredly overtaxed emergency management resources (Figure 1.4).

Finally, messages that focus on *post-disaster recovery behavior*, which tend to appear only in the aftermath of a disaster, teach disaster-affected individuals how best to rebuild their lives. This can include helping people locate government, nonprofit, or international resources dedicated to relief and recovery, and learn how to provide those services for themselves.

FIGURE 1.4   Phuket, Thailand. Tsunami evacuation sign installed in a coastal tourist community hard-hit by the 2004 tsunami.

Goal 3: Warning

The third and final risk communication goal is warning. Warnings are issued to alert an audience about a change in risk concerning an increased or certain likelihood of occurrence, and to provide them with authoritative instruction on appropriate actions they may take in response. Warning messages differ from awareness messages in that they instruct recipients to take immediate action. Like all risk communication efforts, the messages and systems developed to transmit a warning must be designed to reach the full range of possible recipients within the communities, regardless of location or time. Employing multiple systems in collaboration with a full range of public, private, and nongovernmental partners increases the likelihood of a system reaching its target audience. Examples of the various groups that must be considered in planning for hazard warnings include individuals:

- At home
- In school
- At work
- In public spaces
- In their cars
- Who are disabled
- Who speak different languages
- Who are uneducated or have little education
- Who are poor

In order to be effective, warnings must inform people of the impending nature of the hazard or disaster and must also provide instructions about what to do before, during, and after the events occur (see Sidebar 1.3). These warnings might include information about how citizens can get more information, such as a Website address, a radio station frequency, a television channel, or a telephone number. Public warnings are more than simple messages; together with the infrastructure that transmits them and the science that informs them, they are complex systems designed for the specifics of each hazard, population, and environment. Comprehensive warning systems seek to do most or all of the following, in order:

1. *Detect the presence of a hazard:* This step involves collecting data from a number of possible pre-established sensing and detection systems, including weather sensors, water flow sensors, seismicity and ground deformation sensors, air and water monitoring devices, and satellites, for example.
2. *Assess the threat posed by that hazard:* All hazards include some variable component of risk likelihood, which changes through

time as more information becomes available. The data collected from the sensing and detection systems allow issuers to update their assessments of the hazard and then consider how their recipients would be affected.

3. *Determine the population facing risk from that hazard:* The most effective warnings are those that target populations according to their risk, which is typically a factor of geographic location. Targeted warnings also allow responders to focus their assistance on those people with the most pressing needs. Warnings transmitted to people who are not at risk or without information that distinguishes the at-risk population can result in unintended consequences that hinder the efforts of responders or possibly even result in the creation of new risks. This is because some members of the warned yet "not at risk" population will take action in response to the warning that is unnecessary even if understandable.

4. *Inform the population:* One of the most difficult decisions disaster managers make is whether to issue a warning. Many hesitate over fears that recipients will panic if told about a disaster, or that they will accuse those responsible of "crying wolf" if the hazard fails to materialize. However, research has found that both these unwanted outcomes rarely materialize in practice. Moreover, if the issuing entity has followed established risk assessment guidelines and warning protocols, the decision to issue the warning is as justifiable as it is responsible.

5. *Determine appropriate protective actions that may be taken:* Using their updated assessment of the situation, program planners must determine which protective actions they will instruct recipients to take, and these need to be in line with accepted protocol as warnings may be coming from multiple sources. There have been instances where chemical releases have occurred, for example, where people in the affected areas have been instructed to both evacuate and to shelter in place (remain at their indoor location while sealing off the outside environment as much as possible) by different communicators.

6. *Direct recipients to take those actions:* Through previous risk communication efforts, those exposed will likely have an existing awareness of the hazard and will be somewhat knowledgeable about actions they can take when confronted with a warning. Those issuing the warning must determine the best course of action and relay that information to their recipient population through established mechanisms. A warned audience, whether the general public or otherwise, will seek information on what to do next and it is important that a clear message is given to guide them.

7. *Support the actions being taken by recipients:* Actual response assets (such as police and fire officials, emergency management officials, volunteers, organizations' internal crisis response teams, or other established responders) should assist the exposed population in following any broadcasted instructions; for instance, facilitating evacuation efforts.

Warning systems are much more than the application of technology and last-minute decisions. An effective warning system involves three distinct processes that are crucial so that recipients will actually take appropriate action. The three processes are:

1. *Planning:* During this first phase, program planners must consider what hazards allow for warnings, how and when target audiences will be warned, what the target audience can do in response to those warnings, what terminology will be used, and what authority and equipment are needed to issue the warnings.

2. *Public education:* Program planners should not assume that target audiences will respond automatically to any siren, announcement, or any other form of warning they receive just because it has been issued. Studies have shown that even with education about warnings, only as few as 40% of the recipients take appropriate action. Without having previously been instructed on what to do, in fact, it should be assumed that few will respond appropriately. Such information needs to be communicated to recipients prior to the event and on a periodic basis, irrespective of whether that involves incorporation into regular public disaster education campaigns or is part of company hiring practices. This information might explain what the warning will sound like, what the warning or different warnings mean, where can more information be obtained, and what actions might be taken in response to them.

3. *Testing and evaluation:* Testing and evaluation ensure that an actual disaster is not the first time recipients are exposed to the sound of the warning or the processes involved in its issuance. Testing also allows recipients to experience the warning in a low-stress environment, and to hear the actual sound or wording of the warning at a time when they are neither anxious nor scared. It also allows those tasked with issuing the warning to ensure that their assumptions about the system and its processes reflect what will actually occur during a real emergency or disaster event. And evaluation of the warning system helps to ensure that the system is as effective as it can be whether during tests or actual disasters.

SIDEBAR 1.3   THE WORDS OF WARNING

Many different words are used in warnings to describe the severity of an impending hazard or emergency situation. Confusion about these words may cause recipients to respond with either too much or too little action, so clarity and consistency are important. Common terms used to describe the severity of an emergency situation include:

- *Warning:* The hazardous event is under way or is highly likely to occur soon. Generally, an immediate threat to life and property exists. The public should take immediate protective action.
- *Advisory:* Advisories, like warnings, are given for events that are currently occurring or are about to occur. Advisories apply to events that are less severe than those that merit warnings in terms of the expected consequences to life and property. However, action to protect life and property are strongly recommended.
- *Watch:* Watches are issued when the likelihood of a hazardous event has increased significantly, but where and when the event will occur is uncertain. Watches are issued so that recipients may begin taking precautionary measures as far in advance as possible, even though there is a significant chance that the event may not materialize.
- *Outlook:* An outlook is a prediction of a hazardous event in the near future, based upon conditions that are beginning to look favorable for the onset of that event. Outlooks do not usually include action information or recommendations to prepare for the possible event.
- *Statement:* Statements are not warnings themselves but are used to provide detailed follow-up information to warnings, advisories, or watches.

Source: Coppola, Damon. 2015. Introduction to International Disaster Management, 3rd Edition. Elsevier. Burlington.

Other Risk Communication Goals

Like all other forms of public education, disaster preparedness campaigns seek to accomplish several goals simultaneously, often in addition to the three primary goals listed previously. Goals serve to help planners focus their efforts and ultimately determine if their campaign was successful in achieving what it set out to do. Goals should be basic, should be attainable, and should complement one another. They should also be consistent with the communication theory and practice employed in the campaign. Through the actions that are taken to meet these goals, public knowledge and skill are increased and resilience results. Additional goals that address specific needs of an identified and assessed problem, a profiled population, and a developed message (as identified by the CDC [1995] and other sources [Baker 1990]) are as follows:

1. Increase or enhance knowledge
2. Refute myths/misconceptions
3. Influence attitudes and social norms
4. Develop skills
5. Reinforce knowledge, attitudes, and behaviors
6. Suggest/enable action
7. Show the benefits of a behavior
8. Increase support or demand for services
9. Coalesce organizational relationships

Each of these goals is relevant to the campaign, and therefore important, only if it contributes directly to what the campaign is ultimately seeking to achieve, namely:

- Hazard awareness and accuracy of information
- Behavior change
- Individual and population-wide resilience (i.e., vulnerability reduction)
- Sustainability

Priorities and Goals of Risk Communication Recipients

Risk exists in many forms, as experienced and perceived by individuals. In a study performed by risk communication expert M. Granger Morgan and his colleagues, citizens were asked to make lists of risks that concern them the most. The responses ranged from threats that would result in injury or death, such as accidents, disease, and crime; to economic risks that would result in a financial loss for the individual; to risks of a personal nature, such as love-life problems or problems in school or at work, among others. Only 10% of the risks that were cited related to natural or technological hazards. Morgan and his team found that "whereas professional risk experts devote many hours to considering rare and unusual hazards, most people do not share this preoccupation. With jobs, family, friends, and the other demands of daily living, their lives are filled with more immediate concerns." The authors summarize this statement in saying, "The time that most people can devote to rare or unusual risks is usually very limited" (Morgan et al. 2002, p. 2).

For some of the hazards people face, such as those associated with health (e.g., smoking) or safety (e.g., driving), there is a certain amount of control that individuals possess to directly minimize their risk. For other hazards, people can only indirectly minimize their risk, such as by influencing social processes (i.e., voting for certain risk controls or mitigation measures). However, the authors write that:

> In all cases, [people] need a diverse set of cognitive, social, and emotional skills in order to understand the information that they receive, interpret its relevance for their lives and communities, and articulate their views to others. They can acquire those skills through formal education, self-study, and personal experience. However, as diligent as they might be, individuals are helpless without trustworthy, comprehensible information about specific risks. (p. 2)

Target populations, like risk communication program planners, have their own goals that frame and influence how they interface with the disaster preparedness efforts. Although there will always be a certain segment of the target population that pays absolutely no attention to risk communication messages, most will recognize how the messages pertain to their own lives and seek more information upon which they will base any future action. How they go about doing this and what kind of information they seek will differ among the different issues they face. For those who do elect to pay attention to the risk communication message, there are generally three areas that describe their intentions:

1. *Advice and answers:* This group consists of people who want only to be told exactly what to do. They need step-by-step instruction on how to address the problem of which they have just been informed. This group of people would rather receive the product of analysis than be given all of the necessary information to draw such conclusions themselves. This can be compared with the faith individuals have in advice provided by a trusted doctor, lawyer, or other confidant (see Figure 1.5).
2. *Numbers:* There are certain people who will not take advice at face value. Rather, this group would prefer the option of drawing their own conclusions about what they need to do from a body of statistical evidence that the risk messages provide. This group would rather be faced with quantitative summaries of expert knowledge than be fed step-by-step instruction offering little room for individual analysis and perspective.
3. *Process and framing:* This group comprises those individuals who prefer to fully analyze as many factors relevant to the problem as

FIGURE 1.5   A sign indicating the location of a public emergency assembly point at a public park in Singapore.

possible, assuming full ownership of their actions and any likely outcomes that result. Members of this group generally require three primary data points with which to shape future action:

a. The costs associated with inaction versus those associated with the actions prescribed by communicators
b. The statistical likelihood of falling victim to a disaster and the probable consequences should victimization occur
c. The actual or expected reduction in risk that would be achieved through each of the actions offered

This group is the most motivated and capable of the three and is interested in learning not only how vulnerabilities are created through their own or their community's actions but also how they or their community can control that risk. Using that information, they understand that they will be able to assess their personal circumstances, make individual identifications and assessments of risk, and devise self-tailored solutions.

Program planners must also be aware that the priorities and goals of their target audience may not closely match their own. In fact, some recipients' goals may be directly opposed to those of the program planners, and may even run counter to risk reduction in general. For instance, individuals who seek a waterfront view for their home typically place themselves in locations associated with direct exposure to the damaging forces of hurricanes, storm surges, and erosion. While full risk avoidance would entail removing such an individual from the source of risk (the ocean-front property), any such action is likely to be in direct opposition to their wants and needs and will thus fail to elicit adequate behavioral changes. By identifying and accommodating the goals of recipients, and developing and communicating strategies that offer solutions cognizant of those goals, program planners will achieve much greater success overall (even if the prescribed solutions would not have achieved as significant risk reduction than might occur under more ideal circumstances) (see Sidebar 1.4).

SIDEBAR 1.4   THE VARIOUS PUBLICS

Public disaster preparedness education can be a powerful tool in helping not only individuals to change but also groups, communities, and even whole societies. The following list, compiled by the National Institutes of Health, illustrates the different ways in which risk communication can affect different segments of society in an effort to bring about change:

- *Individuals:* The interpersonal level is the most fundamental level of risk-related communication because individual behavior most profoundly affects individual vulnerability. Communication can affect individuals' awareness, knowledge, attitudes, self-efficacy, skills, and commitment to behavior change. Activities directed at other intended audiences for change may also affect individual change, such as training employees in how to apply at-work preparedness measures to their home life.
- *Groups:* The informal groups to which people belong and the community settings they frequent can have a significant impact on their personal vulnerability and propensity to participate in preparedness behavior. The groups include relationships between customers and employees at a salon or restaurant, members of the same gym or social club, students

and parents in a school setting, or employees at the same work site. Risk communication is easily passed from a direct recipient to others within his or her informal social networks. In fact, activities that are aimed at informal settings often enjoy much greater success than those relying solely upon direct formal communicator-to-recipient patterns.

- *Organizations:* Organizations are groups with defined structures, such as associations, clubs, or civic groups. This category also includes businesses and government agencies. Organizations can carry preparedness messages to their constituents, provide support for preparedness communication programs, and make policy changes that encourage individual change.
- *Communities:* Community leaders and policymakers can be effective allies in influencing change in policies, products, and services that can hinder or support people's actions. By influencing communities, disaster preparedness communication efforts can promote increased awareness of existing hazards, changes in attitudes and beliefs, and group or institutional support for desirable behaviors. In addition, communication can advocate policy or structural changes in the community (e.g., floodplain management and mitigation grant funding) that encourage resilient behavior.
- *Society:* Society as a whole influences individual behavior by affecting norms and values, attitudes and opinions, and laws and policies, and by creating physical, economic, cultural, and information environments. Public disaster preparedness education aimed at the societal level can change individual attitudes or behavior and thus change social norms. For instance, greater awareness of the terrorism hazard brought about by the September 11 terrorist attacks resulted in public support for much greater funding for local first responders.

Source: HHS (United States Department of Health and Human Services), *Making Health Communications Programs Work*, National Institutes of Health, Bethesda, MD, 2002.

SEEING THE BIGGER PICTURE: COMMUNICATION AS ONE COMPONENT OF A LARGER SOLUTION

Disaster preparedness campaigns are conducted to address existing hazard vulnerabilities. Like all public education efforts, when properly conducted, they can be highly effective in limiting behaviors that foster vulnerability and promoting those that reduce it. Conducted in a vacuum, however, these efforts rarely succeed because vulnerabilities tend to have much deeper social roots that extend far beyond a simple lack of knowledge (Paton and Johnson 2001).

To maximize the effectiveness of a disaster preparedness campaign, planners should view it as one attack in a battle that is being conducted on several fronts. In the planning process, as is detailed in Chapters 3 and 4, the roots of target audience vulnerability must be assessed. These factors are often social (e.g., cultural, religious), economic (e.g., poverty, personal spending habits), or of some other origin. Likewise, as is true with all social problems (e.g., crime, health, unemployment, homelessness), communication programs should be integrated as much as possible into any larger, comprehensive efforts that are currently addressing or that plan to address the same problem from a similar or different perspective.

Most campaigns that seek to change behavior will need to provide more than just information if they are to achieve positive changes in behavior. Planners need to keep in mind that the social, economic, and other vulnerabilities that together contribute to a person's risk may also prevent them from having the capacity to take action to reduce that same risk. For instance, a person with no disposable income with which to assemble three days' worth of food and water is not likely to build an emergency kit simply because they are given a list of suggested contents. People who lack the strength to secure their furniture to their walls are not likely to go to extraordinary lengths to address this risk simply because they've been provided with technical instructions or even the hardware itself. Planners must therefore understand and accommodate to the best of their abilities the greater range of needs their target audiences face, and incorporate any relevant support into their existing or ongoing efforts to ensure that action is possible. Sometimes this is simply a factor of pointing people in the right direction, while other times it means providing those resources as a component of the campaign.

As is the case with any public education effort aimed at influencing or guiding positive changes in the behavior or a target audience, disaster preparedness campaign planners must investigate the need for and incorporate as necessary each of the five pillars of effective public education campaigns, which are:

- *Communication:* Communication, as subsequent chapters illustrate, can come in many forms and by many different channels. The target of these communication messages includes not only the vulnerable population but also the general public, educators, the media, emergency services, nongovernmental organizations (NGOs), policymakers, or anyone else who either needs to make a behavioral change or can facilitate one.

- *Facilitation:* Facilitation involves helping members of the target population take necessary action to reduce their vulnerability. Oftentimes facilitation is necessary because certain individuals are able to receive and understand the messages program planners are sending them but are unable to act upon them without outside assistance. Facilitation can also be a way to prompt reluctant individuals who are otherwise able to take action to do so. Facilitation differs from communication in that the facilitators are actually performing or assisting others in performing the tasks required to change vulnerable behavior or helping them to gain the necessary skills to respond effectively (e.g., training employees in fire suppression by allowing them to extinguish a controlled fire with actual fire extinguishers).

- *Funding and financial incentives:* Not all vulnerability reduction solutions touted by disaster preparedness campaigns carry financial costs for recipients, but most do. Sometimes these costs are the single greatest obstacle to action, even when those costs are very low. By providing a grant or other financial incentive program (like tax breaks or insurance discounts) to the target population, it is often possible to prompt those for whom only money is a restrictive factor into action. In many cases, even for those individuals who can afford the risk reduction measures but choose not to out of ambivalence or some other self-limiting factor, the chance to gain something for free or at a significantly reduced cost is enough to initiate action. Examples include free canvas bags designed to hold emergency "go kit" items or free smoke-alarms that recipients can install in their own homes.

- *Policy change:* Policies (public or otherwise, and inclusive of laws, ordinances, standards, regulations, and operating procedures) that seek to guide resilient behavior greatly strengthen any preparedness message. Policy action is best suited in several different types of situations, such as when social barriers prevent individuals who would otherwise prepare for a hazard from doing so (e.g., requiring the posting of evacuation signs in hotels), when a recognized safety standard is known but not yet required in private life or on private property (e.g., building codes, seat belt laws), or when implementing such laws or requirements would bring greater benefit to the greater good of the public (e.g., obligatory first aid education in public school). Policies also help to create a preparedness culture, as has already become the case with occupational health and safety for private-sector enterprises. For instance, many organizations in the health care industry, such as hospitals, have begun requiring that employees maintain household emergency plans as a matter of policy.

- *Technology:* Technology alone is rarely an answer in the emergency management world, but by harnessing technological advances and devices, emergency managers have been able to significantly increase their ability to reduce death and destruction among the affected population. This also applies to public disaster preparedness efforts, in that technology can help break down existing barriers and improve the effectiveness of other efforts. For instance, various monitoring and detection systems have allowed more accurate mapping of hazard risk, which in turn has allowed people living or working within those risk zones to better understand their exposure. Technology research has also helped to develop cheaper and easier-to-use mitigation and preparedness devices that allow the public to reduce risk on a personal level. Widespread use of the National Oceanic and Atmospheric Administration (NOAA) weather radio is a perfect example of how technology has improved preparedness (see Sidebar 1.5).

SIDEBAR 1.5   NOAA WEATHER RADIOS

NOAA Weather Radio All Hazards (NWR) is a nationwide network of radio stations broadcasting continuous weather information directly from the nearest National Weather Service office. NWR broadcasts official Weather Service warnings, watches, forecasts, and other hazard information 24 hours a day, 7 days a week. Working with the Federal Communication Commission's (FCC) Emergency Alert System, NWR is an "All Hazards" radio network, making it the single source for comprehensive weather and emergency information. In conjunction with federal, state, and local emergency managers and other public officials, NWR also broadcasts warning and post-event information for all types of hazards, including natural (such as earthquakes or avalanches), environmental (such as chemical releases or oil spills), and public safety hazards (such as AMBER alerts or 911 telephone outages).

Known as the "Voice of NOAA's National Weather Service," NWR is provided as a public service by NOAA, part of the Department of Commerce. NWR includes more than 985 transmitters, covering all 50 states, adjacent coastal waters, Puerto Rico, the U.S. Virgin Islands, and the U.S. Pacific Territories. NWR requires a special radio receiver or scanner capable of picking up the signal. Broadcasts are found on the VHF public service band at seven frequencies between 162.400 and 162.550 MHz.

NOAA broadcasts cannot be heard on a simple AM/FM radio receiver. However, many receiver options range from handheld portable units that pick up only NWR to desktop and console models that receive NWR in addition to other broadcasts. The National Weather Service does not manufacture, sell, or endorse any particular make or model of receiver. Receivers can be found at many retail outlets, including electronics, department, sporting goods, and boat and marine accessory stores and their catalogs. They can also be purchased via the Internet from online retailers or directly from manufacturers. Many municipal mitigation and preparedness programs have used grant funding to supply residents with receivers free of charge, in conjunction with training in how to operate them. The following are the types of NWR receivers:

- *Stand-alone:* While these receivers might also come with AM/FM bands, their primary use is to receive NWR broadcasts. Buyers can choose between handheld and desktop models, depending on the portability desired. Prices range from around $20 to over $100.
- *Multiband/function:* These receivers bundle a number of features, and NWR is just one of possibly many frequency bands included. This includes AM/FM radios, shortwave receivers, CB radios, VHF marine radios, scanners, and more.

The following are features typical of NWR receivers:

- *Tone alarm:* The National Weather Service will send a 1050-Hz tone alarm before most warning and many watch messages are broadcast. The tone will activate all the receivers that are equipped to receive it, even if the audio is turned off. This is especially useful for warnings that occur during the night when most people are asleep.
- *SAME technology:* SAME, or specific alert message encoding, allows users to specify the particular area for which they wish to receive alerts. Most warnings and watches broadcast over NWR are county based or independent city based (parish based in Louisiana), although in a few areas of the country the alerts are issued for portions of counties. Since most NWR transmitters are broadcasting for a number of counties, SAME receivers will respond only to alerts issued for the area (or areas) selected. This minimizes the number of "false alarms" for events that might be a few counties away from where users live.
- *Selectable alerting of events:* While SAME allows users to specify a particular area of interest, some receivers allow users to turn off the alarm for certain events that might not be

important to them. For example, if you live in a coastal county, but not right at the beach, you might not care about coastal flood warnings.

- *Battery backup:* Since power outages often occur during storms, having a receiver with battery backup can be crucial.
- *External antenna jack:* While most receivers come with a whip antenna that can usually be extended out from the unit, depending on location users may need an external antenna to get good reception. Some receivers come with an external antenna jack that allows users to connect to a larger antenna.

Source: NOAA, *NWR Receiver Consumer Information*, NOAA, 2008. http://www.nws.noaa.gov/nwr/nwrrcvr.htm

Unfortunately, a great many disaster preparedness campaigns are conducted wholly independent of any other supportive approach that would likely have increased the desired change significantly. Without such support, campaign planners set unrealistic expectations for what they can ultimately accomplish. In most cases, the noncommunication components of a preparedness campaign are already being conducted or are available to recipients; however, planners are simply not aware of them and are therefore unable to link their efforts. Thorough investigation in the design phase can help to locate as many of these other options and ensure they are incorporated into the greater campaign strategy.

For example, imagine a campaign that is being developed in order to increase the use of household smoke detectors in order to prevent fire-related injuries and deaths (which include over 4000 fatalities and tens of thousands of injuries each year in the United States alone). Through effective risk communication, residents are informed that they are at risk from house fires, told how that risk applies to them, and given appropriate information about the value the use of a smoke detector could provide in terms of giving them early warning about a fire in their house. Even if translated into all applicable languages and broadcast on all appropriate channels, using all necessary communication campaign components (as described in this text), this communication effort alone is likely to do little more than raise greater awareness of the hazard. Such a limited campaign is unlikely to increase the number of homes that use smoke detectors significantly above rates that were seen prior to the campaign. By understanding why people might not be using the devices, and what else can be done to increase their use through the application of a more comprehensive preparedness campaign, it is possible to achieve much greater results. For instance, it is often the case that there exist residents who, for one reason or another, lack the financial means to purchase the devices. Through a simple need-based grant program, communicators can provide additional information about how to acquire free smoke detectors, thereby eliminating the financial burden. Another obstacle might originate from a lack of residents' ability or time to install smoke detectors in their homes. By promoting or creating a home inspection and smoke detector installation program, especially one that carries no associated cost, another major roadblock will have been eliminated. By advocating or calling attention to local laws that mandate the use of smoke detectors in the home, it may be possible to reach those who are reluctant to install smoke detectors for any number of reasons. Finally, by promoting the many technological advances that have been made in the smoke detector industry, including systems that contact the fire department directly when triggered and others that are able to alert people who are deaf or are sleeping, vulnerability is decreased even further (see Figure 1.6).

- To see an evaluation of a community-based program that offers smoke detectors free of charge, managed by Haines City Fire and Rescue in Haines City, Florida, visit http://bit.ly/1obAgkB.
- To see an example of a program that offers funding for smoke detectors for hearing impaired citizens, managed by the Mesa

FIGURE 1.6   A comprehensive smoke detector safety campaign.

(AZ) Fire Department and the Arizona Commission for the Deaf and the Hard of Hearing, visit http://bit.ly/1PmHuZX.
- To see an example of legislative action taken to drive the use of smoke detectors, passed in Baltimore City, Maryland, visit http://bit.ly/1QgPgnZ.

The key to ensuring a comprehensive campaign is not necessarily carrying out each of the components discussed previously. Rather, it is contingent upon the communication campaign planners to recognize these other noncommunication needs, to identify existing or likely sources to accommodate them, and to incorporate them into the overall preparedness effort. This is described in detail in Chapter 4.

CAMPAIGN REQUIREMENTS

Although there is no single recipe by which all preparedness campaigns are developed, there do exist essential ingredients without which success will range from difficult to nearly impossible (see Sidebar 1.6). Perhaps the most obvious requirement is that of trust in the source of the message. Recipients of risk information are unlikely to heed any instructions they hear or read if they do not personally consider the source of those instructions to be credible. However, trust only opens the door—there follows a full range of factors by which the message itself is judged by target populations that further dictate how it is received. Consider each of the following characteristics of effective communicators and messages, each of which has been identified and verified through years of research and practice in the health communication field:

- *Trustworthy:* Disaster preparedness messages ask people to alter their behavior. This is a very personal request, and one for which a great deal of trust is involved. If communicators cannot be believed, few will follow their instructions. Their message is held to the same standard. One of the most effective means of establishing trust is to involve an organization or institution that is highly regarded in the community or popular community members in the communication effort.
- *Authoritative:* Message recipients must have confidence that the communicator is qualified and sufficiently informed to tell them what to do.
- *Free of personal gain:* In a capitalist society, people receive a barrage of advertising and consumerist information on products and services. There is an inherent skepticism among the public that nearly everyone is out for personal gain. Communicators must

be able to convince the public that their message is conveyed only to serve the public good, not to gain anything in return. This can be difficult to do, especially in instances where preparedness requires recipients to purchase something or otherwise spend their money.

- *Accurate:* Communicators must always assume that their target audience will verify any information that is communicated to them prior to acting on that information. It is therefore vital that any statistical or factual information be highly accurate and as current as possible. For specific statistical information, it is necessary to cite a credible reference to back up whatever claim is being made.

- *Consistent:* Disaster preparedness campaigns are rarely just one-off broadcasts of an informative message. Rather, campaigns seek to repeat their message or messages to ensure they are received over a wide enough segment of the target population, and so they become memorable to those who hear them. If a transmitted message is not consistent over time, the benefit of this repetitiveness is lost. This is especially true when catch phrases are used (e.g., "Stop, drop, and roll"). If the main point or argument of a message changes, it will seem less credible to the recipient audience. This same requirement also stands when the message is transmitted over multiple channels. For instance, a message that is broadcast over the radio should match messages in print, on the Internet, and elsewhere, or else recipients who make contact with multiple channels will likely become confused. Finally, if different speakers present the message, each must be consistent with the others, even if they are speaking to multiple distinct target populations.

- *Repetitive:* As the previous requirement suggests, recipients must experience multiple exposures to a message before they are able to learn from it. As is true with product marketing, the more exposure a person has to a message, the more memorable that message becomes.

- *Easily understood:* Naturally, message recipients must be able to understand a message if they are to act on it. There are many facets to this requirement. First, it must be received in a language they speak fluently or well enough to understand correctly what is being said. Second, it must match their level of education (which could range from using technical language for highly educated populations to simple concepts for grade-school children). It should also be relevant to situations and scenarios that are understandable to the audience in light of their gender, culture, age, geographic grouping, or other relevant demographic features.

- *Rational:* In addition to being understood, the message must make sense in a rational and logical sense. Arguments should be as clear as possible for the audience targeted, and defensible justifications must be presented to support the measures advocated. The message might include concrete information about the addressed hazards, including mortality rates, affected area, hazard time frame, population affected, and others.
- *Accessible:* All people receive their information in a unique manner, based upon their preferences, access, social networks, and other factors. Program planners must ensure that, within this realm of information reception, the message is easily accessible to the audience being targeted. This may require multiple channels if the population is a diverse group or if their patterns of learning dictate such measures. More information on channels is provided in Chapter 4.
- *Solution-oriented:* To be truly effective, a communication message must not only inform members of the target population about their hazard risk but also inform them of realistic and affordable solutions by which they may reduce their personal vulnerability. This was one of the greatest early criticisms of the now defunct Homeland Security Advisory System (HSAS) which used five color codes to indicate terrorism hazard risk. Devoid of any real behavioral modifications or solutions to individual vulnerability, the warnings did little to adjust preparedness behavior among the targeted general audience. Therefore in 2011, the HSAS was replaced by the new color-code-free National Terrorism Advisory System which instead issues detailed warning messages.

SIDEBAR 1.6 CHARACTERISTICS OF AN EFFECTIVE CAMPAIGN

Among successful disaster preparedness efforts, one can identify a number of common characteristics. While by no means requirements for success, these characteristics have been found to increase the likelihood that campaign goals are met in an effective and efficient manner. The University of Wisconsin (1995) developed the following list which includes many of these characteristics of campaign success:

- Long-term rather than short-term.
- Built-in evaluation of effectiveness in the mid-term.
- Incorporate the educational infrastructure, from primary schools to university level.
- Use the mass media to reach the majority of the audience.

- Use folk or alternative media to reach other sections of the population.
- Aim at both the general public and the special publics (i.e., minorities in the population).
- Aim at official and quasi-official levels.
- At first, begin in an area with recurring disasters or hazardous conditions, where there is some incentive for the population to react favorably to the program.
- Later, establish a truly national program welded into the educational and communicational aspects of national development.
- The program should be national, regional, or local in character to increase the motivation of those taking part in the program, as well as their knowledge about the hazards.
- It should be an extension of the public information program.
- It should take advantage of normal conditions of life, normal modes of behavior, normal sources of information, and so forth in the preliminary stages.

Source: University of Wisconsin. 2005. Disaster Preparedness. Online Course. Lesson 8: Public Awareness and Warnings. Madison, WI.

THE DANGERS OF FAILED RISK COMMUNICATION

Individuals and organizations embarking upon a risk communication effort are assuming a great responsibility with many moral implications. They are asking their target audience to trust that the content of their messages will improve their safety and security. They are creating a working relationship in which the recipient becomes willing to dedicate limited time and resources to the advice of the communicator. For these and other reasons, communicators need to do their research. They must be certain that their messages and strategies are accurate and effective not only in a general sense but also in a specific sense with regard to the particulars of the target audience. They must be sure that their target audience easily understands the messages and channels through which they communicate risks to the public. And they must be sure that they have verified their methods through testing both prior to and over the course of implementation as described in Chapter 5. The risk of neglecting these requirements is too great, as failed communication can result in any or all the following:

- Waste the target audience's time and resources
- Waste resources dedicated to the risk communication effort
- Disempower individuals that sought to manage their own risk
- Instill resentment toward communicators and authority figures
- Foment controversy and conflict

- Create threats larger than those posed by the risks the campaign sought to minimize
- Undermine effective decision-making
- Increase confusion and misunderstanding
- Increase vulnerability

Such failures are almost never deliberate, resulting instead from some failure by program planners to grasp the complexity of the message they are attempting to convey to the lay public.

CONCLUSION

Program planners embarking on a disaster preparedness campaign must understand the difficulty of the task they are assuming and appreciate the consequences of failure. Thanks to the trove of research and practice amassed by professionals in the emergency management, public health, and communication science fields, they need not pursue their efforts blindly. By following a systemic approach, like the one presented in this chapter and detailed in those that follow, communicators can feel confident they are taking the right steps to understand the problem at hand, learn the particulars of their target population, design their messages correctly, select appropriate channels, test and pretest their methods, and ultimately to motivate disaster-resilient behaviors.

REFERENCES

Baker, Frank. 1990. Risk communication about environmental hazards. *Journal of Public Health Policy.* 11(3), 341–359. Autumn.

CDC (Centers for Disease Control and Prevention). 1995. *Guidelines for Health Education and Risk Reduction Activities.* Atlanta, GA: CDC.

CDC (Centers for Disease Control and Prevention). 2015. *Fact Sheet: Tobacco-Related Mortality. Smoking & Tobacco Use.* CDC Website. http://1.usa.gov/1KTLYbt.

Coppola, Damon. 2015. Introduction to International Disaster Management, 3rd Edition. Elsevier. Burlington.

HHS (United States Department of Health and Human Services). 2002. *Making Health Communications Programs Work.* Bethesda, MD: National Institutes of Health.

Library of Congress. 2000. Civil Defense Era Poster. http://bit.ly/2imlfJL.

McGuire, W. J. 1968. Personality and attitude change: An information processing theory. In *Psychological Foundations of Attitudes,* A. G. Greenwald, T. C. Brock, and T. M. Ostrom, Eds., San Diego, CA: Academic Press, pp. 171–196.

Morgan, M. Granger, Baruch, Fischhoff, Ann, Bostrom, and Cynthia J. Atman. 2002. *Risk Communication: A Mental Models Approach.* Cambridge: Cambridge University Press.

NHTSA (National Highway Traffic Safety Administration). 2014. *2013 Motor Vehicle Crashes: Overview.* Traffic Safety Facts Research Note. DOT HS 812 101. http://bit.ly/1FxJxuH.

NOAA. 2008. *NWR Receiver Consumer Information.* NOAA. http://www.nws.noaa.gov/nwr/nwrrcvr.htm.

NSC (National Safety Council). 2007. What Are the Odds of Dying?. NSC Website. http://bit.ly/2iiV4Z4.

Paton, Douglas and David, Johnson. 2001. Disasters and communities: Vulnerability, resilience, and preparedness. *Disaster Prevention and Management.* 10(4), 270–277.

The American Red Cross and The Weather Channel. 2013. *Coastal Hurricane Preparedness Poll.* Telephone Survey Report. http://bit.ly/1K0dRRm.

University of Wisconsin. 2005. Disaster Preparedness. Online Course. Lesson 8: Public Awareness and Warnings. Madison, WI.

Walsh, Diana Chapman, Rima E. Rudd, Barbara A. Moeykens, and Thomas W. Moloney. 1993. Social marketing for public health. *Health Affairs.* 12. 2, 104–119.

CHAPTER 2

Managing Risk, Emergencies, and Disasters

INTRODUCTION

Disasters have maintained a constant presence throughout our historical record. In response, individuals, organizations, and whole societies have struggled to reduce their vulnerability to hazards in order to maximize their likelihood of survival. Great efforts have been taken to reduce the occurrence of disasters, and for those that strike, systems and structures have been put in place to effectively respond and recover. Together, these elements form the disaster risk management (or more simply, "disaster management") discipline.

As civilizations evolved and governments assumed increasingly greater stewardship over the hazards that threatened their constituents, formal disaster management structures emerged. In contemporary society, almost every nation's government maintains a unique office or agency dedicated to disaster prevention and response—commonly referred to as emergency management or civil defense. Many governments have gone as far as implementing statutory structures through which hazard risk management is standardized, regulated, and adequately funded. Several nations' governments, including that of the United States, have even allowed for full decentralization of this emergency management capacity, thereby empowering each local government with the ability to tailor their emergency management needs to the specific hazards that exist in the community.

Through science, technology, and innovation, nations have further contributed to an overall increase in human disaster resilience. The development of new and improved mitigation techniques has enabled us to more effectively manage risk by decreasing the chances that hazards result in actual disasters and minimizing the consequences when they do. Hazard detection and warning systems are increasing in their ability to inform us of coming events, sometimes days in advance with hazards like cyclonic storms (hurricanes and typhoons) and blizzards. Coupled with the emergence of increasingly advanced and coordinated response systems, these many accomplishments are improving the odds for the ever-increasing number of people that live in hazard-prone areas.

Despite these achievements, significant risk remains. Each year, more than one hundred million people are affected by disasters, and on average about 100,000 of them lose their lives (Guha-Sapir et al. 2015). Earthquakes, floods, hurricanes, cyclones, tornadoes, landslides, terrorist attacks, and many other hazards that plague us will continue to cause financial and physical ruin due to our propensity to live where they strike—along coastlines, next to rivers, over seismic faults, on the slopes of mountains and volcanoes, and elsewhere. And with climate change altering the intensity and geographic reach of the hydrologic and meteorological hazards we face, we are even seeing reversals in some of our most significant hazard control successes (see Figure 2.1).

For the foreseeable future, disasters will continue to strike with regularity. In the face of conflicting priorities, governments must contend with limited resources, labor, and equipment, and a degree of risk

FIGURE 2.1   Total number of people affected by disasters throughout the world (1900–2015). (From EM-DAT: The OFDA/CRED International Disaster Database [www.emdat.be], Université Catholique de Louvain, Brussels, Belgium.)

acceptance is the result. Inevitably levees fail, warnings come too late (or not at all), buildings collapse, and infrastructure is knocked out. In these moments, the fate of the individual lies in the actions they have taken to ensure their own survival.

This chapter examines basic disaster management concepts and explains how these concepts apply to individual, organizational, and community-based disaster preparedness. Brief discussions about risk, vulnerability, and the history of disaster management are provided for context. An explanation of different public- and private-sector emergency management structures and capabilities follows. Several relevant terms are defined.

FUNDAMENTAL EMERGENCY MANAGEMENT CONCEPTS

The terms and concepts detailed in this section explain the basis of the emergency management discipline.

Risk

The term *risk* in the emergency management context is most simply defined as the chance something bad will happen, and the associated outcome of that possible adverse event. Because everything in life, good or bad, involves risk of some form, risk may be considered unavoidable. Risk therefore affects all people without exception, irrespective of their geographic location or socioeconomic conditions. Individuals and societies alike must constantly make choices that involve known and unknown factors of risk, with absolute risk avoidance generally impossible to achieve. Each of life's decisions—where we live, how we live, what we eat, where we travel, where we work—plays into how much and what kinds of risks we ultimately face.

The concept of risk can have drastically different connotations to different groups, depending upon the context in which it is used. For instance, in the business sector, investment risk may be seen to be an opportunity for profitmaking. A medical patient may see the risk associated with an experimental treatment as the opportunity for a future without some illness that is otherwise incurable. For disaster managers, however, the term's meaning is always negative. Even among risk managers, there exists no single accepted definition of risk. One of the easiest illustrations of the term, preferred by many emergency managers (and which pertains to its use in this text), is illustrated through the equation which states that risk equals the likelihood of an event occurring multiplied by the consequence of that event, were it to occur (Ansell and Wharton 1992).

$$Risk = Likelihood \times Consequence$$

In this equation, likelihood is expressed either as a probability (e.g., 0.15; 50%) or as a frequency (e.g., 1 in 1,000,000; 5 times per year), whichever is appropriate for the analysis being considered. Consequences are a measure of the effect of the hazard on people or property. This equation is useful because it is easy to imagine how the reduction in either the likelihood of a hazard or the potential consequences that might result from it would both result in the reduction of risk. Likewise, any action that increased the likelihood or consequences of a hazard would increase that hazard's risk.

Hazard

All risks are the result of the existence of one or more hazard. The term *hazard*, believed to be drawn from either the French word *hazard* (a game of dice predating craps) or the Arabic *al-zahr* (literally "the die"), is rooted in the concept of chance. Under this interpretation of the word, hazards are events or physical conditions that have the *potential* to cause fatalities, injuries, property damage, infrastructure damage, agricultural loss, damage to the environment, interruption of business, or other negative consequences (Federal Emergency Management Agency [FEMA], 1997; see Figure 2.2). Risk and its associated vulnerability ultimately determine if and when a hazard causes a disaster.

A unique set of hazards termed a "hazard portfolio" influences every individual, family, business, organization, community, or country. There are many methods by which the hazards in this portfolio may be categorized, the most common of which distinguishes them as being natural, technological, or intentional. Some hazards may fit appropriately into more than one of these three groupings. Factors including location, topography, industrial activities (both within and around the community), behaviors, laws, demographics, climate, income, and many others determine not only what hazards fall into this portfolio but also how small or great the risk posed by each will be.

Vulnerability

Vulnerability measures how susceptible an object, area, individual, group, community, country, or other entity is to the consequences of a hazard. Vulnerability, which is closely related to risk but determined by

FIGURE 2.2   Avalanche chute on Cotopaxi Volcano, Ecuador. This hazard is only a risk if humans place themselves or their property in its path (Author photo).

a completely different set of variables, explains how a single event with devastating potential, affecting two individuals or two communities with identical force, presents as a minor issue in one case and a disaster in the other. When assessing hurricane damage, for instance, it is not uncommon to come across a house that has been destroyed immediately adjacent to one that is unscathed. On a larger scale, one can consider how two earthquakes, of almost equal magnitude and intensity, caused fewer than 100 deaths in Los Angeles but more than 20,000 in Gujarat, India.

The etymology of the term *vulnerability* points to the Latin *vulnerabilis*, meaning "to wound." Its measurement is derived from a combination of physical, social, economic, and environmental factors or processes. Vulnerabilities may be decreased through actions that lower the propensity to incur harm, and increased through actions that increase that propensity. For instance, retrofitting a building to withstand the shaking effects of an earthquake will lower that building's vulnerability to the hazard, thereby lowering risk (*resilience*, the opposite of vulnerability, is a measure of propensity to avoid loss). Populations have vulnerabilities as well, which are raised or lowered according to their practices, beliefs, and economic status. Public education is the most effective way to influence the vulnerability of populations and, likewise, individuals.

Disaster

When a hazard risk is realized, individuals and communities are left to manage the consequences. If the event overwhelms the individual's or the community's capacity to respond, the result is a disaster. Not all adverse events are disasters, only those that overwhelm response capacity are disasters. Vulnerability and the capacity to manage consequences (dictated by preparedness and mitigation) determine whether a disaster or an emergency event results. The distinction between an *emergency event* and a *disaster* is important. For instance, a simple house fire requires response by a jurisdictional fire department. There is surely property loss, and likely the possibility of injury or loss of life. However, as fires are routine occurrences that are easily managed, they normally are not considered disasters. In the great Chicago fire of 1871, on the contrary, more than 2000 acres of urban land were destroyed over the course of three days. Overall, the destruction included 28 miles of road, 120 miles of sidewalk, 2000 lampposts, and 18,000 buildings, all totaling more than $200 million in property damage (one-third of the value of all property in the city at the time) (Colbert and Chamberlin 2011). Between 200 and 300 people died. While both events are fires, only the Chicago fire can be called a disaster.

Disasters also grow in intensity as they overwhelm progressively larger response units. When individuals or organizations are unable to manage the consequences of an event, they call upon their local fire department, police department, or emergency medical services (see Figure 2.3). If these agencies are unable to adequately contain the event, they likewise request assistance from mutual aid partners, followed by the state or the provincial government. If assistance from that next-higher level is insufficient to manage the requirements of the event, the disaster becomes national in scope, thereby requiring the intervention of the national government. In situations in which a national government or several national governments are unable to manage the consequences of an adverse event, the event becomes an international disaster, requiring intervention by a range of international response and relief agencies.

Disasters are measured in terms of lives lost, injuries sustained, property damaged or lost, and environmental degradation. These consequences manifest themselves through direct and indirect means, and can be tangible or intangible (see Sidebar 2.1). Disasters may be sudden onset or "creeping." Sudden-onset disasters often happen with little or no warning, and most of their damaging effects are sustained within hours or days. Examples include earthquakes, tsunamis, volcanoes, landslides, tornadoes, and floods. Creeping disasters occur when the ability of response agencies to support people's needs degrades over weeks

FIGURE 2.3   Hotel fire in Bangkok, Thailand. Incidents become disasters only when the capacity to manage their consequences is exceeded (Author photo).

or months, and they can persist for months or years once discovered. Examples are drought, famine, soil salination, epidemics, and erosion.

SIDEBAR 2.1   DIRECT AND INDIRECT LOSSES

Direct losses, as described by Keith Smith in his book *Environmental Hazards,* are "those first order consequences which occur immediately after an event, such as the deaths and damage caused by the throwing down of buildings in an earthquake" (1992). Examples of direct losses are:

- Fatalities
- Injuries
- Cost of repair or replacement of damaged or destroyed public and private structures (buildings, schools, bridges, roads, etc.)
- Relocation costs/temporary housing
- Loss of business inventory/agriculture
- Loss of income/rental costs

- Community response costs
- Cleanup costs

Indirect losses (also as described by Smith 1992) may emerge much later and may be less easy to attribute directly to the event. Examples of indirect losses include:

- Loss of income
- Input/output losses of businesses
- Reductions in business/personal spending ("ripple effects")
- Loss of institutional knowledge
- Mental illness
- Bereavement

Tangible losses are those for which a dollar value can be assigned. Generally, only tangible losses are included in the estimation of future events and the reporting of past events. Examples of tangible losses include:

- Cost of building repair/replacement
- Response costs
- Loss of inventory
- Loss of income

Intangible losses are those that cannot be expressed in universally accepted financial terms. This is the primary reason why human fatalities and human injuries are assessed as a separate category from the cost measurement of consequence in disaster management. These losses are almost never included in damage assessments or predictions. Examples of intangible losses include:

- Cultural losses
- Stress
- Mental illness
- Sentimental value
- Environmental losses (aesthetic value)

Source: Coppola, Damon. 2015. Introduction to International Disaster Management 3rd Edition. Elsevier. Burlington.

Safe

One of the most important, but also one of the most contentious, concepts pertaining to emergency preparedness education is the presumption of safety. While the term *safe* might seem obvious as to require no further clarification, its context with regard to emergency management is not evident without a solid understanding and application of risk. Most people wrongly assume that a reference to something as being "safe" implies all risk has been eliminated. However, because such an absolute level of safety is virtually unattainable in the real world, societies establish thresholds of risk that define a frequency of occurrence below which those societies need not worry about the hazard. A practical definition is provided by Derby and Keeney (1981), who contend that a risk becomes "safe," or "acceptable," when it is "associated with the best of the available alternatives, not with the best of the alternatives which we would *hope* to have available" (emphasis added). We are reminded that all aspects of life involve a certain degree of risk. However, as a global society, we are constantly assessing and reassessing what constitutes acceptable risk for every hazard considering that which science, technology, and law can offer to treat those risks.

THE MANAGEMENT OF RISK

For most of life's risks, management is an individual responsibility and is therefore performed on a personal level. Likewise, the consequences of failing to take adequate precaution by preparing for or mitigating these risks are also personal or small in scale (even if *catastrophic* to the individual). Examples of personal risks are easy to imagine and can be grouped into the following categories:

- Health risks (e.g., eating well, exercising)
- Economic or financial risks (e.g., investments, business ventures, employment decisions)
- Social risks (e.g., public behavior, reputation)
- Physical or safety-related risks (e.g., riding a bike, driving a car, crossing the street, cooking with a gas stove)

On the collective scale, communities, nations, and entire societies face risks posed by a range of hazards whose single events occur on a much larger scale. Earthquakes, floods, volcanoes, terrorist attacks, and pandemics are but a few examples drawn from a much longer list of possibilities. While annually these large-scale hazards generally result in lower absolute (population-wide) consequences than the consequence sum-total from all individually faced hazards, they are nonetheless the focus of emergency and risk managers due to their spectacular nature (wherein individual incidents result in multiple casualties and significant property and environmental damage) and the fact that they may be of such great magnitude as to overwhelm the organization's or the community's response and recovery capacity—a disaster by definition.

When considering large-scale hazards, vulnerability may be reduced through efforts conducted at the community, regional, or national levels, depending on the nature of the hazard. For most hazards (though certainly not without exception), it is the government's statutory responsibility to manage (or at least guide the management of) hazard risk reduction measures. When actual disasters result from these hazards, it is likewise a government responsibility to respond to them and provide recovery assistance.

For businesses, vulnerability and risk reduction is required by law or regulation, such as the case of financial risk measures mandated by the Sarbanes–Oxley legislation. Private-sector risk management is also performed on a voluntary basis by companies interested in protecting facilities, data, people, and operations from physical, financial, or liability risk. Businesses apply both structural and nonstructural risk control measures, and conduct business continuity planning to ensure that effective systems and structures are in place to minimize interruptions.

Despite any perceived or actual responsibility that citizens demand of their elected leadership, or employees demand of their employers, the individual maintains power to reduce further his or her own risk levels—even from the greatest of hazards. Research has indicated that within communities or organizations where individuals take action to prepare for disasters, the community or the company enjoys much greater levels of resilience (and likewise fares much better when impacted by an emergency or disaster). On the individual level, people are responsible for managing the risks they face as they see fit. For some risks, management may be obligatory, as is the case with automobile speed limits and seat belt usage. For other personal risks, such as those associated with many recreational sports, individuals are free to decide the degree to which they will reduce their risk exposure, such as wearing a ski helmet or other protective clothing. This is most apparent in the field of public health, where disease risk clearly affects humans as individuals—prompting a management scheme that promotes management of health risks at the individual level. The public health discipline, for this very reason, is the most experienced with promoting risk management on the personal level. However, by employing the same personal risk reduction philosophy and techniques for all hazards, including the catastrophic ones, individuals will reduce their own and their community's vulnerability to them.

THE MANAGEMENT OF EMERGENCIES AND DISASTERS: EMERGENCY MANAGEMENT FUNCTIONS

Comprehensive disaster management in modern society is based upon four functional components:

1. Mitigation
2. Preparedness
3. Response
4. Recovery

The application of these four functions is often depicted in a cyclical manner, with mitigation and preparedness occurring before a disaster, and response and recovery following it. In practice, however, the actions involved with each function are intermixed with those of the others, and are each performed to varying degrees before, during, and after disasters occur. Disasters are best thought of as occurring along a continuum, with the knowledge and experience gleaned from one disaster influencing preparedness, mitigation, response, and recovery actions taken in the next disaster to occur. Each of these functions is described in the following sections.

Mitigation

Mitigation involves the reduction or elimination of one or both of a hazard's risk components (likelihood and consequence). Sometimes called the "cornerstone of disaster management" (FEMA 2005), mitigation seeks to "treat" hazards such that they affect society to a lesser degree. While the three other components of the disaster management cycle (preparedness, response, and recovery) are performed either as a reaction to hazards or *in anticipation* of their consequences, mitigation measures seek to reduce the likelihood or consequences of hazard risk before a disaster ever occurs. Of course, mitigation is by no means the simple answer to a hazard problem. In fact, because of the difficulties often associated with most mitigation measures, it is only in the last few decades that their full risk reduction potential has been recognized. In practice, mitigation measures tend to be costly, disruptive, time consuming, and socially unpalatable. They usually carry their own inherent risk and do not always work as intended. Political will for mitigation is hard to come by in many situations, and the public's attention span tends to be too short to accommodate the significant life changes that may be necessary for mitigation to work. However, as the practice of mitigation grows, it will continue to emerge as a means of measurably reducing the incidence of many types of disasters.

Preparedness

Preparedness involves equipping people who may be affected by a disaster, or who may be able to help those affected, with the tools to increase their likelihood of survival and to minimize financial and other losses. This is achieved by training and equipping response agencies at each government level, and by educating the public about what actions they can take to reduce their individual vulnerability and risk. Many different organizations and individuals, including emergency response agencies, government officials, businesses, and citizens, conduct disaster preparedness activities. Each has a unique role to play and unique responsibilities to fulfill when disasters strike. The range of activities that constitute the preparedness function is expansive, and these actions are often the primary factors that determine whether the response is successful. The goals of preparedness are (1) knowing what to do in a disaster's aftermath, (2) knowing how to do it, and (3) being equipped with the right tools to do it effectively. Preparedness minimizes hazards' adverse effects through effective precautionary measures that ensure a timely, appropriate, and efficient organization and delivery of response and recovery action. Preparedness actions and activities can be divided according to recipient. The government component, which includes administration, emergency management, public health, and other services agencies, is one group. Individuals and businesses are the second group. Preparedness of the first group is normally defined and conducted through the creation and application of an emergency operations plan (EOP) and bolstered by training and exercises. Public education campaigns guide the preparedness of the second group.

Response

Response is characterized by actions taken to reduce or eliminate the impact of disasters that are about to occur, are occurring, or have already occurred (see Sidebar 2.2). Ultimately, the scale of the disaster dictates the response. These actions are aimed at limiting injuries, loss of life, and damage to property and the environment. Response includes not only those activities that directly address immediate needs—such as first aid, search and rescue, and shelter—but also systems developed to coordinate and support such efforts. Furthermore, this function facilitates the rapid resumption of critical infrastructure (such as opening transportation routes, restoring communications and electricity, and ensuring food and clean water distribution) to allow recovery to take place, reduce further injury and loss of life, and speed the return to a normally functioning society. Response processes begin as soon as it becomes apparent that a hazard event is imminent and lasts until the emergency is declared over. Response is by far the most complex of the four functions of emergency management because it is conducted during periods of very high stress, in a highly time-constrained environment, and with limited information. During response, wavering confidence and unnecessary delay directly translate to tragedy and destruction. Relief, the provision of vital necessities to impacted victims, is a major subcomponent of the response function.

Recovery

Recovery involves the repair, reconstruction, or regaining of what has been lost as a result of a disaster and, ideally, a reduction in risk from a similar catastrophe in the future. The recovery phase generally begins after the immediate response has ended, and can persist for months or years thereafter. In a comprehensive emergency management system, which includes pre-disaster planning, mitigation, and preparedness actions, recovery actions may begin as early as during the planning phase, long before a disaster occurs. The actions associated with disaster recovery are the most diverse of all the disaster management functions. The range of individuals, organizations, and groups that are involved is also greater than in any other function (although these participants are much more loosely affiliated than in other disaster management functions). Because of the spectacular nature of disaster events and because disaster consequences affect so many peoples' lives, recovery generates the greatest amount of interest and attention from the world community as a whole. In relation to the other disaster management functions, it is by far the costliest. Disaster recovery is also the least studied and least organized of all of the disaster management functions, and therefore the most haphazardly performed.

SIDEBAR 2.2   THE DISASTER EVENT LIFECYCLE

The evolution of individual emergency and disaster events can be divided into three phases, each with a corresponding set of preparedness and response activities. These phases are:

1. *Prehazard*: During this period of the emergency, the hazard event is impending and may even be inevitable. Recognition of the impending hazard event may or may not exist.

2. *The emergency: Hazard effects ongoing.* This period begins when the first damaging effects begin, and extends until all damaging effects related to the hazard and all secondary hazards cease to exist. It may be measured in seconds for some hazards, such as lightning strikes or earthquakes. However, for others, such as floods, hurricanes, wildfires, or droughts, this phase can extend for hours, days, weeks, or even years. During this time, responders address the needs of people and property as well as the hazard effects.
3. *The emergency: Hazard effects have ceased.* During this final phase of the emergency, the hazard has exerted all of its influence, and negligible further damage is expected. Responders are no longer addressing hazard effects, so their efforts are dedicated to addressing victims' needs, managing the dead, and ensuring the safety of structures and the environment. The emergency still exists and the situation still has the potential to worsen, but the hazards that instigated the emergency are no longer present.

THE MANAGEMENT OF EMERGENCIES AND DISASTERS: EMERGENCY MANAGEMENT STRUCTURES

In most countries, including the United States, emergency management is practiced at all government levels, whether local, regional (state or province), or national. Hazardous *events*, or those situations that require some form of emergency response, occur daily and include house fires, minor floods, or chemical spills, for example. These events are almost exclusively managed at the local level by the local emergency services, namely, fire departments, police departments, emergency medical services, and offices of emergency management. Each of these organizations, and several other peripheral organizations and agencies that participate in emergency management activities, is discussed in the following sections.

The Fire Department

Fire departments (also known as "fire brigades" or "fire services") are the most common local emergency management structures found throughout the world. Although these agencies were first developed in reaction to structural and other forms of fire (the most common hazard faced by communities on a daily basis), many nations' fire departments have expanded their abilities to address a wider range of both regular and rare hazards. Examples of the actions commonly performed by fire departments include:

- Disaster response coordination
- Emergency management
- Emergency medical services
- Fire and arson investigation
- Fire and structural safety inspections
- Fire suppression (structural, brushfire, wildfire, hazardous material fire)
- Hazard and other warning issuance
- Hazard prevention activities
- Hazardous materials response and cleanup
- Issuance and enforcement of permits
- Public education
- Public relations
- Rescue (urban, swift water, wilderness, cave, airborne, alpine, dive, crack and crevice)
- Terrorism (actual or threatened) response
- Training
- Vehicle extraction

Fire departments may be organized at either the local, regional (county or province, for example), or national level (see Figure 2.4). In the United States, fire departments exist almost exclusively at the municipal and county level. Certain facilities like airports or seaports may also maintain fire departments, as do some large companies. How governmental fire departments are structured often depends on whether personnel are paid or volunteer, and the type of government in place. Fire departments' needs are driven by both community risk and funding access. Funding sources and levels differ from community to community but rarely exist at levels sufficient to fully address recognized fire risk and meet all of a fire department's needs, including:

- Personnel
- Training
- Equipment, namely:
  - Apparatus (vehicles specially designed for the firefighters' needs)
  - Firefighting equipment
  - Personal protective equipment (PPE)
  - Rescue equipment

FIGURE 2.4   Falls Church, Virginia. Fire Department officials perform an emergency response exercise (Author photo).

- Communications systems, namely:
  - An emergency notification system enabling the public to inform the fire department of an emergency (e.g., 911 system)
  - A radio communications system, which allows responders to talk to each other and to their command center
  - A broadcast system, which allows responders to communicate with the public
- Facilities
- Information
- Authority (statutory)

Law Enforcement

Law enforcement agencies, known as police departments or constabularies, are government-sanctioned entities responsible for maintaining law and order within the community. Though crime fighting is their primary responsibility, law enforcement officers regularly participate in all four emergency management functions. Law enforcement emergency management responsibilities may include:

- Assessment
- Bomb removal and disposal

- Crime fighting
- Crowd control
- Disaster scene security
- Investigations
- Search and rescue
- Security at critical facilities
- Traffic control
- Warning issuance

Although law enforcement agencies are most often centralized and managed at the national government level (e.g., France), many governments (especially federalized systems, such as in the United States) maintain locally based and organized forces. Still others, such as Canada, maintain a mixture of organizational police forces (the Royal Canadian Mounted Police have national jurisdiction, while three provinces and several cities maintain their own local forces). In centralized systems, police officers may be based within their local communities or assigned to communities other than their own. Police forces have traditionally enjoyed more secure and greater funding than other first-response officials, including fire and emergency medical departments.

Emergency Management

Offices of emergency management perform mitigation, preparedness, response and recovery planning, and coordination for large-scale events. This unique field is rather new, appearing primarily during the civil defense era of the 1950s when governments began preparing for nuclear war. Over time, these offices began to address other catastrophic hazards, and even assumed response and recovery coordination responsibilities. Today, most countries maintain an emergency management capacity at the national level, which addresses mitigation of and preparedness for major disasters. Several countries, including the United States, have empowered their national emergency management offices with response and recovery capacities as well, usually in support of local efforts rather than in place of them. At the local and regional levels, it is common for the fire or police departments to handle emergency management planning and coordination, although many major cities, and all U.S. states, have created dedicated emergency management offices.

Emergency Medical Services

Emergency medical services, often called EMS or the ambulance service, are a specialized form of medical care performed at the scene of a disaster or emergency event. EMS personnel (or emergency medical technicians [EMTs]) are highly trained professionals who offer medical assistance greatly exceeding basic first aid. EMTs stabilize victims for transport to a hospital, where better equipment and conditions are present. Although many police and fire officials are trained to provide first aid and medical assistance, EMS organizations are usually trained and equipped to go beyond the basics, and may even be certified to perform invasive procedures or to administer a range of drugs. EMS systems differ in their level of training, availability of funding, and quality of equipment. In most countries, EMS services are offered by private agencies and they charge victims a fee for their services. They may be publicly funded and associated with a hospital or a fire department, or be an independent public service. The vast majority of EMS officials are volunteers.

The Military

Almost every country includes the military in its overall disaster management planning and operations process. Though most democratic governments hesitate to utilize their military resources to address domestic issues, such forces tend to be best suited in many ways to meet the requirements when responding to major disasters. They have secure budgets, specialized equipment, and a trained and quickly deployable workforce; are self-sufficient; and have a highly organized, hierarchical structure. The connection between the military and emergency management goes beyond mere coincidence or convenience for many countries. Emergency management grew out of a defensive need, and the military has been involved throughout the course of that evolutionary process. As such, their status as a valuable resource is widely recognized and often seen as the ultimate last resort. One of the primary concerns of involving the military in disaster response is that of authority. Military forces work with a command structure that can be at odds with the chain of command outlined in most emergency response plans. Additionally, military training optimizes behavior appropriate in hostile, foreign environments, so civilian–military interface during disasters can quickly become contentious if the proper mechanisms and training are not in place to guide such action and prevent conflict. In the United States, laws limit the extent of military involvement in disaster response. However, the state governors have been given direct authority over National Guard resources, which they call upon regularly to tap into an extensive inventory of heavy equipment and manpower. Utilization of the U.S. Army, Air Force, Navy, Marines, or Coast Guard is not as simple or direct.

Other Emergency Management Resources

There is a full range of nontraditional government agencies and other resources that address one or more of the four emergency management functions. Why, when, and how these agencies participate is determined by the particular characteristics of each community and each disaster. These agencies and offices are described using a full range of titles, although variants within each government structure perform many of the same or similar activities despite differences in nomenclature. These "other resources," which may exist at the local, regional, or national levels, include (but are not limited to):

- Building or Housing Department or Authority
- Department of the Environment
- Department (Ministry) of Public Health
- Department of Agriculture, Forests, Fisheries, and Food
- Department of Civil Defense
- Department of Communications
- Department of Development
- Department of Education
- Department of Energy
- Department of Foreign Affairs, State, or the Exterior
- Department of Labor
- Department of Public Affairs
- Department of Public Safety
- Department of Public Works
- Department of the Interior or Home Affairs
- Office of the Coroner
- Office of the Lead Government Executive
- Transportation Department or Authority

Private-Sector Emergency and Risk Management Structures

A business or a nongovernmental organization is much more than the land and facilities it occupies, the equipment it utilizes, and the products and services it offers. In the communities where they operate, private-sector entities also provide many or most employment opportunities, generate a significant portion of public-sector tax revenues (in the case of businesses), boost civic vitality, and are oftentimes central to the collective community identity. But these organizations are exposed to many if not most of the same damaging forces that affect citizens, schools, government, and the environment; so any deficiency in private-sector disaster response or recovery capacity jeopardizes the community's economic and social stability.

Many businesses and nongovernmental organizations go to great lengths to minimize disaster impacts and prevent operational disruptions by conducting hazard and risk management activities. There are a number of possible options for managing risk exposure for private and nongovernmental sector entities, including hazard mitigation, conducting business continuity planning and enterprise risk management, and ensuring that employees and their families are prepared for disasters. Protective measures are most effective when implemented prior to a disaster.

Business continuity planning is defined as the process by which organizations of any size identify the risks threatening their operations, determine what solutions exist to either eliminate or reduce the risk and formulate plans and procedures to ensure that critical functions may be maintained or resumed in the event of an emergency or disaster (whether of internal or external origin).

Enterprise risk management is the strategic business discipline that supports the achievement of an organization's objectives by addressing the full spectrum of its risks and managing the combined impact of those risks as an interrelated risk portfolio. Enterprise risk management:

1. Encompasses all areas of organizational exposure to risk (financial, operational, reporting, compliance, governance, strategic, reputational, etc.)
2. Prioritizes and manages those exposures as an interrelated risk portfolio rather than as individual "silos"
3. Evaluates the risk portfolio in the context of all significant internal and external environments, systems, circumstances, and stakeholders
4. Recognizes that individual risks across the organization are interrelated and can create a combined exposure that differs from the sum of the individual risks
5. Provides a structured process for the management of all risks, whether those risks are primarily quantitative or qualitative in nature
6. Views the effective management of risk as a competitive advantage
7. Seeks to embed risk management as a component in all critical decisions throughout the organization (Risk and Insurance Management Society 2014)

Businesses and nonprofits also enhance their own recovery capacity, and by extension that of the community, by supporting pre-disaster preparedness activities. This includes the provision or facilitation of training for employees. Businesses recognize that helping employees to reduce risks at home increases the likelihood that these same employees will remain at work or return more quickly from disaster-related absences. Encouraging employees to avoid the impacts of disasters by stockpiling critical commodities, making household disaster plans, and identifying and addressing household disaster risk has the dual benefit of increasing the resilience of the business and decreasing the burden on local response resources given that many fewer individuals will be overwhelmed by the event.

Any disruption has the potential to adversely impact a business, and a lack of planning leaves them exposed. This is particularly true for small and medium-sized enterprises with few cash reserves. Continuity plans enable business owners and operators to better manage their customers', creditors', and suppliers' needs, while simultaneously guiding the business in assessing and addressing facility, inventory, equipment, and staff recovery requirements.

GOVERNMENTAL PREPAREDNESS ACTIONS

There is a diverse range of activities undertaken by governments to prepare for emergencies and disasters. These actions can be grouped into the following five general categories:

1. *Planning:* In the event of a disaster, each government jurisdictional level will be expected or required to perform a range of tasks and functions in the lead-up to its aftermath. Well in advance of a disaster, governments must know not only what they will need to do but also how they will do it, what equipment they will use, and how others can and will assist them. The most comprehensive methodology used to plan for disasters is the creation of a community or national EOP. These plans can be scaled up or down depending upon the needs of the community and the particular disaster, and can accommodate the complex and diverse needs of a full range of disaster response and recovery actions.

2. *Exercise:* Response exercises allow those involved in emergency and disaster response, as defined in the EOP, to practice their roles and responsibilities before an actual event occurs. Exercises also help agencies find EOP problems in nonemergency situations, and introduce individuals and agencies involved in response.

3. *Training:* Disaster response officials are more effective when adequately trained to do their jobs. Novice or poorly trained responders add to the possibility of a secondary emergency or disaster, and further strain response resources by diverting officials to manage responder rescue and injury care. Though first

responders are likely to have some basic standard of introductory training, the specialized instruction required of disaster response is much more technical and not universally available. Many nations, including the United States, have established centralized or regional training facilities to bring these skills to the local level.

4. *Equipment:* Specialized tools and equipment designed for disaster response and recovery have helped to drastically reduce the number of injuries and deaths and the amount of property damaged or destroyed as a result of disaster events. This equipment has also increased the effectiveness of response agencies by protecting the life of the responders themselves. Access to this equipment depends on the availability of funding. Oftentimes, several neighboring communities will share disaster-specific equipment under mutual aid agreements, thereby extending the reach of rarely used, expensive items.

5. *Statutory authority:* In order to ensure that all individuals and agencies involved in emergency management are able to function effectively, proper statutory authorities must exist. Statutory authorities form the legal framework that ensures emergency and disaster response agencies and functions are properly established and staffed, and that they receive regular funding. These laws and regulations also guide how government response officials and agencies may interact with the public and businesses in a range of situations. Response requires travel over and operation on both public and private land, and statutory authorities allow this to occur without question or unnecessary delay. Mutual aid agreements between neighboring communities, states, or even countries also require a legal contract or similar instrument to guide expectations, command, coordination, and reimbursement for services.

INDIVIDUAL AND ORGANIZATIONAL PREPAREDNESS

In the event of a disaster, it is assumed that governmental resources will be stretched to the limits and even exceed their capacity during the first few hours or days of response. During this time, the public, businesses, and other NGOs must be prepared to provide for their own immediate response needs. At the individual level, public preparedness efforts serve to empower ordinary citizens to help themselves, their families, their neighbors, or complete strangers. Business and other NGO preparedness serves to preserve the integrity and viability of the organization and to protect all human, material, and informational resources.

To be effective, all individuals and organizations involved must do more than simply raise their hazard awareness. A prepared public must also be given the skills that allow them to perform specialized response actions such as search and rescue, first aid, or fire suppression. In recent years, disaster managers have established effective ways to increase public knowledge of disaster preparedness and response activities and got the public to act upon that knowledge. It was long believed that the public was incapable of acting rationally in the face of disaster, but these attitudes have been proved baseless. Studies of actual post-disaster scenarios found that the public acts rationally and effectively, even when frightened or stressed.

JURISDICTIONAL MANAGEMENT AND CONTROL: DEFINING RESPONSIBILITY

Public preparedness education may be carried out by any individual or organization. At the government level, however, such a task may be required or even mandated by local statutes. A community's EOP, or its hazard mitigation plan (HMP), if one exists, may include pre-disaster responsibilities. In most EOPs and HMPs, public education is listed under the responsibilities of a designated official in either the fire department or the Office of Emergency Management. These plans rarely provide any detail about what that task entails, leaving the task for interpretation to the responsible official or agency. With the shortfall of financial and human resources in virtually all emergency services throughout the nation and globally, this function tends to be given low priority or is performed in a cursory fashion. Likewise, many public officials performing this function have not had any training or technical knowledge to perform an effective public education campaign.

Success stories of public education campaigns that are funded, developed, and managed by local government agencies do exist, however. Agencies that recognize the value of public education and possess the resources to carry out an effective campaign have experienced varying yet positive success in their endeavors ranging from good to great. Examples of public education campaigns funded and conducted by government include:

- Washington State "Prepare in a Year" Campaign: Guides personal and family hazards preparedness by promoting a schedule of preparedness tasks that demands no more than one hour per month over a 12-month calendar year (http://bit.ly/1PEKJ12)
- California "Bear Responsibility" Campaign: Promotes a 10-step emergency preparedness program that includes risk identification,

making a plan, making a kit, learning skills, mitigation, and more (http://bit.ly/1KVQCIb)

- Mississippi Emergency Management Agency Preparedness Campaign for Kids: This campaign uses preparedness-themed cartoon animals to communicate preparedness messages to kids. Lessons cover a number of hazards, including earthquakes, floods, tornadoes, hurricanes, and winter weather. Kids who participate in the program can learn how to build their own disaster kit and are awarded a "Disaster Prepared" certificate upon completion (http://bit.ly/1oo5RPK).

More examples of publicly funded and conducted emergency preparedness campaigns can be found in Chapter 7.

Public education is also conducted by the nongovernmental and private sectors. Many NGOs consider disaster preparedness issues as central to their mission, or directly related to their individual programs. For instance, NGOs working with special needs populations, such as the elderly, children, or the poor, might consider the higher vulnerability to hazards typically faced by these groups to be a development issue their expertise could address. Community foundations, to a growing degree, have begun to fund grant requests for projects that seek to increase disaster resilience of one or more groups within the community or of the community as a whole. In addition, several NGOs that have facilitated the long-term recovery in disaster-affected areas are working to decrease the likelihood of a repeat disaster among the affected population by conducting the education necessary to allow victims to help themselves.

Businesses are similarly becoming involved in public emergency preparedness efforts through a sense of civic responsibility to raise the profile of their brand or their products. Businesses are also educating their own employees in recognition that people victimized by disasters are rarely able to return quickly to work. Most businesses participate in these efforts by collaborating with or providing funding to NGOs or government agencies performing public emergency preparedness campaigns in the communities where the businesses operate or where their sales base is located, but some elect to perform the actual education themselves. Either way, their contribution has become a critical element to the greater goal of public emergency preparedness.

Examples of nongovernmental and private-sector public education campaigns include:

- The George Washington University ReadyGW Program—The George Washington University conducts an ongoing disaster preparedness program targeting students and employees. The program includes Web-based information and several on-campus outreach programs. Each year, the Office of Emergency Management holds a Safety Expo on the university grounds that helps connect employees, students, and citizens who live on or near the campus with key preparedness stakeholders like police and fire departments and the National Weather Service, and encourages planning and preparedness activities. The Office of Emergency Management also supports each of the University's departments in their emergency and business continuity planning efforts, and provides a number of training opportunities including disaster exercises.

- Target Corporation, a discount retailer with over 1,800 stores in the United States alone, promotes disaster preparedness among employees and in the communities where it operates. Target provides employees with information about how they can keep themselves and their families safe when a disaster strikes and conducts preparedness drills throughout the year. The company also supports preparedness beyond its fence by supporting the FEMA-managed preparedness program "America's PrepareAthon!" As part of the campaign, Target Corporation supports and engages its employees in community preparedness events throughout the year.

- The Salvation Army, a faith-based international nonprofit organization heavily engaged in emergency management work, promotes disaster preparedness by providing preparedness courses to both affiliated and unaffiliated individuals. The Salvation Army describes the goal of this training to be "to equip individuals to serve during times of crisis." The program, which began in 2004 and which is supported by the Lilly Endowment, covers course topics that include preparedness for senior citizens and people with disabilities, preparing faith-based congregations for disasters, and volunteer management (among many others). Descriptions of all courses can be found at http://bit.ly/1os7WuH.

WHAT IS PUBLIC EMERGENCY PREPAREDNESS?

People in almost all nations, and certainly all of those in the industrialized world, have come to expect that their government will intervene in times of disaster to provide lifesaving assistance. In response, the elected leadership of these nations have taken great measures, in word and in deed, to assure their constituents that response needs would be met should a disaster occur. Despite these promises, the true test of a nation's response capacity comes only when an actual disaster event occurs.

Their success, or lack thereof, is most often a factor of how adequately they have prepared themselves and their public.

Public emergency preparedness equips individuals with the knowledge, skills, or resources necessary to increase their likelihood of survival and to minimize financial and other losses in the event of an emergency or disaster. The justification behind such efforts is the belief that ordinary citizens who are empowered with these tools are better able to help themselves, their families, their neighbors, and their communities. By increasing the resilience of individuals, the collective resilience of the group or population to which they belong also increases.

Individuals take disaster preparedness actions on a daily basis, often without even thinking about them. Glancing at a fire escape diagram upon entering a building, for instance, prepares people with the knowledge required to escape should an alarm sound while they are inside. Scanning the news for weather reports allows people to anticipate any emergency food and water needs. Cutting back overgrown shrubbery around the house provides a firebreak should a wildfire strike. Each of these actions helps individuals to reduce the risk from the unique and wide range of hazards they face.

Preparedness education measures that address disaster risk can range from highly specific, targeting a singular disaster consequence, to more general in nature, encompassing the diverse needs of an all-hazards portfolio. For instance, the Institute for Building and Home Safety (IBHS) is well known for its program that assists day care centers in mitigating the specific consequences associated with seismicity (including falling furniture, books, and fixtures, for instance). On the other end of the spectrum is a FEMA-supported public emergency preparedness initiative called CERT (Community Emergency Response Team) Training. Students enrolled in the CERT course spend several weeks learning the particulars of individual and family planning for emergencies, search and rescue, fire suppression, first aid and disaster counseling, and much more. These skills are designed to prepare students to assist themselves and others in almost any disaster situation they face.

The U.S. Department of Homeland Security (DHS) maintains that public disaster preparedness involves three distinct components:

1. *A kit:* Making a disaster kit that prepares the individual or family to survive emergencies (where essential resources such as water, food, and clothing are in short supply or not available).
2. *A plan:* Making a family disaster plan that allows for family members to locate each other, make contact, join together if possible, access disaster information, and make informed decisions.
3. *Knowledge:* Learning about what hazards exist that affect the individual, how to recognize those hazards when they occur, what the

possible consequences of an associated hazard might be, and what actions can be taken to respond to those various disaster scenarios (e.g., evacuation, sheltering in place, moving to a safer location).

These three steps are reflected in many other campaigns given that the DHS Ready.Gov campaign was designed to serve as a model for state and local emergency management agency efforts in the United States. In terms of preparedness value, the three items include a wide spectrum of activities. However, the most comprehensive campaigns pursue even greater returns by advocating for disaster risk reduction (hazard mitigation) and disaster recovery planning. Unfortunately, the limited time, attention, and capacity of most audiences are significant obstacles that make such lofty goals unreachable.

THE ADVANTAGES OF A TRAINED PUBLIC

Public disaster preparedness education, when successful, is a highly effective way to save lives and reduce property damage. In fact, research has found a positive correlation between increased public knowledge about disaster reduction and preparedness basics and a decreased incidence of death and destruction when an incidence of the particular hazard occurs (Foster 2007). Hazard risk should always be viewed as a dynamic factor (i.e., something that can be altered in a positive or negative way). The action people take will work to either increase or decrease their risk to one or more of the hazards that affect them. By understanding what a hazard is, how to recognize it, and what can be done to mitigate its consequences, individuals can lower their personal hazard vulnerability prior to the occurrence of a disaster. By learning what types of actions can be taken in the event of a disaster, individuals can prepare themselves to respond appropriately to prevent the loss of life and property.

In routine emergency incidents such as car accidents, house fires, and simple criminal acts, local emergency service agencies (fire, police, EMS, and emergency management) are ready and able to assist victims and minimize loss. The magnitude of the consequences associated with major disasters, however, can quickly overwhelm these traditional first-response services, leaving affected residents to fend for themselves for hours or days. By default, these affected individuals become first responders, working to address their own emergency needs and those of their neighbors. Therefore, a prepared public is obviously integral to a community's disaster resilience. When properly informed and educated, members of the general public can learn not only how to recognize a potentially hazardous situation before it occurs but also about what can be done to minimize risk once that disaster becomes imminent.

A disaster-affected population requires an insurmountable measure of supplies and countless skilled practitioners to address their emergency needs. Lifelines will have been cut, critical infrastructure will be damaged or disabled, and a wide range of injuries and fatalities is likely to have occurred in a matter of minutes or hours. The required response capacity of a community's emergency services is directly proportional to the collective response needs of that community. In other words, the greater the vulnerability of the individual citizenry, the greater the burden of the emergency services in the event of a disaster. Likewise, as individuals reduce their vulnerability, so does the community, resulting in less pressure on its emergency services.

Public preparedness efforts empower ordinary citizens to help themselves, their families, their neighbors, and even complete strangers. To be effective, this effort must go beyond simply raising awareness of a hazard and its affiliated risk. Public disaster preparedness education can decrease individual vulnerability in two primary ways—by teaching individuals how to mitigate their hazard risks, and by training them how to respond effectively when a disaster is imminent or has just occurred.

The public can also be provided with skills that prepare them to perform specialized risk reduction actions prior to and during a major disaster. This includes a wide range of functions—from sandbagging to search and rescue, firefighting to first aid, and many other actions that are described in Chapter 3. Until recently, it was thought that the public was incapable of acting rationally in the face of disaster. Response officials feared that victims would panic or would be unable to use preparedness information effectively. However, studies of actual post-disaster scenarios found that the public could act rationally and effectively, even when frightened or stressed. These studies were the ones that first highlighted the need for governments and other agencies to help the public prepare. During its International Decade of Natural Disaster Reduction, the United Nations (UN) introduced the concept that increased disaster risk awareness among the more vulnerable populations of the world is a vital component of any effective national risk reduction strategy. The UN continues this effort through its International Strategy for Disaster Reduction, which identifies public preparedness as one of the four key objectives in establishing greater worldwide disaster resilience.

There have been many situations where an informed public significantly reduced its hazard risk by participating in a public education effort, faring much better than others who did not. Consider the following:

- In 2006, the nongovernmental organization SurfAid began promoting emergency preparedness in 54 tsunami-prone communities in Indonesia. The program, which was funded in large part by an Australian Aid grant of just over $3 million, trained approximately 1,500 volunteers in response actions appropriate for not only tsunamis but also floods, landslides, and epidemics. Topics included first aid, evacuation, basic search and rescue, and others. A warning system which uses large gong-type bells was implemented, and evacuation routes were established. In 2007, when two earthquakes struck, an evacuation was quickly initiated. Over 4,000 structures, including homes, schools, offices, and other community buildings were destroyed, but not one person lost their life—a statistic that the villagers attribute to the preparedness training (Global Education 2017).

- When the 2004 Boxing Day tsunami events struck Southeast and South Asia, more than 200,000 people were killed within several hours. Many fatalities could have been avoided had precursor warning signs been heeded or had there existed widespread knowledge about how tsunamis formed. There were select communities, however, where previously established risk communication was credited for minimizing injuries and deaths as compared with neighboring communities that faced similar impacts. For example, the coastal zones of the Indonesian island Simuelue (population 78,000), which sits very close to the source of the tsunami, were inundated by water only 8 minutes after the magnitude 9.1 earthquake struck that morning. Many of the island's coastal communities were completely destroyed by the rising water and violent waves, but only seven people died. A Humboldt State University geology professor determined that an oral storytelling tradition, which had preserved preparedness knowledge obtained after a 1907 tsunami, had ultimately equipped the local population with the tools they needed to prevent injury and death quickly and effectively (Cairns 2005). The affected local population had learned: "Once in a while large earthquakes are followed by large killer waves, so it's always wise to run to high ground and wait a while, just in case." Other populations had much more time to respond, better telecommunications and warning capabilities, and many more resources at their disposal, but fared much worse, experiencing casualty rates as high as 90% in some regions. Survivors interviewed in those places indicated that they had little or no knowledge of tsunamis, were not aware of what caused them, and did not know what typically preceded them.

- In 2002, Ohio's Van Wert County earned the designation "Storm Ready" by meeting several preparedness and mitigation standards established by NOAA. Part of this certification involved the installation of a public alert system and the carrying out of a public education campaign that instructed residents how to react to warnings. On November 10 of that same year, detection systems indicated a high likelihood of tornadoes, and a warning was issued. Several tornadoes materialized, and 35 people were killed across a number of affected states. Even though Van Wert County fell directly in the path of a particularly destructive tornado, there were no deaths and few injuries. In what became a classic example of the value of preparedness education, all of the employees and patrons of a Van Wert County movie theater destroyed by the tornado survived what would otherwise have been a mass casualty disaster. The theater's employees worked with patrons to move everyone into interior hallways and restrooms as local emergency management officials in the Storm Ready campaign had taught them. When the tornado struck just 28 minutes after the warning was issued, the main seating area of the theater (where more than 50 people had just been sitting) was destroyed. Cars were thrown through the theater walls, landing on several rows of seats, and the theater's roof was torn off (NOAA 2007).

- The CERT program is a U.S. government–supported public disaster preparedness education program that gives detailed mitigation, preparedness, and response training to regular citizens (see Figure 2.5). CERT, which has grown significantly throughout the country since it was created in 1993, helped to significantly bolster the emergency resources available to several of the towns and cities affected by the 2004 hurricane season (Hurricanes Charley, Frances, Ivan, and Jeanne). CERT-trained citizens were put to use by emergency officials in a number of roles, including staffing emergency operations centers and information line phone banks, registering special needs populations for evacuation assistance, performing evacuations, performing traffic control, distributing ice and water, sandbagging, and conducting damage assessments. CERT teams also helped to staff emergency shelters, clear debris on impassable roads, deliver food, and perform many other activities that would likely have been staff deficient were it not for these pre-trained individuals. In total, more than 4,000 trained CERT team members participated in the response to these events (FL Citizen Corps 2004).

- When Cyclone Pam struck the small Pacific island nation Vanuatu with sustained 150 mph winds in March of 2015, almost half of the country's population was affected. Virtually all crops were destroyed, and housing damage was so great as to leave 75,000 homeless. Damage to infrastructure left over 100,000 people without access to water. High levels of disaster preparedness among the population were credited to the

FIGURE 2.5   Charleston County, South Carolina. CERT students practice the use of "cribbing" to remove a trapped disaster victim. (Courtesy of Jim Tarter, Charleston County Emergency Preparedness Division.)

extremely low number of fatalities, which were limited to just 11 people. Preparedness education came from several fronts. To begin with, representatives from local "community disaster committees" that had been established by the UN Development Programme supported by a grant from the NGO CARE visited every household in the affected areas, and explained how and why to prepare (UNDP, 2015).

CONCLUSION

Emergency management is a pivotal function of government. However, the public is an important, if not vital, stakeholder in the process. In fact, experience has proven that individuals possess the capacity to do more to save their own lives and those of their friends, families, and neighbors in the first hours of a disaster than any formal emergency services agency. The roots of emergency management and its associated functions and skills may be ancient, but without effective education and training programs in place, individuals are not likely to incorporate the profession's risk reduction practices into their lives and routines. Governmental, nongovernmental, and private entities have made significant efforts to educate their citizens, employees, or other stakeholder audiences about emergency preparedness, and many of these efforts have resulted in increased resilience that saved lives during disasters. Application of risk communication practices, as detailed in the following chapters, can help organizations of any size achieve the same success.

REFERENCES

Ansell, Jake and Frank Wharton. 1992. *Risk: Analysis, Assessment, and Management*. Chichester, England: Wiley.

Cairns, Ann. 2005. *Disaster Lessons: What You Don't Know Can Kill You*. Geological Society of America. http://bit.ly/2iqsrHZ

Colbert, Elias and Everett Chamberlin. 2011. *The Ruined City*. GreatChicagoFire.Org. Accessed 08/05/2016. http://bit.ly/2aVJKPR.

Derby, Stephen L., and Ralph L. Keeney. 1981. Risk Analysis: Understanding "How Safe Is Safe Enough?" *Risk Analysis*, 1(3), 217–224.

FEMA (Federal Emergency Management Agency). 1997. *Multi Hazard Identification and Assessment*. Washington, DC: FEMA.

FEMA (Federal Emergency Management Agency). 2005. *FEMA Mitigation Directorate*. www.fema.gov/about/divisions/mitigation.shtm

FEMA (Federal Emergency Management Agency). 2017. Federal Insurance and Mitigation Administration. FEMA Website. http://bit.ly/2jKBhC7. Accessed January 2017.

FL Citizen Corps. 2004. *Florida CERT—Makes a Difference in the 2004 Hurricane Season*.

Foster, Chad. 2007. On the Line. *Natural Hazards Observer*, 31(3), 9–11. http://bit.ly/2jCtnXr

Global Education. 2017. *Saving Lives with Disaster Preparedness*. Global Education. http://bit.ly/1PS8yQM. Accessed January 2017.

Guha-Sapir, Debarati, Philippe Hoyois, and Regina Below. 2015. *Annual Disaster Statistical Review 2014: The Numbers and Trends*. Brussels: Center for Research on the Epidemiology of Disasters, Universite Catholique de Louvain.

NOAA. 2007. *"StormReady" Label Proves Correct for Ohio County in Recent Tornado Outbreak*. National Weather Service. http://www.weather.gov/stormready/vanwert.htm. Accessed January 2017.

Risk and Insurance Management Society. 2014. *What Is ERM?* RIMS Website. Accessed 03/2015. http://bit.ly/1AGKUOu.

Smith, Keith. 1992. *Environmental Hazards: Assessing Risk and Reducing Disaster*. New York: Routledge.

CHAPTER 3

The Campaign—Step 1
Early Planning

INTRODUCTION

Successful emergency preparedness campaigns require adequate planning, staffing, and funding, and must be based upon a comprehensive understanding of the target audience. Far too many efforts have failed as a result of a single major flaw in design: an overlooked cultural taboo, a budget that fell short of actual costs, a lack of community support, or an unreceptive audience.

However daunting these requirements may seem, project failure is rarely inevitable. By subscribing to a regimented planning and project management framework, like the one suggested in this text, program planners can ensure that their message coverage and program outcomes are maximized. Well-laid plans, initiated in the earliest stages of the campaign, allow for the flexibilities often needed when variables and assumptions shift, thereby helping the project team to work efficiently through problems as they arise. The adage, "failing to plan is planning to fail" certainly rings true in the realm of communication campaigns. Moreover, although adequate project planning may seem overwhelming at first, there are always ways to make it happen. The NIH writes that:

> Making health communication programs work requires planning, but planning need not be a long-term, time-consuming activity. Nor should all the activities [be conducted all at once], before any other actions are taken. Planning is easiest and best done bit by bit—related to and just in time for the programmatic tasks it governs. For example, you need certain kinds of information about the intended audiences in order to define them, select them, and set objectives. You need different information to guide message development; gather each type as you need it. (National Cancer Institute 2004)

Proper planning can be the dividing factor between an organization that succeeds in influencing peoples' behavior and another that churns out unread brochures. At the project outset, the planning process may take time, but over the course of the campaign, it will ultimately save time by providing much-needed focus and direction, setting the project on an attainable course. Planning should be considered important for all of the following reasons and more:

- It helps you to better understand the hazards and the associated risk.
- It delineates the role your organization is best suited to play in targeting those hazard risks.
- It helps you to better understand who your audience is, why they are at risk, what they know and do not know about their risk, what they can and cannot do to change their risk, and how they learn about risk.
- It helps you to identify solutions that have a high chance of effecting behavioral change.
- It helps you to determine what you will say, how you will say it, and who will do the talking.
- It helps you to manage your project, prioritize tasks, assign individual roles and responsibilities, and budget the funds required to complete the project.
- It helps you to identify obstacles before they derail your successes.

Chapter 3 through Chapter 6 will present and explain an easy-to-follow structure by which emergency preparedness education campaigns may be planned, conducted, and assessed. Chapter 3 describes the early planning phase, beginning with identification of the problem that is to be addressed—namely the hazard or hazards and their associated risk. This is followed by the critical process of target audience identification, which allows program planners to have a sound understanding of those with whom they will be communicating, including their demographics and psychographics (personality and thought characteristics), their vulnerabilities, their perceptions of risk, and the medium through which they are most likely to receive their information. Using this hazard and audience information, program planners will be able to identify appropriate solutions to be communicated, and to establish project goals and objectives. Early planning also involves forming a planning team and coalition, identifying and securing partners and stakeholders, identifying potential obstacles, and planning to manage the project.

DEFINE THE PROBLEM

All public education efforts begin with the identification of a problem or problems that are to be addressed. In the case of emergency management, the problem relates to the vulnerability to a known hazard. Individuals and population groups are often affected by hazards differently due to a variety of social and behavioral factors both at the individual and community level, including physical location, availability and access to resources, knowledge, abilities, perceptions, norms, and others. Therefore, the program planner must first identify and understand the source of the risk as well as the actions and behaviors that contribute to vulnerability, and then determine the most realistic and efficient methods for reducing or eliminating that vulnerability.

The process of defining the problem involves the following steps:

1. Identify and analyze the hazard risk
2. Define the target population
3. Identify appropriate solutions

Identify and Analyze the Hazard Risk

The first step in defining the problem is to identify and analyze the hazard that will be managed. Obviously, program planners need to know exactly what hazard they will be addressing if they are to adequately provide the public with risk reduction information. A *hazard* is defined as any event or physical condition that has the *potential* to cause fatalities, injuries, property damage, infrastructure damage, agricultural loss, environmental damage, interruption of business, or other types of harm or loss. There are many individual hazards that affect us on a personal or family level, such as a fall, minor crime, choking, drowning, or car accident, for example. However, disaster preparedness public education efforts focus on those hazards for which the consequences may be so great as to overwhelm the local capacity to respond. These events, by definition, are disasters. Coppola (2006) classifies common hazards into three categories: (1) natural, (2) technological, and (3) intentional.

1. *Natural hazards* are those that originate from natural processes and include the following subcategories:
   a. *Tectonic hazards* (earthquakes, tsunamis, volcanoes)
   b. *Mass-movement hazards* (landslides, rockslides, debris flows, avalanches, land subsidence, land expansion)
   c. *Hydrologic hazards* (floods, drought, desertification)

    d. *Meteorological hazards* (hurricanes, tornadoes, ice storms, severe weather, hail, extreme temperatures, windstorms, sand storms, wildfires, thunderstorms, fog)

    e. *Biological hazards* (human epidemic or pandemic, animal epidemic, plant epidemic, plagues)

    f. *Other natural hazards* (e.g., meteors, salinization) that do not fall into any of these categories

2. *Technological hazards* are those that are artificial in origin, but for which there is no malicious intent, including:

    a. Transportation hazards (infrastructure failure or damage, airline accidents, rail accidents, maritime accidents, roadway accidents)

    b. Infrastructure hazards (power failure, telecommunications failure, computer network failure, water/sewer failure, gas distribution failure, dam failure, food shortage, overburdened public health system, economic failure)

    c. Industrial hazards (HazMat processing or storage accidents, explosion, fire, raw materials extraction accident)

    d. Structure fires or failures

3. *Intentional hazards* are those for which there exists malicious intent, including:

    a. Terrorism

    b. Civil unrest

    c. Stampedes

    d. Crime

    e. War

Generally, if it is the program planners' intention to address the vulnerability to a single hazard—earthquakes, for instance—then there is no need to conduct a full hazard identification for the community. However, if the goal of the campaign is overall emergency preparedness (for all possible hazards), program planners will need to determine all major hazards that threaten the community. This is performed using any of the following information sources:

- Community historical records
- City or county emergency operations plan
- City or county hazard mitigation plan
- Local emergency management officials
- Local libraries
- Local colleges or universities
- Local or county floodplain manager
- Local chapter of the American Red Cross
- Local emergency planning committee (LEPC)

Once identified, a hazard must be profiled and analyzed to determine the likelihood and consequence components of its associated risk, and to provide program planners with a better understanding of how it affects the community. The more completely a hazard is understood, the better the risk program planners can successfully address it among the target population.

A risk assessment tells program planners how often the hazard will likely occur, and what will happen if it does. Risk consists of likelihood and consequence. The risk component can be expressed as a probability (e.g., 50% chance of occurrence in a given year) or a frequency (e.g., occurs once per decade). The consequence component of risk measures the human (deaths and injuries), structural, economic, and environmental effects that would occur if the hazard resulted in a disaster.

Because few organizations have the time, expertise, or resources to conduct a full hazard risk assessment, it is recommended that organizations obtain hazard analysis information from the city, county, or state office of emergency management. Almost all offices of emergency management—which may be a stand-alone department or part of the fire or police departments—will have conducted such an assessment as required by law, and will likely be willing to share all or relevant excerpts of this assessment for the purposes of a public preparedness campaign. These assessments will likely include much of the information that is needed to complete a hazard profile. The hazard profile is a tool that provides program planners with all the hazard information they need to begin identifying a target population and vulnerability reduction solutions in one place, including:

- The hazard name and description
- The hazard frequency or probability, including historical incidences, predicted future frequency or probability, and magnitude and potential intensity
- The geographic range of the hazard (what is affected in the community), including property, infrastructure, and populations
- Duration of the hazard
- Seasonal or other time-based patterns associated with the hazard
- Speed of onset of the hazard
- Availability of warnings

Define the Target Population

A difficult yet pivotal step in planning any communication campaign is the identification and definition of the population to be targeted by its messages. In the hazard identification and analysis step, program planners identify many different populations and groups that are vulnerable to the effects of the hazard in question. However, each group and individual differs with regard to vulnerability; abilities and capacities to mitigate, prepare, respond, or recover; and methods for receiving and processing information. In other words, there can be no single solution that meets everyone's needs equally.

Generally, program planners should limit their message to a single target audience to which the campaign will be tailored, or define each audience individually in order to tailor solutions, messages, and communication methods to each. Because resources are always limited, and it is therefore impossible to reach all audiences effectively, planners must prioritize the audience that will be the intended target of their message. It is important to note that the designated target audience is not always the most vulnerable group in the broader population. When choosing a target audience for a given campaign, program designers should identify the most vulnerable group *that has the means and the will to benefit from the campaign.* Sometimes, the most vulnerable group is at risk because of their own unwillingness or inability to take the proper protective behavior. For example, members of an extremely religious sector of a particular population may refuse to take protective action because they interpret such action as a challenge to God's will. Although it is certainly possible to design campaign messages to alter risky beliefs and norms, these types of changes are likely to happen very slowly over long periods of time, so a single intervention is unlikely to successfully motivate behavior change in time to mitigate an imminent threat. In this case, although the religious group may be the most vulnerable segment of the population, it may save more people to target a group whose vulnerability stems from simple lack of knowledge or awareness than deep-seated religious beliefs. Therefore, in selecting a target population, program planners must consider the time frame, money, and resources available in order to determine which target audience should be encouraged to enact what behaviors to produce the most "bang" for the campaign's "buck."

In many ways, the particulars of the selected target population determine all other factors—what messages must be developed, how those messages are communicated, what risk reduction options are possible, and what results are likely to be achieved. By learning as much as possible about the target audience, program planners will increase their chances of success immeasurably.

Defining a target population helps to ensure that message content and delivery are best suited to meet the particular needs of the intended individuals program planners hope to reach. In the business sector, this process is commonly referred to as *market research*. Market research is performed to define the individual and social features of a target audience in order to maximize "product sales". In public education, the process is almost identical, with the product being an idea or a way of thinking.

As is true with any product, the sales pitch behind that idea must be designed for the recipient population—their comprehension, attitudes, biases, and purchasing power, among many other factors.

All audiences, small or large, can be subdivided into smaller and smaller definable groups. The more defined a target audience becomes, the more targeted a communication campaign can be tailored to suit those individual characteristics. However, increasing specificity generally raises costs and lowers campaign reach. Program planners must decide how particular they wish to make their audience profile.

Audience profiling is critical because the ways in which people receive messages and interpret information are by no means uniform. For example, while children learn primarily through teachers, peers, and the other members of their families, their parents may be more likely to educate themselves through newspapers, social networks, and television. However, even as a group, parents may differ in how they learn according to their level of education, age, and social networks. It is easy to see how each group can differ so much in its learning mechanisms when one considers all of the possible demographic characteristics that define individual members, including socioeconomic status, education, race, gender, age, and employment.

Audiences are categorized primarily by demographics and defining characteristics. The most basic determination is geography—residents of a community, city, county, floodplain, or state, for example. More often, geography is a secondary defining characteristic from within which a smaller segment of the population is determined. The actual group that is chosen will more likely be determined by the interests of the organization conducting the campaign, a particularly high vulnerability among only certain members of the general population, or some other factor that is of special importance to the organization or group conducting the campaign.

The following list is provided to give a sampling of the more common headings under which the myriad identifiable characteristics describing target populations are found. Ultimately, the chosen target population members will be described using defining characteristics from several of these categories. For example, the selected target population could be "poor families with young children in rural areas of Montana."

Population by location

- Jurisdiction (generally set by political boundaries—either town, city, county, state, or nationwide)
- Risk area (selection may be based on the location of a community in a highly vulnerable and hazard-prone zone, its accessibility in the event of a disaster, its disaster history, and its local resources)
- By place of residence or employment

- *Physical or mental ability:* There are approximately 57 million people in the United States classified as having a disability—nearly one-fifth of the population. Limitations in mobility, seeing, hearing, or learning complicate emergency responses and therefore require extra planning. The Centers for Disease Control and Prevention's (CDC) National Center on Birth Defects and Developmental Disabilities (NCBDDD) developed a Webpage with helpful information about emergency preparedness for people with disabilities as well as emergency managers, responders, service, and care providers (NCBDDD, 2016). It is recommended that program planners reference these resources when planning to target people with specific disabilities. Within the category of disabilities, there are defining characteristics that will guide how messages are formed. For instance, people who are deaf have one set of individual preparedness concerns, and they will receive information one way, while those with a physical handicap such as the loss of one or more limbs will have different concerns and will receive their information (as a group) in a different manner.
- *Urban or rural livelihoods:* The type of communal settlement within which a population resides determines not only its risks but also the means by which its members receive information and what options they have for preparing for disasters. For instance, while residents of cities may benefit from robust media markets, they also face many unique hazard risks not faced by most rural populations (e.g., the presence of critical infrastructure, an increased risk of international terrorism). Rural populations, however, may face risks and conditions unique to their living situation, including fewer emergency management resources and more dispersed social networks. Research has found that natural disasters are more likely to affect nonmetropolitan areas, which make up about 75% of the nation's total land area.
- *Income:* Low-income population groups demand special attention because they often lack access to disaster information through traditional delivery systems like television and radio. Furthermore, low-income groups are more likely to be located in high-risk areas or near infrastructure susceptible to accidents or intentional acts, such as train stations, railroad tracks, and chemical plants.
- *Transience:* Populations that exist within a geographic area who do not consider that area their permanent residence often have special vulnerabilities that differ greatly from that of the general population. Transient populations include tourists, business travelers, student residents, and seasonal workers, for example.

- *Religion:* Members of different religious affiliations will perceive, prepare for, and respond to hazards and disasters in different ways as determined by their religious beliefs and rules. These affiliations will also define how they receive and process information, both important factors to program planners.
- *Age:* Members of different age groups differ greatly from one another in terms of abilities, perceptions, and many other factors. The most common delineations of populations by age include children, adolescents, adults, and seniors, although there are many other groupings that are possible in order to best meet the needs of communicators (see Figure 3.1).
- *Gender:* Although differences between genders are decreasing in the United States with regard to emergency preparedness, there are still differences in the ways that men and women receive and process information, as well as how they perceive risks.
- *Literacy:* Program planners must have an understanding of the education levels of target audience members, as this will help them to design their message content and means for delivery.
- *Ethnicity:* Ethnicity can be an important factor in determining spokespeople, as members of ethnic groups may hold an inherent

FIGURE 3.1   Fire and police department officials are especially effective communicators for transmitting preparedness and prevention messages to children (Author photo).

trust or distrust in certain sources of information (government officials or police officers, for example).

- *Employment or school status:* This characteristic is important because it can help program planners better understand target population members' financial or time resources, and help them determine the best means to reach them. Examples of subgroups under this heading include the employed, the unemployed, retirees, workers in specific occupations, and students.
- *Psychographics:* People differ greatly in terms of their psychological profiles. This can include their attitudes, outlooks, self-image, opinions, beliefs, values, and many other personality traits.
- *Health:* People who enjoy good health can differ from those with general or specific ailments with regard to their perception of risk, their ability to change behavior, or other factors.
- *Language:* Language is one of the most fundamental requirements of communication. Program planners must have a full understanding of the language abilities of their target population in order to determine what language is most appropriate for campaign messages.

Other defining characteristics include housing type, family status, preferred method of transportation, business affiliation, culture, and behavior. The number of defining characteristics is almost limitless. While it is important to define the target audience as fully as possible, it is also important not to define it so narrowly that there are few individuals who fit the defined profile.

The most comprehensive source of data and information available to drive the process by which audiences are defined is the U.S. Census. Conducted every 10 years, and estimated periodically between official counts, the official census can provide a wide range of information on populations within given jurisdictional and administrative boundaries. These data are especially useful in determining income, age, gender, household, employment, ethnicity, and many other demographic factors. However, the census will not give program planners psychographic information that helps them understand audience perceptions, attitudes, learning patterns, and other important factors. To acquire this kind of information, program planners will need to rely upon other methods of information collection. The best way to ensure that your program messages are audience appropriate is to include members of the target audience in the program planning process. Other ways to collect this information include:

- Interviews with members of the target population
- Group meetings with representatives from the target population

- Meetings with or assistance from individuals, organizations, or agencies that regularly serve or work with the target population (e.g., teachers, NGOs, religious organizations, service organizations, corporations, foundations, fire departments, counselors, newspapers)
- Social science research publications
- Data maintained by polling companies or depositories of polling information
- Chambers of commerce
- Advertising agencies, newspapers, and radio and television stations (for media-use data and buying and consumption patterns)

Once the primary audience has been identified, program planners begin to profile the members of this group in order to learn as much as they can about their particular needs, preferences, and characteristics. The more that is known about the primary audience, the better the message can be designed, delivered, and timed. To ensure maximum impact, planners should try to establish a baseline by answering the following questions:

- What people make up this group? Are they children, adults, senior citizens, students, homemakers, business executives, blue-collar workers, single, or married?
- What are the special characteristics and needs of this group? Consider such factors as age, education and literacy levels, gender, occupation, motivations, cultural and social interests, activities, and preferred entertainment options.
- What specific hazard consequences (from the hazard in question) affect members of this group?
- How are members of this group at particular risk from the consequences of the hazard (vulnerability)?
- Risk perception (see Sidebar 3.1):
- What does this group already know about the hazard?
- What disaster knowledge do they lack?
- What misinformation (inaccurate beliefs) do they possess?
- How does this hazard measure up in comparison to the concerns and fears they hold for all hazards?
- What specific characteristics of this audience place them at an increased risk from the hazard (see Figure 3.2)?
- What abilities does this group have to address risk and vulnerability?
- What desires does this group have to reduce their vulnerability?
- What social, cultural, or economic obstacles does this group face in minimizing vulnerability?
- What social or cultural factors would help to affect change or influence message delivery?

FIGURE 3.2   Fire danger signs in Western Australia placed along high-traffic routes and in public parks help alert citizens to current risk factors (Author photo).

- What benefits do members of this group associate with behavior change?
- From what sources does this group typically receive information? This could include newspapers, television, radio, mail, town meetings, informal social networks, parents, and peers.
- When are members of this group most receptive to messages?
- Where are members of this group most apt to receive information?
- Who are the most influential voices for this group (e.g., role models, teachers, parents, relatives, leaders, etc.) Are there other people in this community to whom this group listens and respects (e.g., elders or clergy), often called *gatekeepers*?

SIDEBAR 3.1 RISK PERCEPTION

The branch of science that studies why people fear the things they do (and why they do not fear other things) is called *risk perception*. Understanding trends in public risk perception helps to explain why, for instance, millions of people in the Washington, D.C., metropolitan area were so disproportionately afraid of the Washington, D.C., sniper in 2002 even though they were statistically less vulnerable to that than, for instance, automobile accidents, food poisoning, heart disease, or cancer. Risk perception is a primary factor, though not the only factor, that determines whether people prepare for the hazards they face.

In their article, "Rating the Risks," Slovic et al. (1979) stated, "People respond to the hazards they perceive." These scientists discovered that people tend to misjudge their risk according to four risk perception fallibility conclusions, namely:

1. Cognitive limitations, coupled with the anxieties generated by facing life as a gamble, cause uncertainty to be denied, risks to be distorted, and statements of fact to be believed with unwarranted confidence.
2. Perceived risk is influenced (and sometimes biased) by the imaginability and memorability of the hazard. Therefore, people may not have valid perceptions even for familiar risks.
3. Risk management experts' risk perceptions correspond closely to statistical frequencies of death. Laypeople's risk perceptions are based in part on frequencies of death, but there are some striking discrepancies. It appears that for laypeople, the concept of risk includes qualitative aspects such as dread and the likelihood of a mishap being fatal. Laypeople's risk perceptions are also affected by catastrophic potential.
4. Disagreements about risk should not be expected to evaporate in the presence of evidence. Definitive evidence, particularly about rare hazards, is difficult to obtain. Weaker information is likely to be interpreted in a way that reinforces existing beliefs (Slovic et al. 1979).

People tend to fear a hazard risk less as they become better informed with more specific details of the risk. However, the amount a person can discover about a risk will almost never be complete, as the actual likelihood or consequence most risks pose cannot be quantified in a way that addresses the specific threat faced by individuals (even well-known risks such as cancer or heart disease) (Ropeik 2002). The more uncertainty a risk poses, or as Slovic, Fischhoff, and Lichtenstein state, "the more of a gamble something is," the more people will fear it. In the face of uncertainty, people will consciously or subconsciously make personal judgments based upon imperfect information in order to establish some individual concept of the risk they face (Slovic et al. 1979). These judgments, based upon uncertainties and imperfect information, often cause people to wrongly perceive their own risk, more often in a way that *overstates* reality.

People are more afraid of those things that they can imagine or that they can remember. These easily *available* risks, as they are

called, tend to be overestimated regarding their likelihood of occurrence. For instance, we rarely hear about a person dying from a common cause such as a heart attack, unless somebody close to us dies
of that specific cause. However, the media will often heavily report on
a death that is the result of an uncommon cause, like the West Nile
Virus. The result tends to be that people underestimate common risks
and overestimate rare risks. Generally, people fear what they hear
about repetitively or constantly. This phenomenon is referred to as
the *availability heuristic*, which states that people perceive an event
to be likely or frequent if instances of the event are *easy to imagine
or recall*. This is a perception bias that can be correct when considering events that are, in fact, frequently observed, such as in the case
of those who believe that automobile accidents are common because
almost everyone they know has been involved in one. However, when
a risk that is spectacular but not necessarily common receives constant media attention, such as high school shootings did in the 1990s
(in particular, the Columbine attack), people often wrongly assume
that similar events are very likely to occur.

It can be difficult for people to understand the statistics they are
given, and even more difficult for them to conceptualize how those
statistics apply to them personally. Furthermore, statistics tend to do
little to affect the way people perceive the risks that are calculated.
This is not to say that the average person lacks sufficient intelligence
to process numbers; it is just that the numbers are not the sole source
of influence on public risk perception. It has been discovered through
extensive research that people use other, more heavily weighted,
qualitative factors in addition to the quantitative likelihood of a hazard
resulting in personal consequence when ranking their risks (Slovic
et al. 1979). People are usually more concerned with the consequence
component of risk than they are about the likelihood component.

Slovic, Fischhoff, and Lichtenstein, in their article, "Facts and Fears:
Understanding Perceived Risk," proposed that there are 18 risk characteristics that influence public risk perception (Slovic, et. al. 1980). Of these
characteristics, 17 fall under two subgroups called *factors*: factors related
to dread (Factor 1) and factors related to how much is known about the
risk (Factor 2). Using these 17 characteristics, they examined public perceptions of 90 risks and plotted their findings on a two-dimensional graph
depicting Factor 1 on the x-axis and Factor 2 on the y-axis.

Factor 1
  Dreaded versus not dreaded
  Uncontrollable versus controllable
  Global catastrophic versus not global catastrophic
  Consequences fatal versus consequences not fatal

Not equitable versus equitable
Catastrophic versus individual
High risk to future generations versus low risk to future
    generations
Not easily reduced versus easily reduced
Risk increasing versus risk decreasing
Involuntary versus voluntary
Affects me versus does not affect me
Not preventable versus preventable

Factor 2
Not observable versus observable
Unknown to those exposed versus known to those exposed
Effect delayed versus effect immediate
New risk versus old risk
Risks unknown to science versus risks known to science

Risks that are typified by the first-listed characteristic (on the left) in each factor-pair listed above are seen as more dangerous than those that are exhibited by the second-listed characteristic (on the right). For example, uncontrollable risks are more feared than controllable ones.

Slovic et al. (1979) state that "people's beliefs change slowly and are extraordinarily persistent in the face of contrary evidence. New evidence appears reliable and informative if it is consistent with one's initial belief; contrary evidence is dismissed as unreliable, errone-ous, or unrepresentative." They add that "convincing people that the catastrophe they fear is extremely unlikely is difficult under the best conditions." This stoicism is compounded by the fact that once people make their initial judgments, they believe with overwhelming confidence that their beliefs are correct. This phenomenon, called the "overconfidence heuristic," states that people often are unaware of how little they know about a risk, and how much more information they need to make an informed decision. More often than not, people believe that they know much more about risks than they actually do.

Risk perception factors into what is called a "worldview." Worldviews are conceptualized as "...general societal, cultural, and political attitudes that appear to have an influence over people's judgments about complex issues" (Slovic 1999). Studies have found strong correlations between worldviews and risk perceptions (e.g., Dake 1992; Jenkins-Smith 1993). Some specific worldviews that have been investigated (e.g., Buss et al. 1986; Dake 1991; Jasper 1990) are the following:

- *Fatalism:* Characterized by those who feel that they have little control over their own fate.

- *Hierarchy:* Typifies those who prefer to leave risk decisions to the experts.
- *Individualism:* Associated with those who believe that those with greater ability should earn more.
- *Egalitarianism:* Describes those who feel that the source of many of the world's problems is inequality.
- *Technological enthusiasm:* Depicts those who trust in advances in technology to improve health and societal well-being.

While these categories are not mutually exclusive and this list is certainly not exhaustive, the purpose of their inclusion in this chapter is to emphasize the importance of doing formative research about the characteristics of one's target audience that shape their perceptions of risk before trying to craft messages to change their risk-related behaviors. An in-depth discussion of all findings associated with differential risk perceptions is outside the realm of this book, but practitioners can greatly benefit from conducting their own literature searches involving their specific population of interest before designing campaigns. Several theories of communication and psychology provide lists of important elements to consider when engaging in this type of formative research. See Chapter 4 for further discussion.

In relatively recent years, researchers have called attention to the limitations posed by assessing risk strictly in terms of quantifiable scientific certainties. Risk communication scholars emphasize the importance of considering risk perceptions, intuitive risk judgments that citizens rely on to evaluate hazards, in addition to the technologically advanced methods used by analysts when making risk assessments. As argued by renowned risk communication scholar Paul Slovic (1987):

> Lay people sometimes lack certain information about hazards. However, their basic conceptualization about risk is much richer than that of experts and reflects legitimate concerns that are typically omitted from expert risk assessments. Efforts are destined to fail unless they are structured as a two-way process. Each side, expert and public, has something valid to contribute. Each side must respect the insights and intelligence of the other. (p. 285)

Of the variety of audience characteristics that are important to planners, there are some that may facilitate change; others that may hamper it; and yet others that, while they seem important, may have little overall impact. The ability of the planning team to analyze these audience characteristics, and to identify the strengths, weaknesses, opportunities, and obstacles regarding how that audience receives and retains information, is key to the campaign's outcome. The following examples illustrating how particular audience characteristics can influence public education is adapted from Bernstein, et al. (1994, 627 and 631):

1. *Age:* Younger people are more likely to change their attitudes than older ones, perhaps because they are more receptive to opinions and input from others, and have yet to build a base of experiences that may firm up their own attitudes. The receptivity of children to developing positive attitudes toward emergency preparedness can have a substantial influence on overall community disaster education efforts. An application of this principle can be found in emergency preparedness educational efforts in schools, which can have a powerful effect on how children approach disaster hazards at home.

2. *Intelligence:* Some argue that highly intelligent audiences will understand the persuasive arguments, and thus be more likely to change their attitudes and behavior. Others suggest that such individuals will challenge the logic of the arguments (i.e., "counter-argue") and will be more likely to find flaws in the presentation, and therefore not change at all. Research suggests that the degree to which people focus on understanding and enacting the recommendations rather than counter-arguing against the recommendations is a function of the extremity of the position taken in the argument and how involved audience members are with the topic. Audience intelligence alone is not a reliable correlate with susceptibility to persuasion. However, if the recommendation is not promoting a severe change and if the audience does not seem to hold a firm position on the topic, people of higher intelligence are probably more likely to successfully follow the plan.

3. *Self-esteem:* Those with low self-esteem tend to value the attitudes of others more but at the same time may be incompletely attentive to events around them. Thus, while susceptible to persuasive arguments, those with low self-esteem may not think about them enough to effect change. In contrast, those with high self-esteem pay attention to others, but their self-confidence precludes susceptibility to change. The American Red Cross recommends personalizing the disaster preparedness issue by reinforcing for people that they can effectively prepare for a disaster. "Tell them: 'You can do this; you can get ready; it's something you can do now.' People get more involved when they feel they are in control over their situation"

(American Red Cross 1992, p. 80). This technique can also increase self-efficacy (discussed in Chapter 4).

4. *Relevance of the topic/involvement*: If the topic being discussed is highly relevant to the audience, they are more likely to pay attention to the message. Strongly presented arguments are thought to increase source credibility, thereby increasing the effectiveness of the message. Therefore, in most cases, the more important the topic is to those in the audience, the more they will be receptive to strongly presented arguments. However, the increased attention that comes with high involvement is also associated with greater scrutinizing of the message. Therefore, weak arguments are more likely to be rejected by highly involved audience members than by those to whom the topic is not relevant. In contrast, as noted in Chapter 1, those who are not highly involved with the issue are more likely to be persuaded by simple heuristic cues such as the number of arguments presented (regardless of their strength) and the credibility of the speaker.

Program planners often seek to address two very different audience types when they set out to affect a behavior change in a population. In both groups, program planners are trying to bring about a certain behavior, but the type of behavior sought is what places individuals in one group or the other. The first and most obvious group is called the *primary intended audience*. This audience includes those individuals whose hazard vulnerability program planners are trying to reduce. There may be one primary intended audience, or several different primary intended audiences, depending on how much segmentation is performed by planners (see Sidebar 3.2). *Secondary intended audiences*, or gateway audiences as they are also called, are those with influence on the primary intended audiences or those who must do something to help cause the change in the primary intended audiences. This group also requires behavior change, but the type of behavior relates to their interaction with the primary intended audience, not with their hazard vulnerability. For this reason, it is often the case that different kinds of messages and tools need to be developed if program planners decide to utilize the assistance of this valuable (and sometimes vital) resource.

SIDEBAR 3.2   SEGMENTATION

Defining subgroups of a population according to common characteristics is called *segmentation*. Segmentation can help program planners develop messages, materials, and activities that are relevant to the intended audience's current behavior and specific needs, preferences, beliefs, cultural attitudes, knowledge, and reading habits. It also helps to identify the best channels for reaching each group, because populations also differ in factors such as access to information, the information sources they find reliable, and how they prefer to learn. Program planners may increase a program's effectiveness by developing strategies that are attuned to the needs and wants of different intended audience segments. In fact, given the diversity of the public, trying to reach everyone with one message or strategy may result in an approach that does not effectively reach those most able or ready to change. Be aware, though, that moving from a mass-market strategy to a differentiated strategy will add economic and staff resource costs for each additional segment. The key to success is to segment the intended population on characteristics relevant to the disaster preparedness behavior to be changed. A logical starting point is the behavior itself. When possible, compare those who engage in the desired behavior with those who do not and identify the determinants of their behavior. Many planners simply rely on demographic, physical, or cultural segmentations. However, people who share these characteristics can be very different in terms of preparedness behavior.

Identify Appropriate Solutions

Once the hazards have been identified and the target population has been defined, program planners need to begin formulating the solution they intend to communicate. This solution will be a preparedness measure, a mitigation measure, or a combination of both. Moreover, while there are several possible solutions to each hazard vulnerability, the chosen solution will be the one that, given the particular characteristics of the target audience, is most likely to succeed.

Defining solutions understandably requires a working knowledge of both the hazard and the population vulnerable to it, as was determined in the previous two steps. Program planners begin to identify the most appropriate solution by identifying all possible solutions. From this list, they weigh the benefits, costs, and likelihood of audience members taking the proposed actions, in order to select the best alternative.

Mitigation solutions work by decreasing either the likelihood of a disaster occurring or the consequences of a disaster should one actually occur. Preparedness measures allow an individual or group to respond more effectively to a disaster once it happens, through action or equipment. In selecting the appropriate solution, program planners will need to fully understand not only how the mitigation or preparedness option works (from conception to implementation, including maintenance) but also how these factors are influenced by the particular characteristics of the target population.

Each mitigation or preparedness option may be analyzed according to the following factors, as each relates specifically to the target population:

- Benefit (the amount of actual vulnerability reduction)
- Cost (in financial terms, to the individual)
- Time (required to implement or maintain the solution)
- Availability (of materials, resources, and expertise that are required to implement the solution)
- Secondary negative consequences
- Sustainability
- Target audience obstacles (problems—ideological, cultural, technical, or other—that the population will have with the solution)
- Feasibility obstacles (problems that are independent of the target population that would make implementation of the solution difficult or impossible)
- Likelihood that individual members of the population will take the mitigation or preparedness action
- What, if any, segment of the population is already taking this action, and their successes and failures in doing so

This is the point of program development in which communication theory may first provide insight as well. When considering the most desirable solution to promote through the program, it is important to consider *why* the target population is not already engaging in protective behavior against the hazard. Is it a simple lack of awareness that they are at risk, or is it something deeper such as a cultural norm or a widespread fear that will need to be addressed within the program's message? The behavioral theories detailed in Chapter 4 of this book list constructs that may serve as a checklist that program planners may use to identify barriers to the recommended behavior among the target population. Consideration of these barriers and the time and resources that would be necessary to break them down should factor into the process of identifying an appropriate and realistic solution.

Based upon these assessments, program planners are able to make more informed decisions about what actions will have the greatest overall effect in reducing population vulnerability. Remember that there is no perfect solution, so the option that brings about the greatest change is preferred above the rest.

With the hazard identified, the target population defined, and the most desirable solution singled out, program planners will have successfully defined the problem to be addressed. The entire program will be built upon this foundation. It is not difficult to understand how a lack of knowledge in any of these three areas could make for potentially devastating setbacks later on.

MARKET RESEARCH

At each step in the campaign process, from planning to assessment, there will become a need for program planners to gain more insight and to test the validity of their assumptions and proposed methods. The most effective way to do this is to work directly with a sample group from the target population itself. This is often referred to as *market* or *communication research.*

Market research provides program planners with a much deeper understanding of how the issues with which they are dealing apply to the target audience in particular. When program planners make decisions regarding hazards, solutions, communication methods, and other aspects of the campaign, they are making assumptions about how these issues apply to or affect the target audience. For instance, program planners may need to find out how members of the population feel about making the behavior change they have chosen. If they assumed that the population's members would be receptive to the idea, but through market research discover members of the target population are vehemently opposed to it, they will have saved themselves considerable time and money by having the option to change course at this early juncture. By failing to conduct such testing, they may not find out about these attitudes until the campaign has begun and resources have already been dedicated.

Working directly with members of the audience may confirm or invalidate assumptions, thereby providing program planners with more realistic impressions of what needs to be done; how successful their efforts, methods, or materials will be in practice; or how successful their conducted efforts have been in affecting change. At this early point in the process, program planners use market research methods to learn more about their proposed solution. In order to take the next steps—namely developing a message and choosing communication methods—it is key to understand as much about the knowledge, attitudes and feelings, misperceptions, and assumptions that the audience holds with regard to the proposed mitigation or preparedness solution. It is within these bounds that the communication campaign will be designed, taking advantage of these factors in planning rather than encountering them unexpectedly along the way.

There are several ways in which market research can be conducted, with the chosen methods a factor of capacity, time, and available funding. Surveys are the most common, but other highly effective methods include the following:

- *Focus groups*: A qualitative research technique in which an experienced moderator guides approximately 8 to 10 participants through a discussion of selected topics, allowing them to talk freely and spontaneously. Focus groups are often used to identify previously unknown issues or concerns, or to explore reactions to potential actions, benefits, or concepts during the planning and development stages.

- *In-depth interviews*: A type of qualitative research in which a trained interviewer guides an individual through a discussion of a selected topic, allowing the person to talk freely and spontaneously. This technique is often used to identify previously unknown issues or concerns, or to explore reactions to potential actions, benefits, or concepts during the planning and development stages. In-depth interviews are preferred over focus groups when the topic of interest may be considered private, politically charged, or otherwise sensitive such that participants may not be comfortable discussing it in front of others.

- *Theater-style testing*: Individuals typical of the intended audience are invited to a conveniently located meeting room. The room should be set up for screening a television program. Participants are generally not told the real purpose of the session, only that their reactions to a television program are being sought. At the session, participants watch a television program. The program can be any entertaining video approximately 15 to 30 minutes in length. The videotape is interrupted about halfway through by a sequence of four commercials. The emergency preparedness message should be inserted between the second and third commercials. At the end of the program, participants receive a questionnaire and answer questions designed to gauge their reactions, first to the program and then to the advertisements. Finally, the ad is played again and participants complete several questions about it. The majority of these questions should be closed-ended to enable an easy and accurate summary of participant responses.

In recent years, researchers and campaign designers have increasingly examined social media and web 2.0 platforms to assess public sentiment and interest in a particular topic. For example, Twitter data have been used to track users' interests and concerns related to particular public health issues (e.g., Signorini et al. 2011); Google Trends may be used to estimate the spread of illness throughout a region (e.g., Ginsberg et al. 2009), as well as assess issue salience and public opinion (Zhu et al. 2012). Companies such as CrowdTangle.com provide customers with information about how often a Web link of interest has been shared, who shared it, and what they said about it, providing information about public interest and issue salience. These types of sources analyzed qualitatively may provide a useful jumping-off point for program planners who are looking to gain insight into public sentiment about a given issue in a particular region. Analyzing these data using statistical procedures that can be generalized to a larger public requires a specialized skillset, so program planners looking to hire specialists to do formative for summative evaluation using this type of data should look for someone experienced in analyzing "big data."

EXISTING PROGRAM RESEARCH AND GAP ANALYSIS

Before going about planning the campaign from the ground up, it is always wise to identify and assess what has already been done to address the issue, what is currently being done, and what the outcomes of these actions are (in terms of vulnerability reduction and behavior change). There is no sense in repeating the work of others. Nor is it wise to conduct a campaign whose message differs from or even contradicts the message of another campaign without first planning how you will explain the differences. In many cases, even when no other organization or agency has addressed the problem in exactly the same way, it has tackled some part of the problem or addressed similar issues with the same population. Existing program research is conducted for the following reasons:

- To avoid reinventing the wheel
- To build upon the successes of other programs and benefit from the trust they have gained
- To find collaborative opportunities
- To understand and learn from the failures of other programs
- To understand any misconceptions, mistrust, or other incorrect or negative feelings that may exist because of a prior communication attempt

When program research is conducted to determine the individual communication needs or actions lacking within the greater spectrum of communication efforts currently underway, it is called a *gap analysis*. Gap analysis looks for specific areas where messages are not reaching audiences. This could be a factor of segments of the population or it could relate to components of the message received by all members of the population.

DETERMINE PROJECT FEASIBILITY

In Chapter 1, the many possible components of a comprehensive disaster preparedness campaign were described, including communication, facilitation, funding and financial incentives, policy change, and technology.

With a full comprehension of the problem in hand, and a better understanding of how the target population is affected, program planners can better determine which of these components will be necessary to actually bring about measurable vulnerability reduction. If communication alone will do little to change attitudes in the absence of a change in policy, and no effort to bring about a policy change exists within the campaign strategy, it would be better to change the campaign goals to something more achievable than trying to go ahead with the campaign as is. On the contrary, if the target population lacks only the funding and knowledge to bring about change, and a partner organization or sponsor is willing to assist by helping those unable to afford the necessary measures (such as purchasing a weather radio, go-kit, or smoke detector), then this combination would likely bring about much greater change than communication alone.

Once you have determined that your proposed solution has the potential to bring about actual change, there are a few final factors that must be considered before setting out on the full campaign effort. These include the following:

- Does your organization have the necessary expertise and resources to conduct the campaign? If not, can these be acquired?
- Does your organization have the necessary authority or mandate to bring about the changes or measures being proposed?
- How much time does your organization have to dedicate to campaign planning and implementation?
- What, if anything, can be accomplished in that time?

ESTABLISH REALISTIC GOALS AND OBJECTIVES

With the wealth of information program planners have gained in these initial steps, they will finally be able to begin establishing a campaign goal and objectives. The goal and objectives will be used to guide the campaign design and methodology as it progresses. In fact, the purpose of the initial research (the problems, the audience, and the solutions) was primarily to establish exactly what program planners are setting out to achieve (the goal) and how they plan to go about doing it (the objectives).

The campaign *goal* is defined as the general emergency preparedness outcome that the communication team hopes to create. An example of a campaign goal is:

> To encourage college freshmen at the University of California to plan and prepare for earthquakes.

All aspects of the campaign will be designed to meet this central goal. The goal does not indicate how, to what level of success, or in what time frame this outcome will be achieved.

Campaign *objectives*, on the contrary, are specific, plainly measurable action points that the communication team hopes to achieve in its drive to meet the goal. They are more specific than goals in that they offer some quantifiable target outcome involving specific knowledge, beliefs, attitudes, or behaviors of intended audience members. The CDC offers guidance for writing realistic and measureable objectives (Public Health Information Network Communities of Practice, 2015). They recommend all objectives be written in SMART format (see Sidebar 3.3). An example of a SMART campaign objective that relates to the preceding goal could include:

> To increase by 10% the number of UCLA students who have secured furniture to walls, using anchors, one year after the program launches.

Note that while the use of furniture anchors by *every* student at the university would be optimal, the long-term objective of the campaign is only to *increase* the number by 10%. It is unrealistic to expect that any single campaign could completely solve a problem. The NIH suggests that practitioners seek the guidance of statisticians or emergency preparedness experts to help to determine realistic rates of change before setting quantifiable communication objectives. The organization points out that even commercial marketers consider a 2–3% increase in sales to be a great success.

SIDEBAR 3.3   WRITING SMART OBJECTIVES

The CDC's Division for Heart Disease and Stroke Prevention put out a guide to help states write realistic and measureable objectives. They recommend all objectives be written using the acronym SMART. Objectives should be:

- *Specific: What exactly will be done for whom?* An objective should identify the target population or setting and clearly specify the action to be taken.
- *Measurable: How exactly will the objective be measured?* In order to maintain objectivity in process and program evaluation, objectives and their results should be able to be quantified. If the objective specifies that something will change over time (e.g., the number of students who have secured furniture to the walls, using anchors, will increase by 10%), a baseline measurement

must be established first so that it may be compared with the outcome measurement. If no baseline is known during the program planning process, taking a baseline measurement should be included as the first *short-term objective* of the program.

- *Attainable/achievable: Can the objective be met within the time frame provided with the resources available to those who are implementing the campaign?* As explained previously, it is important to set realistic expectations for a single program.
- *Relevant: Does meeting this objective bring us closer to meeting the program's stated objective?* Long-term objectives should link directly to the program's stated goals; short-term objectives should link directly to longer-term objectives that ultimately lead to the program's stated goals.
- *Time-bound: When will this objective be accomplished?* Because there are often delays associated with access to funding and other unanticipated barriers to program launch, it is recommended that program planners specify time in terms of years, months, weeks, or days after the program launch date, rather than specifying an exact month and year. For example, the sample objective listed previously sets a time frame of one year after program launch instead of specifying a particular month and year. This allows for program launch delays without having to change the months and years listed in the objectives.

Preparedness programs are often composed of a number of short-term objectives that ultimately lead to attaining at least one long-term objective, which is directly related to the program goal. Short-term objectives do not necessarily have to be so closely linked to achievement of the goal, as long as their action ultimately leads to it. One or several short-term objectives may be necessary to meet before members of the target population can take action to achieve the long-term objectives. Often, short-term objectives are related to the theory that is being used to guide in program design (discussed in Chapter 4). Theory provides program planners with insight into *why* members of the target population are not taking action to prepare for an emergency despite having knowledge of how the action may be protective for them. For example, UCLA students may be aware that securing furniture to their walls using anchors will help to protect them in the event of an earthquake, but they may not be taking action because they *don't know how* to anchor their furniture. If this is the case, a short-term objective might be set to increase the percentage of students who *know how* to anchor furniture to the wall. This objective alone will not bring about the overall campaign goal (as knowledge does not necessarily lead to action) to fruition, but it is necessary before the long-term objective, to increase the number of UCLA students who secure their furniture to the walls with an anchor, which *is* directly related to the goal, can be met. When writing long-term and short-term objectives, it is important to remember that 100% compliance is never a realistic expectation. Therefore, program planners must take some attrition into account at each step of progression from short-term to long-term objectives. For example, knowing *how* to secure furniture to the walls is a necessary precursor to actually taking action to do so, but not ALL students who learn how to secure furniture should be expected to do so. Some students may opt not to secure their furniture because they do not have enough money to buy anchors; others may decide it isn't worth the hassle because they intend to move within the next few months anyway; some may fully intend to secure their furniture but simply never get around to it. Therefore, in order to increase the number of UCLA students who actually secure their furniture by 10%, the increase in the number of students who learn *how* to secure their furniture should be even higher—perhaps 20%. When writing a series of short-term and long-term objectives, each subsequent objective should project a smaller portion of the target population to comply.

If a single target audience has been selected, then objectives will pertain entirely to this audience. However, if segmentation is used and several audiences are to be targeted, then each may require its own unique set of objectives. Each of these objectives, in turn, will be achieved through the performance of one or more tasks, to be described in the project planning phase.

Without objectives, it is impossible to truly measure whether the project has achieved what it had intended to, which makes it extremely difficult to report successes to supporters, partners, and other stakeholders. Often, there is a tendency to see outcomes in terms of what we hope them to be, rather than as they truly are. Setting measurable objectives before the start of the campaign keeps us honest with others and ourselves in determining if the campaign achieved what it set out to do. Therefore, it is vital that these objectives be reasonable and realistic in order to give the campaign a fair chance at being deemed a success (see Sidebar 3.4).

SIDEBAR 3.4   SETTING REASONABLE AND REALISTIC OBJECTIVES

The NIH recommends that communication campaign objectives be assessed to determine how reasonable and realistic each is concerning the organization's capacity to achieve it. The following is an adaptation from these recommendations:

Be reasonable: Objectives describe the intermediate steps that must be taken to accomplish broader goals; they describe the desired outcome but not the steps involved in attaining it. Develop reasonable communication objectives by looking at the program's goal and asking, "What can communication feasibly contribute to attaining this goal, given what we know about the type of changes the intended audiences can and will make?"

Communication efforts alone cannot achieve all objectives. Appropriate purposes for communication include:

- Creating a supportive environment for a change (societal or organizational) by influencing attitudes, beliefs, or policies
- Contributing to a broader behavior change initiative by offering messages that motivate, persuade, or enable behavior change within a specific intended audience

Raising awareness or increasing knowledge among individuals or the organizations that reach them is also feasible; however, do not assume that accomplishing such an objective will lead to behavior change. For example, it is unreasonable to expect communication to cause a sustained change of complex behaviors or compensate for a lack of basic emergency services.

The ability and willingness of the intended audience to make certain changes also affect the reasonableness of various communication objectives. Your objectives will be reasonable for a particular intended audience only if audience members are able and willing to make the recommended behavior change.

Be realistic: Once reasonable communication objectives are developed, determine which of them are realistic, given your available resources, by answering these questions:

- Which objectives cover the areas that most need to reach the program goal?
- What communication activities will contribute the most to addressing these needs?
- What resources are available? Include:
  - Staff and other human resources
  - Committee members, associates from other programs, volunteers, and others who have the requisite skills and time
  - Overhead resources such as computer time, mailing costs, and printing

- Services available from another source, such as educational materials available free or at cost and the effort by other organizations willing to help
- Information about the issue, the intended audience, the community, and media structures, or about available educational materials
- Budget available to fund the program
- Time (weeks, months, or years available to complete the program)
- What supportive factors exist (e.g., community activities, other organizations' interests, positive community attitudes)?
- What barriers exist (e.g., obstacles to approval, absence of funding, sensitivity of an issue, intended audience constraints)?
- Which objectives would best use the resources your program has identified and fit within the identified constraints?

Your answers to the last question should become your priority objectives. Sometimes you may feel so constrained by a lack of funds that proceeding appears impossible. An honest assessment may lead you to conclude that a productive communication effort is not possible. However, creative use of the resources already identified may enable you to develop a communication program that can make valuable contributions.

FORM THE PLANNING TEAM AND COALITION

Once goals and objectives are set, program planning can begin. Task generation, assignation of responsibility, delineation of timelines, and dedication of resources together make up the campaign planning process that is discussed in Chapter 4.

Operational campaign planning begins in earnest with the formation of a planning team or a planning coalition. The myriad tasks that are generated and driven by this planning effort are generally too broad in nature to be effectively conceived of and outlined by just one person, and the value of added perspectives that are gained through the input from a diverse team of planners cannot be underestimated. The utilization of a planning team or coalition also allows communicators to allocate appropriately individual task responsibilities (such as market research or strategic plan development) to those individuals, groups, or organizations most capable of handling such tasks—thereby increasing the quality of each distinct campaign function.

The process of forming a planning team begins with the selection or appointment of a project leader, who is normally chosen from within the organization leading the communication effort. The project leader, in turn, leads the development of the full team. Because the quality of the planned campaign will always be reflective of the diversity, knowledge, perspective, and experience of the planning team, the team should be composed of individuals who together satisfy all perceived needs. There are many stakeholders in every communication project, including facilitators, recipients, potential partners, and many others involved in the management of the hazard and its associated risk; each has an important perspective that merits attention and inclusion.

The selected or appointed project leader can begin forming the project planning team by generating a list of all parties and individuals believed to have an interest or stake in the project's outcome. At this point, it must be decided whether the planning effort will remain within the organization or open up to include outside organizations in the form of a coalition. The project leader should consider what each project partner is able to offer in terms of expertise or knowledge on the preparedness topic, time and effort (volunteer or otherwise), relevant skills, access to contacts and other professional networks, sponsorship, financial support, and more (see Sidebar 3.6).

If it is determined that a coalition is a wise choice, then the planning team leader uses the extensive list of potential partners or external planning participants to determine those individuals and organizations whose assistance would be most useful *and* appropriate (keeping in mind the need to maintain representation from the greatest number of stakeholders), and who would be dedicated to the project and work collaboratively with all other team members and partners. Project leaders may then invite members of this culled list to join the planning coalition, thereby giving them the opportunity to contribute to the campaign planning effort. Keep in mind that these invitees need not be public education or emergency management professionals, although it is almost always of benefit to include such experts (e.g., firefighters). The coalition may also include teachers, respected community officials, business people or leaders, concerned parents and volunteers, and others representative of the target audience. Involving people with different backgrounds and experiences has many advantages, including:

- Access to a wider range of ideas, perspectives, and expertise
- Greater access to the target audience
- Access to additional partners
- A minimized risk of faulty assumptions and methods
- Shared work responsibilities among several people
- Expanded networks of potential contacts, supporters, and sponsors
- Increased access to project funding, labor, and other resources
- Increased message credibility

- Increased message coverage
- Increased levels of trust and attention from target audiences
- Expanded support for priority activities

Coalitions, like partnerships, bring together the knowledge, resources, and commitment of multiple organizations—in this case, members or leaders from different organizations with a stake in emergency preparedness. Ultimately, the attention those organizations pay to the improvement of public preparedness becomes institutionalized for long-term action. For this reason, the strongest potential partners are most likely to be interested in joining a project planning coalition. The NIH recommends using the following guidelines to create a successful coalition (also see Sidebar 3.5):

- Formalize the relationship to create greater commitment: Formal arrangements include written memoranda of understanding, by-laws, mission statements, and regular reminders of the coalition's purpose and progress.
- Make sure that the responsibilities of each organization and its staff are clear: In particular, staff members need to know whether to take direction from the coalition chairperson or from the agency that pays their salary.
- Structure aspects of the coalition's operation: Elect officers. Form standing committees. Have regularly scheduled meetings with written agenda and minutes. Expect and support action, not just discussion, at these meetings. Circulate action items resulting from meetings among coalition members. Establish communication channels and use them frequently.
- Ensure the involvement of representatives who show leadership characteristics, such as the ability to obtain resources, problem-solve, and promote collaboration and equality among members—Members with political knowledge, administrative or communication skills, or access to the media and decision-makers are also valuable.
- Create and reinforce positive expectations by providing information on the coalition's progress—Optimism and success sustain member interest.
- Formalize accountability and develop criteria for judging whether coalition members are honoring their commitments.
- Be flexible—Losing prospective partners can limit a program's effectiveness.
- Provide training to help members complete their tasks—For example, coalition members may need training in how to be effective advocates for your program's issues.

- Give members a stake in the coalition and an active role in decision-making.
- Seek external resources to augment member resources.
- Evaluate the effectiveness of the coalition periodically and make necessary changes—This should include process evaluation of the coalition's functioning and assessment of the coalition's impact on the health problem being addressed.

Tucker and McNerney (1992) describe four kinds of coalitions. The FEMA Emergency Management Institute provides examples of how each may relate to a public disaster preparedness education campaign:

1. Representatives of different groups who have grown weary of costly confrontation. They need to build consensus, using a specific issue as common ground. Example: *Various voluntary community groups, competing to garner the most support from private and corporate donations, might instead combine efforts on the topic of community preparedness, and share otherwise limited resources to achieve a wider level of preparedness.*
2. Representatives of different groups who, although of different missions or opinions, realize that they share a common perspective on a specific issue. Example: *Insurance companies and emergency preparedness authorities might have different goals (selling insurance to cover disaster claims versus providing adequate responses in a major population emergency), but both will benefit if the community is prepared (less damage/less claims, and less dependence on limited police/fire/ambulance resources in a disaster).*
3. Representatives of groups with varied goals and perspectives who are more likely to be sensitive to the specific point of view. Example: *A municipal health department with oversight for ambulance, public health, hospital, and clinic services might be sensitive to community emergency preparedness because the public's health needs in an emergency will affect the agency by demanding a response for many who, if not prepared, might otherwise become injured, need medical services, or become homeless.*
4. Representatives of varied groups might share a position that already has widespread acceptance. Example: *Businesses, service organizations, and governmental agencies all might climb on the bandwagon to publicize a smoke detector installation campaign in residences. Such efforts can sell detectors, reduce overall insurance liability, limit loss of life and property, and make the jobs of fire departments safer and more effective.*

SIDEBAR 3.5   SIX STEPS TO FORMING A COALITION

FEMA describes six steps that may be used to build and organize coalitions. The following is an adaptation of these steps:

1. *Develop a position*: Evaluate the importance of the preparedness issue, who is driving it, and who is likely to be affected or think they will be affected by it. Create a position that will benefit your organization's success with the program, as well as those you are trying to educate.
2. *Create a strategy for pursuing your position*: Questions to consider include:
   a. How can you accelerate the opportunity to enhance community preparedness?
   b. How can you make adjustments to adapt to the community's need or capitalize on a given trend?
   c. Is there a mutual benefit for the community and for businesses to promote preparedness education and activities?
   d. Can you get a major organization to back the concept or offer incentives for those taking specific training or actions?
   e. Is there a sense of ownership among participants?
      A key strategy is to help develop a sense of ownership of specific outcomes among coalition participants. The partners must understand and embrace these outcomes as goals they want to achieve.
3. *Identify coalition participants*: For each organization considered, planners should think about the following questions:
   a. What are their positions?
   b. How credible is the organization/individual with other organizations or individuals?
   c. Will they want to be the official sponsors of the effort?
   d. Who are the leaders of those organizations?
   e. Will they participate themselves or will they recommend someone who will?
   f. How can I work with others within those organizations or who have influence on them to help shape their opinion and see the preparedness point of view more favorably?
4. *Conduct research*: Try to get a baseline on the level of community preparedness before beginning a campaign. This evidence is used to support the need for your preparedness education programs.
5. *Organize your meeting*: Try to find common ground among invited coalition members. Where do we agree and disagree? Where can we work together? Try to identify common

philosophical values and look for misperceptions and unrealistic expectations. With groups of differing perspectives, building consensus will not be easy. Participants will need to work through the process, so everyone must be able to let his or her positions be known.

6. *Plan the campaign.*

Planners should be aware that there can be drawbacks to including partners in the planning process and in the facilitation of the campaign itself, but awareness of these issues can help them to be minimized. Drawbacks to including partners can include:

- Identifying partners, persuading them to join your efforts, waiting for them to make a decision, training them in the relevant issues, and coordinating with the additional team members often serve to increase the burden of time involved in planning.
- The different wants, needs, perspectives, experiences, capabilities, and ideals of each partner can require that the nature of the campaign be altered to ensure that all partners are satisfied.
- Partner organizations may try to use the program for their own needs or take credit for the program's successes beyond the contribution they provided.
- Staffing problems, funding shortages, or mismanagement in partner organizations can all lead to delays, mismanagement, or complete failure of the campaign.

For these reasons, planners must be sure that they are prepared to work with the partners they recruit, and that those partners are willing and able to do so (and for the right reasons). They must have a solid understanding about how flexible they are willing to be with the campaign to meet the wants of their partners, and how much support they are willing and able to provide them if and when they require it.

The makeup of the team that results from this effort must consist of enthusiastic supporters who can help plan and promote the public education effort. Ideally, representatives from the target audience are included as full members or in advisory roles, to verify assumptions and provide subject matter expertise. It is equally important to involve community organizations that typically work with the target audience, primarily to prevent redundancy of effort, provide the mutual benefit of collaboration, and allow for the sharing of ideas and experiences (as well as access reputation and trust they enjoy among message recipients). Although it is important that at least two or three people in the core planning team are able to provide leadership and continuity throughout the planning and implementation effort, it is okay if some planning team members rotate in and out as appropriate (with some available only for the initial planning meetings and others helping out only during implementation).

The target audience profile will heavily influence the team's membership. For instance, businesses and industries can serve as effective conduits for sharing disaster information among their employees, if their employees are among those targeted. Businesses typically have phone trees established and methods for disseminating information to staff. Furthermore, many companies have already established disaster education programs that the planning team can tap into (such as emergency drills and annual training sessions). Government agencies and other community organizations are also important partners in public education. School systems, for example, can help educate children and young adults about hazards in their areas and appropriate preparations and response measures. Many government emergency management offices have already assessed the hazards in the community, and may have even developed guidance on how to educate their constituents.

One of the greatest benefits of including a wide range of stakeholders is that each will provide important input into the process specific to his or her individual perspective, and will likewise become a vocal advocate for preparedness in general and the project at hand. The following are examples of stakeholders that may be included in a public education planning effort:

- Emergency responders (fire, police, EMS) and emergency managers
- Local, state, and federal governmental agency officials
- Private-sector/business/industry leaders
- Volunteer organization representatives
- Community and faith-based organization leaders
- Elected officials
- News media representatives (television, newspapers, radio, Internet)
- Representatives from the target audience
- Educators and school administrators (from schools, colleges, and universities)
- Concerned individuals
- Civic and business organizations
- Businesses
- The Chamber of Commerce and the area Council of Governments
- Local community centers
- Religious organizations
- Youth clubs
- Women's clubs and organizations
- Trade enterprises and associations
- Banks and credit unions

- Health centers, hospitals, or clinics
- Sport clubs
- Libraries, cinemas, theaters, or circuses
- Utility companies
- Red Cross chapters

Encouraging Partners to Join the Planning Team

The inclusion of partners can be the most effective way to expand the scope and reach of the campaign. In exchange for the benefit of participating, partners bring to the project skills, labor, equipment, audience access, credibility, materials and supplies, space, experience, and much more (see Sidebar 3.6 for examples of benefits gained through partnership). How and when partners are identified and approached is always at the discretion of the organization conducting the campaign. In some cases, if your organization has little or no experience with public education, it may be preferable to include partners from the very beginning of the planning process before the problem is fully defined or the audience is profiled. However, in most cases it is preferable that there be structure to the project so that partners may know in what they are agreeing to participate.

SIDEBAR 3.6   PARTNER ORGANIZATION CONTRIBUTIONS

Partnering organizations bring to the program a much wider range of skills, abilities, and resources than are possessed by any single organization. The addition of these attributes allows planners to consider many more options than they otherwise could. The skills and resources a partner organization can bring to a public disaster preparedness education campaign might include:

- Graphic design software, skills, and equipment
- Printing materials and equipment
- Advertising space or time
- Endorsement
- Sponsorship or inclusion at events
- Specialized knowledge of or access to the target audience
- Specialized skills
- Additional people to communicate the public education message
- Space to hold events and equipment required to do so
- Food, drinks, and other supplies to draw people to events

- Storage, transport, or distribution of materials
- Experience with the hazards addressed
- Increase in the number of messages the program is able to transmit
- Training resources

Expanded support for your organization's priority activities

With luck, partners may jump at the chance to participate in your project as proposed. This is most typical for organizations that regularly work with the target audience and when these partners are required to dedicate little or no resources of their own. However, most potential partners will need convincing before they agree to join. The planning team leader must therefore be able to present to these organizations and individuals the benefits each stands to gain through their participation. Such benefits could include:

- The opportunity to share credit for success
- Membership and participation in a forum whereby community problems are discussed, addressed, and resolved
- The opportunity to foster good community relations
- Increased awareness of the hazards faced by community residents and businesses
- The opportunity to improve the working relationships between government and civil society
- Local and collective ownership for the resolution of community problems
- Increased visibility and credibility in the community
- The opportunity to build organizational capacities and other skills
- Networking opportunities
- Increased positive media coverage, perceived credibility, and community visibility
- Access to data and experience
- Assurance of message accuracy

Among the wide variety of options for partnership opportunities, there are subgroups within this body that can be approached for specific reasons. Major subgroups of partners in the community include the following:

- *Local businesses*: There are two primary reasons why local businesses participate in community projects like a preparedness education campaign. The first is that these businesses depend upon their good reputation among community members. A project such as this can significantly raise their profile within the community, as its goal is to reach as many members of an audience as possible. The second reason is one of corporate responsibility. Many businesses feel they should give back to the communities that make their success possible. Preparedness education projects in general can require a significant amount of skills, equipment, and materials, all of which are provided by different members of the local business community. By partnering with these organizations, it is possible to acquire access to these skills, equipment, and materials as an in-kind donation in exchange for the positive publicity that comes through shared project credit. Through creative planning, it is often possible to gain these items through no extra cost on the part of the partners. For instance, grocers, hardware store owners, and other merchants in your community may be invited to put preparedness messages on shopping bags, store windows, or marquees outside their stores (see Figure 3.3). Local businesses may agree to work with you to set up displays inside their stores featuring key items shoppers might need as they put together a family emergency supply kit. Local merchants might also be interested in sponsoring contests on preparedness in the schools and donating prizes for kids. Other examples of opportunities for partnership roles for local businesses include:

- Local utilities (telephone, water, electric, gas) can include emergency preparedness and mitigation messages or literature in customer bills or newsletters.
- Businesses can be encouraged to distribute disaster preparedness information to employees, and hold preparedness workshops with employees and their families during business hours.
- Graphic design, printing, and other businesses with related capacities can design and print hazard and basic preparedness fact sheets and brochures.
- Local organizations and businesses can donate space upon which a poster may be hung or where brochures may be distributed to customers.
- Businesses with a large customer base may allow access to their customers by permitting the organization to host in-store workshops or other events.
- Restaurants or fast-food chains may want to donate food or refreshments at events.
- *Community organizations*: Community organizations include youth clubs, Red Cross chapters, NGOs, law enforcement

FIGURE 3.3 Tulsa, Oklahoma, Mayor's Citizen Corps received donated space on food tray liners from the McDonald's Corporation for printing emergency preparedness education materials for disaster education. (Courtesy of Tulsa Mayor's Citizen Corps and the Oklahoma Department of Emergency Management.)

organizations, women's groups, veteran's groups, religious organizations, and others. While these organizations are rarely able to provide financial assistance to the project, they can often provide two equally important resources: people and credibility. Community organizations tend to have deep roots in the community and may enjoy an even higher level of recognition and trust among community members in general or the target population in particular. Members of these groups work to help their community in a variety of ways, and when the public education project is compatible with those goals, they are likely to pay close attention. By accessing the networks each of these groups has established, your team can greatly extend the reach of its disaster awareness and preparedness message. Some ideas of partnership roles for community organizations include:

- Organizations that hold meetings with members of the community or some other target population can present disaster preparedness and mitigation workshops at one of these meetings.

- Organizations that hold periodic fairs, festivals, or other events can include a segment or booth on disaster preparedness.
- Organizations that work with the target population can incorporate disaster preparedness into the services that they regularly offer.
- Organizations with a wide volunteer base can offer the time or skills of their volunteers for the planning or facilitation of the campaign.
- Organizations may contribute space to hold meetings, store equipment and supplies, or host people working on the project.
- Organizations may provide equipment such as computers, software, printers and plotters, audio and video recording and display devices, and so on.
- Organizations may agree to include information about your preparedness program and perhaps even a link to your program's Website or other online presence through their Website, or social media account such as Facebook, Twitter, or Instagram. Because people are more likely to check their Website or be linked to their social media accounts, this will increase the reach of the preparedness program as well as enhance the credibility of the message.

- *Public safety organizations*: The various public safety organizations that operate in the community already have a vested stake in the preparedness of the community populace. These organizations may even have public education campaigns in place that are operational. By working with them, planners will tap into a great amount of community-specific knowledge regarding hazards, solutions, and audiences. Additionally, the credibility these organizations hold within the community is rarely surpassed. The range of contributions these organizations may provide is limited primarily by the available time of their members, and their resources. However, as the vast majority of public safety organizations depend upon financial contributions from the community, they are likely to participate in any event or project that can increase their likelihood of receiving grants or donations. Creativity on the part of the planning team, and the ability of the planning team members to tap into their very limited time, will be the key to their involvement. Some ideas for partnership roles for public safety organizations include:
  - Firefighters, policemen, emergency managers, or EMTs may present public safety campaign messages through

presentations at schools, civic group meetings, or other venues (see Figure 3.4).

- Public safety organizations can offer sponsorship to a campaign, thereby lending a great deal of credibility to the message.
- Public safety organizations may have valuable information that can be used to define the hazard, possible solutions to the problem, or information specific to the target audience.
- Public safety organizations may have unique access to members of the target audience (e.g., they may have an e-mail list or phone numbers of people signed up to receive e-mails or text messages from their organization) or authority to conduct specific tasks (such as home safety inspections).
- Public safety organizations may agree to promote your message or program through their online or social media

FIGURE 3.4 Emergency services departments can combine annual fundraising efforts with public education campaigns by holding family preparedness fairs that encourage children and families to prepare by showcasing the resources and capabilities of the department (Author photo).

presence similar to what was described above with community organizations.

- *Partnering with schools*: Schools provide quite possibly the best access to any target audience that includes children or families. The environment found within schools is perfectly suited to foster learning, so any message conducted within this setting is likely to benefit (see Figure 3.5). In addition, schools already participate in many other public health education campaigns, so the structures are in place to transmit the disaster preparedness message. Through school-based associations, including parent–teacher groups or sports teams, planners can extend their message reach. Students are often enthusiastic about participating in public education projects and can be relied upon to echo preparedness messages throughout the community. Local merchants might even be more likely to participate if they know that schools are involved, because of the wider customer base that is reached and the credibility that is gained. Examples of partnership roles for schools include:
  - Schools can hold poster competitions, with prizes (donated by local businesses, for instance) for contest winners.
  - Schools can incorporate a disaster preparedness workshop into their regular parent and teacher meetings.
  - School teachers can incorporate a disaster preparedness message into their lesson plans.

FIGURE 3.5 A fourth grader at Painted Rock Elementary School dons firefighter gear during a FEMA for Kids presentation in Poway, California, February 13, 2008 (John Ashton for FEMA 2008).

- Schools can assign at-home projects that involve family disaster preparedness activities.
- Schools can pass along program materials and messages by e-mailing parents directly or posting information on their Websites or social media pages.

- *Target audience leaders*: Often, planners are not necessarily experts on the issues faced by the special populations their public education efforts are targeting. By involving leaders and members of these target groups in the planning process, they are not only ensuring that all of the important topics and issues are at least considered but they are also helping to establish trust and buy-in among the targeted individuals. Examples of partnership roles for target audience members and leaders include:
  - Audience members and leaders can assist with the development of a target audience profile.
  - Audience members and leaders can participate in the pre-testing of messages and materials before they are distributed among the greater target audience.
  - Target audience leaders can endorse the project, lending significant credibility to the campaign.
  - Target audience members and leaders can help the organization to assess the progress of the campaign and to make required adjustments.
  - Target audience members can raise awareness about the program and recruit others to get involved through their personal social media accounts, as they are likely to be a direct link to members of the target audience.

The Media as a Partner

In most public disaster preparedness endeavors, a partnership with the news (mass) media will be paramount, offering quite possibly the most important and influential contribution an organization can gain through its partnership endeavors. News media outlets, which include television, print (newspapers), radio, and Internet-based companies, already play a significant role in disaster and emergency management both before and after disasters occur. The media, for instance, are lauded for the valuable service they perform during the initial critical moments of a disaster when emergency response efforts are first mobilized, and media organizations serve to transmit warnings, evacuation orders and instructions, the location and availability of medical care and shelter, and where to go for more specific information.

In the preparedness phase of emergency management, the primary public education tasks assumed by the media are very similar (if not identical) to what you are likely to be performing yourself, including raising citizen awareness to the presence of hazards and providing information to those citizens regarding prevention or protection measures. The media have established themselves within modern society such that, as a general population, citizens turn to them more than any other source to obtain information, including that which relates to hazards (Walsh 1996). FEMA mitigation specialists even go so far as to claim that the media role in community and citizen preparedness is critical if such efforts are to succeed (FEMA 1998).

The media role should not be overestimated, however, as it is not absolute. While it has been found that personal preparedness is most likely to be undertaken by people attentive to the news media, this tendency is usually accompanied by other behavioral characteristics that support preparedness actions and attitudes (e.g., personal experience and expendable income). In this sense, the media role should be seen as an important *supplemental* component in your preparedness campaign, not the answer to its problems. Campaigns that rely too heavily on the media without addressing the reasons why people do not or are unable to prepare will not succeed. Other specific problems associated with media participation in public disaster preparedness education campaigns include the following:

- Although the media is effective at raising awareness about issues and communicating degrees of urgency, they often avoid contributing solutions to problems.
- The media is often unable to educate the public about risk in such a way as to give citizens an accurate perception of personal vulnerability.
- The media often speaks to a general audience rather than addressing the specific needs of a more focused target population.

The mass media is diverse in character, utilizing print, broadcast, and other methods of transmission, and existing at the local, regional, national, and international levels. It is a well-established institution operating in a predictable manner. With the right strategy, planners can tap into these resources and channels to reach wider audiences easier and quicker than they ever could by other means. FEMA proclaims in the publication *Project Impact: Building a Disaster Resistant Community*,

> You will want to target print, radio, and television outlets at planned intervals with your messages. As gatekeepers to your community, the media affect and shape our opinions and our behavior. They influence

our preferences and our choices. By encouraging reporters to write or broadcast your messages, you will generate awareness and interest.

FEMA claims that a targeted, comprehensive media list, containing all of the important and relevant media outlets that reach the target audience, is the "most essential tool of any successful media campaign." The planning team can create a media list through cooperation with local government agencies and other organizations that maintain regular contact with members of the mass media. Sources of greatest value will likely be those that cover community affairs, natural disasters, or the metro desk, for example. Outlets that should be included in the media list are found in Sidebar 3.7.

You must always remember that members of the media are not public education experts, and their goal is not to inform the public but rather to increase the ratings of their media outlet. Therefore, careful attention must be paid when fostering partnerships with the media to ensure that their inclusion does not backfire and end up hurting rather than helping your cause. Peter Sandman, an acclaimed risk communication expert, describes 11 ways for those performing preparedness education to help reporters understand the technical aspects of a story or message. They are (Sandman 1992):

1. Don't assume knowledge
2. Guide the interview
3. Avoid jargon
4. Simplify content
5. Anticipate problem areas
6. Provide written back-up information
7. Be alert for signs of confusion
8. Check for understanding
9. Suggest other sources
10. Offer to look at a draft or check quotes
11. Encourage specialized reporting

Media partners can disseminate preparedness messages through various means, which may include articles, feature stories, editorial coverage, or donated advertising space. In its *How-To Guide for State and Local Mitigation Planning*, FEMA describes various ways in which a planning team can work directly with the media to promote the risk communication messages it has developed, such as (FEMA, 2002):

- Include a special insert in a local newspaper
- Broadcast public meetings on a local access channel or through public service announcements

- Produce a video to be broadcast on local access channels
- Use news releases or information contained in press kits to create feature stories or reports. Press kits are folders summarizing the key information about your goals and actions, information that helps to pique interest in your program, and information that provides reporters with accurate details about the hazards and what can be done about them.
- Announce an upcoming meeting or event
- Attend a meeting or event to highlight your cause
- Provide viewers with contact information or other important data that will help them locate preparedness instruction and information.

The planning team can also contact local broadcasters and offer interviews with disaster safety experts. Television stations frequently need guests to fill slots in early morning or weekend shows. Radio talk show hosts may welcome the chance to interview an emergency preparedness expert provided by the team, because the topic is always timely. The team can also arrange visits to the editorial department of local newspapers to gain print coverage. Experts could include representatives of the local or regional Red Cross, Salvation Army, emergency management office, National Weather Service, or fire department rescue team. The team may also want to have the expert write an opinion piece or a letter to the editor to be submitted to the newspaper.

FEMA provides some caution for working with the media. It states,

> [w]hile the media is a good source for getting information to the public, you do have to be careful. Sometimes the media can distort the information you give them or give it a different spin. The media likes attention-grabbing headlines so they may try to make your plan controversial in some way. You should work on establishing an honest, working relationship with a local reporter so that each of you has someone to turn to when you need to gather or provide information to the community.

Almost every major news outlet now includes an online component, most of which allow readers to offer comments and to share the article both privately through e-mail and text and publicly on their own social media pages. Stories that are more often selected and shared by users will expose more people to the message. Researchers have identified characteristics of news stories and social media posts that make them more likely to be selected, shared, and "go viral." These characteristics are discussed in Chapter 4.

SIDEBAR 3.7   MEDIA CHECKLIST

Media lists should include:

- Newspapers (dailies, weeklies, monthlies, college/university papers, and community newsletters)
- City and regional magazines
- Local trade and business publications
- State bureaus of national wire services, such as the Associated Press (AP), Reuters, and United Press International (UPI)
- Local radio and television stations (including college/university networks)
- Local cable stations
- Public broadcasting stations (which may have community affairs programming)
- Public information officers at military bases, if applicable (many military housing areas have broadcast stations and newsletters that may reach the entire families of service members)

Regardless of the medium, for the most part your media list will consist of the following types of reporters:

- Metro desk/city reporters—interested in news around town
- Public affairs reporters—interested in civic and legislative issues
- Business reporters—interested in hard news involving regional business, local economy, and economic/community growth (e.g., impact on sales, environment, address changes)
- News assignment editors

Public service announcement directors.

Source: FEMA (Federal Emergency Management Agency), *Making Your Community Disaster Resistant: Project Impact Media Partnership Guide*, FEMA, Washington, DC, 1998.

DRAWING UP PARTNERSHIP PLANS

Projects run more smoothly when everyone involved assumes his or her role with an accurate impression and full understanding of what he or she is expected to contribute. This certainly holds true with partners. Partnership plans and agreements can be drawn up to manage expectations. These agreements not only ensure that partners understand what role they are expected to play but they also help to prevent them from overstepping their bounds and taking too much control of the project. Project managers can easily lose control and ownership if any one organization begins working far beyond the expectations of the original partnership agreement, and the partnership plan is a good reference that keeps these risks in check.

PROJECT MANAGEMENT

All complex projects require project management. The project management effort depends upon a project manager who is able to direct all players and resources according to the tasks required and the timetable desired. Project management must cover the project from planning and development, through implementation, to evaluation. The most effective method of maintaining project management is to create a visualization of each of these elements. Identifying and describing all tasks at the start of the project is very effective in ensuring that the project does not run into hidden or unexpected overruns in time or cost.

One very effective tool for managing a project is a program logic model. A logic model is a picture of the program that links all program resources and activities to short-term and long-term objectives and goals, and indicates how each will be measured and evaluated. Figure 3.6 offers one way to set up a logic model and describes what should be included in each box. This figure is based on logic models shown in the W.K. Kellogg Foundation's *Logic Model Development Guide*, which can be downloaded from the resource section of the W.K. Kellogg Foundation Website (W.K. Kellogg Foundation, 2004).

Logic models can be useful during several different phases of an emergency preparedness program. During the *planning phase*, logic models can be used to generate an exhaustive list of resources, activities, and output measurements required to achieve long-term and short-term objectives. This helps program planners to ensure that the scope of the project falls within any time and budgetary constraints. Program planners may start by filling in the last two boxes of the model that are reserved for goals and objectives. They may then work backward within the model to complete the "outputs," "activities," and "resources" boxes.

To begin filling in the output box, for each objective, program planners should ask, "What data are necessary to determine whether or not this objective has been met?" Each data point required to determine whether the objective was met should be listed in the "outputs" box. This will include baseline and completion measurements. For example, if a long-term objective is "To increase by 10% the number of UCLA students who have secured furniture to walls, using anchors, one year after the program launches," the corresponding

Resources (Inputs)
List all materials and resources necessary to carry out the activities listed below. Examples of resources might include: money, time, staff, meeting space, partners, etc.

Activities
List all actions that must be taken throughout the course of the program. Examples of activities might include: hire staff, create program materials, distribute program materials, meet weekly with stakeholders, take baseline measurements, take evaluation measures, etc.

Outputs
List all forms of data that will be used to determine whether or not the proposed activities have been accomplished and whether or not objectives have been met. Examples of outputs might include: number of staff members hired, number of campaign materials created, number of campaign materials distributed, number of weekly meetings held, number of members of the target population engaging in the recommended behavior at baseline, number of members of the target population engaging in the recommended behavior at the end of the timeframe specified in the program objective

Short-and long-term objectives
State all short- and long-term objectives

Impact
State the program goal

FIGURE 3.6   Example of a Gantt chart used to organize and illustrate the tasks of a preparedness campaign.

"outputs" to list would include "baseline number of UCLA students who have secured furniture to their walls, with anchors," and "number of UCLA students who have secured furniture to their walls, with anchors, one year after program launch."

Next, program planners should look at each objective and output individually and ask "What needs to be done in order to bring about each objective and to collect the corresponding data listed in the output box?" Each step needed to meet these objectives and take these measurements should be listed in the "activities" box. For example, if a short-term objective is to increase the number of UCLA students who know how to anchor furniture to their walls within six months of program launch, the corresponding activity to meet this objective might be to hold workshops on campus over the course of this six-month period. Examples of activities associated with this objective might include: "schedule workshops";

"create workshop curriculum and materials"; "recruit and train five workshop facilitators"; "create and distribute promotional materials for workshops"; and "hold the workshops."

Once the "activities" box is complete, planners may need to return to the "outputs" box to add in data needed for process evaluation. For example, an additional output based on the activities listed in the previous paragraph might be "number of workshops held during the fall semester."

Finally, program planners should use all outputs and activities listed to make a determination about all resources needed to carry out the program's activities. In keeping with the anchoring furniture example, the workshops listed in the activities box might require all workshop materials, a lecture hall to hold the workshops, facilitators to teach at the workshops, and materials for promoting the workshop. The baseline and final measurements listed in the outputs box might require a schoolwide survey, incentives for survey completion, the school's e-mail listserver for survey distribution, and password-protected computers for storing and analyzing survey responses.

Logic models should be seen as dynamic guides that may be adjusted several times throughout the course of the program. They may be used as a reference over the course of the program to keep all personnel on the same page about how the program is scheduled to run and to guide in process as well as summative evaluation, which are discussed in greater detail in Chapter 5.

The tasks involved in a public disaster preparedness education campaign are not conducted in a purely linear fashion. Often, different members of the campaign conduct many tasks at once. To increase the efficiency of time, labor, and resources, and to minimize the time required for project development and campaign facilitation, the project manager will need to be aware of each task and its current status. This is usually conducted with a task list.

Task lists are most effective when they are ordered by start date, with the anticipated time to conduct the task noted. An effective means to illustrate the task list is a cascade Gantt chart, so called because of its waterfall-like appearance. An example of a Gantt chart is provided in Figure 3.7. A timeline is drawn to each task (respective to all other tasks), responsible individuals or organizations are assigned, and resources are noted.

The project manager, who is responsible for assigning people and organizations to tasks, can use a Gantt chart or a similar illustrative task list to ensure that no one is double booked, and that all resources are identified, acquired, and assigned to no more than one task. These figures also make it easier for the project manager to ensure that tasks are being conducted on time and in the order in which they are needed.

ID	Task name	Start	Finish	Duration	2008				2009				2010	
					Q1	Q1	Q2	Q3	Q4	Q1	Q2	Q3	Q1	Q2
1	Project kickoff	12/1/2008	12/1/2008	1d										
2	Define campaign strategy	12/2/2008	12/15/2008	2w										
3	Select settings, channels, and methods	12/15/2008	1/9/2009	4w										
4	Select communicators	1/12/2009	2/6/2009	4w										
5	Design/develop message content	2/9/2009	4/17/2009	10w										
6	Create campaign materials	4/20/2009	7/10/2009	12w										
7	Pretesting and materials adjustment	2/9/2009	7/10/2009	22w										
8	Campaign launch	7/13/2009	7/13/2009	1d										
9	Campaign implementation	7/13/2009	4/16/2010	40w										
10	Campaign evaluation	7/13/2009	4/16/2010	40w										

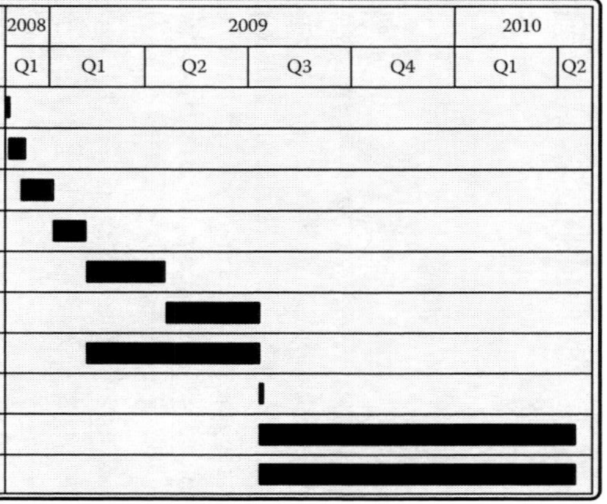

FIGURE 3.7 Logic model guide.

While by no means required, there exists off-the-shelf software, like Microsoft Project or EasyProjects.net, which guides the project management process. Whatever method is used, it should be flexible enough to allow for changes as the project progresses, and the true completion dates and costs become apparent.

CONCLUSION

Emergency preparedness public education campaigns may be complex, but with proper planning, staffing, and funding, and with a comprehensive understanding of the target audience, they can be very successful. Campaign planners are wise to dedicate as much time as possible to the planning phase—often as much or even more time as the actual campaign itself. The next two chapters describe the process by which these plans become practice, and the public is educated about the actions it may take to reduce its hazard risk.

REFERENCES

American Red Cross. 1992. *Community Disaster Education Guide.* Washington, DC: The American National Red Cross.

Ashton, John. 2008. FEMA Media Library. http://bit.ly/2jdKT7U.

Bernstein, D. A., A. Clark-Stewart, E. J. Roy, T. K. Srull, and C. D. Wickens. 1994. *Psychology*, 3rd ed. Boston, MA: Houghton Mifflin.

Buss, D. M., K. H. Craik, and K. M. Dake. 1986. Contemporary worldviews and perception of the technological system. In *Risk Evaluation and Management*. V. T. Covello, J. Menkes, and J. L. Mumpower, Eds. New York: Plenum, pp. 93–130.

CDC (Centers for Disease Control and Prevention) and NCBDDD (National Center on Birth Defects and Developmental Disabilities). 2016. *Emergency Preparedness and Response for Special Groups.* https://www.cdc.gov/ncbddd/disasters/index.html

CDC Public Health Information Network Communities of Practice. 2015. *Evaluate a CoP.* http://www.cdc.gov/phcommunities/resourcekit/evaluate/smart_objectives.html

Coppola, D. 2006. *Introduction to International Disaster Management.* Burlington, MA: Butterworth Heinemann.

Dake, K. 1991. Orienting dispositions in the perceptions of risk: An analysis of contemporary worldviews and cultural biases. *Journal of Cross-Cultural Psychology,* 22, 61–82.

Dake, K. 1992. Myths of nature: Culture and social construction of risk. *Journal of Social Issues,* 48, 21–37.

FEMA (Federal Emergency Management Agency). 1998. *Making Your Community Disaster Resistant: Project Impact Media Partnership Guide.* Washington, DC: FEMA.

FEMA (Federal Emergency Management Agency). 1998. *Project Impact: Building a Disaster Resistant Community.* Washington, DC: FEMA.

FEMA (Federal Emergency Management Agency). 2002. *How-To Guide for State and Local Mitigation Planning.* Washington, DC: FEMA.

Ginsberg, J., M. H. Mohenni, R. S. Patel, L. Brammer, M. S. Smolinski, and L. Brilliant. 2009. Detecting influenza epidemics using search engine query data. *Nature,* 457(19), 1012–1014. doi: 10.1038/nature07634.

Jasper, J. M. 1990. *Nuclear Politics: Energy and the Slate in the United States, Sweden, and France.* Princeton, NJ: Princeton University Press.

Jenkins-Smith, H. C. 1993. *Nuclear Imagery and Regional Stigma: Testing Hypotheses of Image Acquisition and Valuation Regarding Nevada.* Technical report Institute for Public Policy, Albuquerque, NM: University of New Mexico.

National Cancer Institute. 2004. *Making Public Health Communications Work: A Planners Guide.* Washington, DC: National Institutes of Health.

Ropeik, D. 2002. *"Fear Factors" in an Age of Terrorism.* October 15. http://www.msnbc.msn.com/id/3077306/

Sandman, P. M. 1992. *Helping Reporters Understand a Technical Story.* Conference Handouts. http://www.psandman.com.

Signorini, A., A. M. Segre, and P. M. Polgreen. 2011. The use of Twitter to track levels of disease activity and public concern in the U.S. during the influenza A H1N1pandemic. *PLoS One,* 6(5), e19467. doi: 10.1371/journal.pone.0019467.

Slovic, P. 1987. Perception of risk. *Science,* 236, 280–285.

Slovic, P. 1999. Trust, emotion, sex, politics, and science: Surveying the risk—Assessment battlefield. *Risk Analysis,* 19(4), 689–701.

Slovic, P., B. Fischoff, and S. Lichtenstein. 1979. Rating the risks. *Environment,* 21, 14–20, 36–39.

Slovic, P., B. Fischhoff, and S. Lichtenstein. 1980. Facts and fears: Understanding perceived risk. In *Societal Risk Assessment: How Safe Is Safe Enough?* New York: Plenum.

Tucker, K. and S. L. McNerney. 1992. Building coalitions to initiate change. *Public Relations Journal,* 48(1), 38–40.

Walsh, J. 1996. *True Odds: How Risk Affects Your Everyday Life.* Santa Monica, CA: Merritt.

W.K. Kellogg Foundation. 2004. *Logic Model Development Guide.* http://www.smartgivers.org/uploads/logicmodelguidepdf.pdf

Zhu, J. J., X. Wang, J. Qin, and L. Wu. 2012. *Assessing public opin-ion trends based on user search queries: Validity, reliability, and practicality.* Paper presented at the Annual Meeting of the World Association for Public Opinion Research, Hong Kong, June 14–16. https://www.researchgate.net/publication/265946891_Assessing_Public_Opinion_Trends_based_on_User_Search_Queries_Validity_Reliability_and_Practicality.

CHAPTER 4

Step 2—Develop a Campaign Strategy

INTRODUCTION

The second step in the preparedness campaign process focuses on the development of a campaign strategy and a communication plan. In this step, the planning team works together to determine how they intend to communicate the risk reduction solutions identified in Step 1. Campaign strategy development, which draws primarily from the market research conducted in preparation for the communication campaign, involves the selection of appropriate communication settings, channels, and methods, each of which is described in this chapter. The spokespeople who will be transmitting the messages must be identified and recruited, and the timing of communication events and message transmissions must be planned. Campaign messages and materials are developed, which is perhaps the most complex element of the communication effort. Finally, a communication plan is created, and staff is trained, thereby paving the way for the actual communication efforts.

PROJECT KICKOFF

Projects that rely upon a cooperative effort almost always stand to benefit from a milestone event marking their commencement, and public emergency preparedness efforts are certainly no exception. It is common practice for a project manager to hold a project kickoff meeting that serves to (among other things, of course) give all project stakeholders a sense that planning and operational efforts are officially under way. In order to generate excitement among participants, this event is generally celebratory in nature, is oftentimes catered with food and drinks, and adorned with banners and other decorations, and may even include prizes and incentives like logo-bearing, project-related giveaways that help to raise excitement and morale among all participants. With proper foresight and planning, these important events can also provide much more than simple ceremony, including public recognition and the development of strong partner relationships from which the public education effort will grow. Moreover, for most projects, the kickoff meeting is the first opportunity for all stakeholders to gather, giving the project manager a controlled opportunity to bestow a first impression of trust and confidence in all participants.

The adage "the more the merrier" holds true with project kickoff meetings. In fact, attendance should be inclusive of everyone involved in the planning and operation of the project, or at minimum a representative from each group and organization if the project effort is an especially large one. This could include:

- The project manager
- Representatives from the lead organization
- The full project planning team
- Members of partner organizations who might not be involved in the planning effort
- Businesses that are lending support to the campaign
- Project sponsors
- Organizations or individuals who will provide training to team members
- IT and other support staff
- Target audience leaders
- Consultants and contractors

The kickoff meeting serves as a venue for several important project tasks that must occur early in the project. However, for any of the individuals or groups that are participating in the project for the first time, the amount of uncertainty will be high, as will be the learning curve of knowledge and understanding. The project manager can help to ensure that the meeting is effective in addressing these concerns by using a structured organization, guided by an agenda provided to all participants in advance. Kickoff meeting participants who are part of the project planning team or coalition should be provided (if they have not already) with a packet containing information about the project and all participants and partners (including names, phone and fax numbers, and email and mailing addresses). Tasks that should be covered in the meeting include (but are not limited to):

- Introduction of all participants to one another
- Sharing and verification of all contact and communication information
- Setting in motion the official start of the project

- Communication of project purpose, goals, scope, and timelines (perhaps with the assistance of a logic model and Gantt chart, both introduced in Chapter 3)
- Presentation on the intended audience, their vulnerabilities, and proposed solutions
- Communication to all partners of their roles, responsibilities (tasks), and resources
- Voicing of all partner assumptions and concerns
- Discussion of the project budget
- Discussion of project risks
- Discussion of training needs

The project manager can commence this meeting with a prepared motivational statement, and provide all facilitation of the meeting as dictated in the agenda. If there are any conflicts between partners, concerns of participants, or other input or suggestions, this is a great opportunity to identify and manage them early on, before actual project development has begun. Again, it is the impression of organization and control that are of the utmost importance at this initial meeting.

THE CAMPAIGN STRATEGY

In order to begin developing the campaign in a structured, organized fashion, a campaign strategy must be drawn up. A campaign strategy profiles the processes and procedures by which a communication program intends to achieve its risk reduction goals. The strategy, which is created in consideration of resources available to program planners, restrictions in time, and logistical capacity, outlines the guiding principles behind all of the campaign's messages, materials, events, and activities. Ideally, the strategy provides readers with sufficient detail about the target audience's profile, the hazard risk being addressed, the desired behavioral changes and benefits expected as a result, and the actions that can be performed to bring about those changes, to ensure that all program elements are compatible with the campaign goals and objectives (and with each other). It gives the program's creative staff the direction they need to develop the messages and materials that will convey the campaign messages. It must be developed in the best interests of the target audience and should be favorably viewed by that audience should members be given a chance to examine it. The NIH details the components of a campaign strategy as follows:

- A definition and description of the intended audience
- A description of the action the intended audience members should take as a result of exposure to the communication

- A list of any obstacles to taking action (including external influential variables—see Sidebar 4.1 and Sidebar 4.2)
- The perceived benefit (among target audience members) of taking the action
- A description of the support that will make the benefit, and its ability to attain it, credible to the intended audience. (In this case, support is something that can be provided through hard data, peer testimonials, demonstrations, or statements from organizations the intended audience finds credible.)
- The settings, channels, and activities that will reach intended audience members, particularly when they will be receptive to or able to act upon the message
- The image your program plans to convey through the tone, look, and feel of messages and materials. NIH writes that the goal should be to convey an image that (1) convinces intended audience members that the communication is for them and (2) is culturally appropriate. For instance, printed materials convey image through typeface, layout, visuals, color, language, and paper stock used. Web materials convey image through design, typeface, color, layout, and ease of use. Audio materials convey image through voices, language, and music; in addition to these details, video materials convey image through visuals, characteristics of the actors (including their clothing and accessories), camera angles, and editing.

The following is an example of a campaign strategy:

- *Strategy:* Hold flood mitigation training sessions for property owners in the National Flood Insurance Program (NFIP) Special Flood Hazard Area (SFHA).
- *Intended audience:* Low- to middle-income business owners and homeowners whose properties lie at or below the floodplain mitigation goal of base flood elevation (BFE) plus 2 feet.
- *Objectives:* (1) to understand the mitigation options available that would make their structures resilient to flood risk, (2) to understand the NFIP and the options for flood insurance, (3) to obtain and understand a FEMA elevation certificate, and (4) to select and invest in flood mitigation options that provide the greatest increase in protection for their structures for the money spent.
- *Obstacles:*
  - Unavailability of financial resources
  - The lack of technical knowledge required to fully understand certain mitigation options
  - Misperceptions of risk (feelings that "it can't happen to me")

- Undesirable aesthetic changes to homes or businesses
- Loss of use of certain parts of the structure
- Low self-efficacy
- Lack of time
- Competition with other structural improvement needs
- *Key promise:*
  - If I maintain adequate flood insurance for my flood-prone structure, my losses will be covered in the event of a disaster, and I will not be disqualified for future emergency assistance.
  - If I mitigate my structure to at least BFE + 2 feet, my flood risk will decrease significantly and I will enjoy much lower flood insurance premiums.
  - By mitigating my structure from flood risk, I will be much less likely to suffer the long-term negative effects of a flood disaster, will be displaced from my home for a much shorter period of time, will suffer much less of a business interruption, and will have far fewer financial and physical losses.
- *Support statements:*
  - Every year, flooding causes more than 90% of the disaster-related property damage in the United States, and accounts for more than 75% of all presidential disaster declarations. Floods are one of nature's most powerful destructive forces, and they cause more damage than all other forms of disaster in the United States combined.
  - If your home or business has been threatened or damaged by a flood or severe storm, and you have not made any changes to the structure that protect it from water damage, you are probably still at risk for similar or worse consequences when flood events occur in the future.
  - Through engineering, architecture, and sheer determination, it is possible to reduce, or even eliminate, your chances of falling victim to flooding.
  - The NFIP is a federal program that enables property owners to insure their property against flood losses, most of which are not covered under regular business, renter, and homeowner insurance policies.
  - Structures that are mitigated from flood risk have a much higher resale value than those that are at risk of flood damage.
  - Structures located within the NFIP SFHA are legally required to have flood insurance if they are purchased with a federally backed mortgage.
- *Tone:* Urgency without fear; empowerment

- *Channels:*
  - Interactive training sessions of no more than 10 attendees per session, with PowerPoint presentation, Q&A opportunities, and speakers from the NFIP, the County Floodplain Administrator's office, and community organizations
  - Descriptive, easy to understand flood mitigation guidebook
  - Flood mitigation fact sheets
  - Flood mitigation helpline
- *Media:*
  - Local television public service announcements (PSAs)
  - Radio PSAs/live announcer scripts
  - Posters
  - Newspaper ads
  - Billboard and metro transit ads
  - Website
  - Articles in local newsletters
- *Settings:*
  - Rush hour commute
  - Evening news
  - Sunday real-estate section of the newspaper
  - Day, evening, and weekend training sessions
- *Creative considerations:*
  - Solutions must be adaptable to local needs and capacity.
  - Certain mitigation measures may be regulated by floodplain management ordinances.
  - Some property owners may have taken mitigation measures that brought their property into compliance with older flood maps, but under new BFE measures, they are no longer compliant.

This example shows a brief strategy statement. Depending upon the complexity of the campaign, strategy statements of greater detail and length may be warranted to account for multiple projects being performed under the same program umbrella. They may also contain additional background information about the hazard, its risk, the affected target population, and other factors that will assist planning team members in developing the campaign along a unified front.

SIDEBAR 4.1   RISK COMMUNICATION OBSTACLES AND EXTERNAL INFLUENTIAL VARIABLES

Risk communication is as recognizable for its importance as it is for the complex challenges associated with it. While the World Bank claims that "awareness programs addressing existing hazards and physical and social vulnerabilities are often central to social risk reduction" (World Bank 2002), the National Research Council (NRC) Committee on Risk Perception and Communication writes, "risk messages are difficult to formulate in ways that are accurate, clear, and not misleading" (NRC 1989).

Countless risk communicators have experienced project failure caused by obstacles they could not overcome, for which they did not plan, or of which they were simply unaware. These obstacles have included internal and external political affairs, sociocultural issues, and economic constraints of both communicators and recipients. In addition, while some obstacles may be obvious and even well documented prior to initiation of the campaign, many may not appear until well after the campaign has begun implementation. Program planners must always understand that, even with the best-laid plans, the effectiveness of risk communication can and often does fall short of the communicator's expectations because of the presence of obstacles (Morgan et al. 2002). If obstacles are not considered in the planning stages, program planners may face insurmountable problems in the execution of their project. It is therefore vital that planners prepare themselves to identify and manage obstacles as they arise.

Successful risk communication tends to be highly situation dependant, and practitioners who succeeded in reaching target audiences with their intended messages and effecting change are those who have sufficiently identified and mitigated for situational obstacles. Obstacles differ from audience to audience, and community to community. As such, educators working in rural communities may encounter obstacles not typically encountered in urban communities, for example. Some of the obstacles that should be factored in to risk communication projects are reviewed in the following.

- *Literacy and education:* An estimated 781 million adults over the age of 15 are illiterate, two-thirds of whom are women (United Nations 2015). Illiteracy severely limits how risk communication can be conducted. There are countless ways a message can be distributed through written media, such as leaflets, newspapers, billboards, and informational booklets, among others. However, these tools are virtually ineffective if the target population is unable to read the message being transmitted to them. Poor levels of education can also act as an obstacle to effective risk communication. Deprived of basic numeracy skills, for example, a person will be unlikely to understand the statistics included in a risk communication or the specific risk factors being explained to him or her.

- *Language:* Language is an obvious obstacle to risk communication, as it is with all communication topics. It would seem
that one would need only to learn the language of the target
audience to mitigate this issue, but the answer is not always
so straightforward. In many communities, there are several
languages spoken and several dialects of each language.
Throughout the world, there are more than 6,000 recognized
languages. It is a common misconception that all people of
one ethnic group or nationality will speak the official language
of their particular group or country. Such a misconception
can easily lead to risk communication not reaching target
audiences. Unfortunately, even if one does learn the target
population's language, there may be particular abstractions
and colloquialisms that cause common terms and phrases to
have vastly different meanings between two speakers of the
same language. When such misunderstandings occur in risk
communication, the result can be counterproductive at best,
and deadly at worst. In the wake of Hurricane Mitch, 1998,
the nonprofit organization World Vision distributed powdered
chlorine to many villages in Central America for purifying
water. There was found to be widespread appropriate use
of the chlorine in villages where Spanish was the primary
language, but inquiries revealed that indigenous villagers
(whose first language was not Spanish) were using the chemical to wash their clothes. Because the powdered chlorine was
distributed to these indigenous villages without instructions
in their native language, they were unable to properly utilize
the preventive measure. In this instance, the primary outcome
was many gastrointestinal illnesses that probably could have
been avoided. Nevertheless, consequences could have been
much worse if villagers had ingested the chlorine in deadly
doses because of poor risk communication (Swanson 2000).
- *Access to technology or the media:* Risk communicators
regularly employ the media to convey a message to a target audience. This is particularly true during sudden-onset
disasters, where the media become the primary, if not only,
source of communication between emergency responders
and the public. Understandably, this form of communication
is only possible if the target audience has access to television, radio, newspaper, or the Internet. When access is sub-
standard or nonexistent, risk communicators are presented
with a formidable obstacle. The Internet, for instance, which
digitally connects the world's population at ever-increasing
rates, is a newer communications form that has rising

(yet far from blanket) rates of coverage. In addition, while the Internet is an effective risk communications medium, there are certain demographic groups that do not yet enjoy equal or regular Internet access (e.g., the elderly, the poor, recent immigrants, and transient populations). In poor rural areas, lack of access is evident in older communications technologies as well, including radio, television, and telephone. While they may be the message vehicles of choice for risk communicators, researchers, and the media, these forms of communication may not be effective in all communities and for all audiences. Therefore, to mitigate this obstacle, it is important to identify and utilize alternate, nontechnical forms of risk communication.

- *Class structure:* Social scientists have focused considerable research upon the study of community stratification (Cockerham et al. 1986). *Social stratification* refers to the way certain societies' populations are divided into hierarchical groups based upon inequality. Every society has some form of social stratification, the United States included. The way in which select communities practice this discrimination and oppression effectively limits access for each successive drop in class ranking. These institutionalized hierarchical systems have remained steadfast for decades, if not centuries. Their effect has gone beyond the basic socioeconomic factors of wealth and power, and has created a psychological reality that cannot be underestimated by outsiders who may not fully understand their influence. Program planners attempting to transfer their message effectively to populations with such forms of class structure will face a formidable challenge. They will likely need to garner an authoritative grasp of the history and culture of their target audience, much of which may not be formally recorded. It is likely that they will encounter strong resistance unless they can find a diplomatic way to appease all groups while still achieving their stated goals. Furthermore, they will find resistance to change if the risk reduction message requires people to behave unlike one in their caste would (even if that behavior would reduce personal risk).
- *Poverty or the effects of poverty:* Poverty, as it influences behavior, access, and opportunity, is an obstacle to risk communicators almost everywhere. Poverty and disasters are intimately connected, as poverty is often the cause of disasters by means of forcing poor populations to live under conditions that directly place them at great risk, and limiting their access to vulnerability reduction measures. These poor

often live in precarious conditions because they have no other viable, easily identifiable alternatives. Sometimes, even when their vulnerability to disasters is extreme, little is done to mitigate hazard risks despite extensive knowledge about them. People living in extreme poverty are often unwilling or unable to participate in conventional risk reduction measures that do not fully account for their poverty. If risk communicators do not consider the economic means and monetary constraints of the people to whom they are communicating the risk, their message will surely fall upon deaf ears. Many poor people live in riskier places because they cannot find alternate housing, not because they do not know the risks. Simply informing them that they are at high risk from landslides or floods, for instance, would do little—even if alternatives are offered—unless those alternatives are viable within their financial bounds.

- *Cultural understanding:* Incorporating cultural context into risk communication can be very difficult. Risk communicators must fully understand the ways in which not only their words but also their actions, tone of voice, gestures, dress, and approach to discussion, among others, will influence the efficacy of reducing risk. With all population groups, especially those of uniform backgrounds, cultural sensitivity to group-specific attributes must be observed. Not doing so can result in a myriad of negative outcomes, from a communication breakdown to anger, insult, or an increase in risk. However, cultural barriers are not impenetrable if risk communicators avoid ethnocentrisms and utilize creative measures that accommodate local norms.

- *Cultural and social norms:* In addition to understanding how the communication message is received and interpreted by a target audience, program planners must also understand how their proposed solutions mesh with the audience's culture and way of life. Oftentimes, behaviors that contribute to risk are not performed out of ignorance of their negative impact, but rather because they serve some long-standing cultural significance that is not easily abandoned. Program planners must understand the origin of beliefs and behaviors in order to devise solutions that accommodate them.

- *Lack of community sponsorship:* Effective risk communication is undoubtedly enhanced by the official support of a local community and its government, even if that support is marginal. This enhancement is pronounced if there is great trust in the government or community organizations and officials who champion the cause being communicated. Agencies and organizations can show their support by performing actions ranging from making official statements of endorsement to passing laws requiring or prohibiting certain activities. However, if the community or its government does not support the public information message, that stance becomes a severe detriment to communicators.

- *Denial or apathy:* Denial is common, but it can be overcome. People tend to construct psychological barriers to preparedness, either minimizing the likelihood of a threat by assuming it will not affect them if the threat becomes a reality or feeling that there is little they can do to mitigate the consequences of a disaster. By concentrating on the survivability of people in the event that realistic hazards do occur, preparedness education emphasizes positive steps for positive outcomes. The assumption is that people can learn to prepare, and those who do will cope with the disaster better. Apathy differs from denial in that individuals simply lack the motivation to change their behavior despite knowledge of its risk reduction potential. Complex psychological and social processes, in addition to a simple unwillingness or true lack of care, can cause apathy.

- *Risk perception and heuristics:* In order to manage a risk, one must also be able to judge the relative seriousness of that hazard in comparison with other hazards. Risk analysis is what disaster managers use to compare and rank community hazards. For laypeople, however, in the absence of such technical and involved analysis, the mechanisms by which they *perceive* the hazards that threaten them can be very different and very complex. Risk perception is a field of study that attempts to explain why people fear the things they do (and why they do not fear other things). Risk perceptions more often than not differ significantly from actual statistical risks, causing people to fear most things that are statistically unlikely to harm or kill them, while risks that are more probable are of no concern. *Heuristics*, which are types of thought processes that influence the ways people perceive and analyze information and experiences (oftentimes called rules of thumb), have a similar effect on communication efforts. Several heuristics must be considered. For instance, once people make an initial judgment (i.e., first impression), they believe with overwhelming confidence that their beliefs are correct. This phenomenon, called the *overconfidence heuristic*, is the result of people being unaware of how little they know about a risk, and how much more information they need to make an informed decision. More often than not, people believe that they know much more about risks than they actually do. Risk perception and heuristics are described in detail in Chapter 3.

One of the greatest risk communication obstacles comes from the uncertainty, complexity, and incompleteness of statistical data associated with disasters (Covello and Sandman 2001). The uncertainty component of natural and technological hazards is what distinguishes the issues managed by emergency management communicators from those of the public health community (who work with risks for which there exists much greater understanding of associated likelihood or consequence). To make effective mitigation or preparedness decisions, emergency managers rely upon risk assessments that have far fewer data points, and they must rely upon a significant amount of expert judgment (over clinical experience, for example). Covello and Sandman contend that such a lack of more concrete data presents a critical challenge, primarily because the communicators may only be able to state that the risk in question falls "somewhere between serious and nonexistent" (e.g., earthquake risk).

INFLUENTIAL EXTERNAL VARIABLES

In addition to obstacles that get in the way of communication efforts, there is another set of factors that influences how messages are received and perceived by recipients. These factors exert pressure and interference on one or more of the stakeholders in the campaign (including both the communicators and the recipients). Unfortunately, communication cannot be performed within the confines of a controlled laboratory where all factors are restricted in a manner that maximizes the transfer of messages from communicator to recipient. In the real world, there are competing interests, a multitude of voices, and a full gamut of individual agenda.

External variables can exert both positive and negative pressures on a communication campaign. The key is being aware of the variable and planning for it as best as possible either to capitalize on the benefits or to minimize the impediments. Negative influence most often comes in the form of information or belief that opposes or contradicts a key campaign message. This form of outside influence can originate from a multitude of sources, including private interests (businesses), cultural behaviors or histories (including customs and traditional behavior), popular attitudes and beliefs, and many others. The more a planning team is able to identify these factors and adjust for their presence accordingly in their messages, channels, and methods, the less of a detrimental effect they will have on the outcome of their efforts. Each will represent a conflict between the program message and the will of the audience to comply. By directly addressing the concerns or misperceptions of the audience that pertain to these factors through the content of the message, the influence of many if not most of these negative variables can be reduced or avoided.

Outside variables may also have a positive effect on the outcome of the campaign, especially if they are properly identified and appropriately utilized. For instance, the occurrence of a disaster anywhere in the world can have the positive effect of raising awareness both inside and away from the disaster area. During these so-called windows of opportunity, even those who are unaffected are more apt to pay attention to disaster preparedness messages. How much they actually change their behavior will rest upon the abilities of the campaign team to seize upon the increased salience and get their point across effectively. The program may benefit considerably by latching on to the positive or parallel nature of these factors.

It is key to identify both positive and negative external factors as early as possible in the planning process. The difficulty in achieving such early recognition is a matter of access to the information sources by which such discovery is possible. This could be as simple as performing a basic Internet news search or interviewing members of a certain population. The following list of categories of external influential factors is representative of what may be encountered and is by no means exhaustive:

- Current events
- History
- Timing
- Media interest
- Public policy
- The three agenda (government, public, media)
- Competing messages
- Popular culture
- The economy
- Audience characteristics (described in Chapter 3)

SIDEBAR 4.2   PARENTAL INSTINCT PRESENTS AN UNFORESEEN OBSTACLE TO EVACUATION PREPAREDNESS AND PLANNING

A survey conducted in the summer of 2008 found that 63% of parents faced with an evacuation order would disregard those instructions if their children were in school at the time. These parents indicated that rather than flee the area in danger, they would immediately drive to their children's schools to pick them up themselves. Such behavior would likely further hinder both general evacuation efforts by causing more traffic, and the organized evacuation efforts at the individual schools. The survey, which was commissioned by the Columbia University Mailman School of Public Health and the Children's Health Fund, found that nearly 45% of parents did not know to where their children would be evacuated by the schools, which could help explain a certain amount of the anticipated resistance. However, emotional factors would also play a strong role, as indicated by a mother of three who was quoted by the Associated Press as stating, "As a mom, you wouldn't be able to keep me away from picking up my children. My first instinct would be to get them at all costs. I would literally run the entire distance to get them. I believe most parents would feel the same." It is important and even more revealing to note that this individual is also the author of a disaster preparedness book entitled *Your Home Office Recovery Plan*, a fact that emphasizes the strength of the emotional obstacle.

Source: Matthews, K., *Survey Finds Holes in U.S. Disaster Preparedness*, The Associated Press, 2008, http://bit.ly/2jq1JgV.

SELECTING APPROPRIATE SETTINGS, CHANNELS, AND METHODS

Program planners must design their message within a framework that accommodates the ways in which their target audiences acquire information in general and specifically as it pertains to hazards and risks. Each audience will be unique in this regard as a feature of their means, culture, social networks, and other factors as described in Chapter 3. For example, people living in poverty or who are marginalized in society often gather information to make decisions through informal social networks rather than from newspapers, official government sources, or other formal communication methods. Members of these groups may mistrust government and other "official" information sources, leading them to ignore or disregard their messages. Another group, transient populations (e.g., tourists and business travelers), tends to be limited in both time and motivation when learning about particular hazard risks simply because they are outside their normal social and physical environment (and therefore less likely to perceive a hazard risk that might not be readily apparent). Special needs populations, which include the elderly, young children, the disabled, and the illiterate, for example, must each be approached in a manner that addresses their particular method of perception and learning.

These preferences are identified through market research and defining the target audience.

Program planners should consider three factors when determining how to deliver a message to a target audience. They are:

1. Settings
2. Channels
3. Methods

Settings

Settings are the situations in which communication occurs (see Figure 4.1). Learning is not uniform in all situations. Some settings hinder the communication process; others foster message receipt and understanding. It is not hard to imagine the difference in success of learning for students in the classroom as compared with in an arcade, for instance. Identifying appropriate settings for message delivery increases the probability of program success.

Three primary factors distinguish a setting:

1. *Time*
   - Time of day (e.g., morning, afternoon, evening)
   - Day of the week (e.g., weekday, weekend, Sunday)
   - Time of year (e.g., hurricane season, during summer vacation, wildfire season, early winter)

FIGURE 4.1 Preparedness campaign billboard in western New York uses a fear appeal to urge commuters to visit the campaign Website to gain information about emergency preparedness.

2. *Location* (e.g., at home, at work, in school, while on vacation, in a car or other form of transportation, at the doctor's office, in a store, at a community center)
3. *Situation* (e.g., while having dinner, while gathering with friends or peers, while shopping, while attending a school assembly, while visiting a county fair)

Obviously, people are most receptive to preparedness messages when the disaster poses an imminent threat, which lifts the topic to the forefront of the public and media agenda. However, various nondisaster times also occur throughout the year when public interest in the topic of preparedness may be raised to a comparable degree. During these key times, the news media recognize the salience of the issue and are therefore more likely to pay attention to events, use material from press releases, request interviews from key officials in the organization, and attend preparedness-related events. A campaign kickoff event, in which a key official announces the start of a preparedness or other effort at a planned ceremony, can be very effective at drawing positive media attention. National Preparedness Month is probably the single greatest time of the year for an organization to hold a disaster-related kickoff event (see Figure 4.2). Of course, any time of the year is appropriate, as long as there is a campaign, event, or other news to announce. Disaster seasons allow another opportunity to garner public and media attention. While not all hazards have designated times of year when their likelihood goes up, many do. For example, a set hurricane season runs each year from June 1 to November 30. The media grasp upon the opening of this season, which provides an excellent opportunity to draw attention to the event. Other examples of hazards with seasons include wildfires and severe winter weather. Anniversaries of major disasters, especially in the first years following that disaster, can draw equal (if not more) attention as disaster seasons. Fifteen years after the September 11 attacks in New York and Washington D.C., there is a marked increase in media attention to terrorism during the weeks surrounding that important date. Late August has drawn attention to hurricane preparedness every year since Hurricane Katrina. The flurry of preparedness activity surrounding the 100th anniversary of the Great 1906 San Francisco Earthquake demonstrates that events do not need to be recent. Finally, there is the ever-present availability of "piggybacking" activities. Piggybacking is achieved by injecting a preparedness message into another important event or activity that is salient and therefore in the media spotlight.

The key to selecting a setting is to determine not only where and when you can best reach the target audience but also where and when they are most likely to attend to, receive, understand, and act upon your message. The best places are those that help to establish message credibility.

FIGURE 4.2   Oakland, California, September 18, 2007—As part of the National Preparedness Month, FEMA employees manned information booths to help build public awareness and provide booth visitors with preparedness materials for home, family, school, businesses, and individuals with disabilities and special needs. (*Source:* FEMA News Photo.)

Unfortunately, times, places, or situations that are ideal for reaching the audience are not always ideal for delivering the message. For this reason, we must also consider communication channels.

Channels

A channel is the route or mechanism through which a message is delivered. Within each broad channel category, communicators can reach their target audience through many different individual sub-channels. The five primary message channels, and examples of sub-channels within each category, are listed in the following:

1. *Interpersonal channels (face-to-face):* Interpersonal channels rely upon the direct personal interaction between a communicator and an audience member. Often, the spokes people are people who are highly trusted by the audience member, who serve

as authority figures, or who are in some way influential to the audience member. As such, interpersonal communication channels tend to be the most effective at motivating people to change. The human interaction helps to mobilize people and can provide social support to maintain the behavior changes that are advocated. However, because of their reliance on high-effort one-to-one interactions, they do not necessarily have the immediate and broad reach of other channels such as, for instance, the mass media.

2. *Group channels:* Communication methods included in these channels are those that create or exploit gatherings of target audience members, whether to discuss the intended message or for another reason entirely. Like interpersonal channels, group channels can help communicators to enjoy some of the trust and influence that exist within the group, but by talking with several individuals at once, the message reach is much greater. In addition, by creating discussions among peers with similar wants and needs, many doubts can be alleviated not only by the spokesperson but also by peers themselves (thereby lending more credibility to the message). However, these methods are also similar to interpersonal methods of communication in that they require significant effort to reach larger audiences over time.

3. *Organizational and community channels:* Communication methods included in these channels include those that rely upon official, established entities operating within the community that are able to interact with members of the target audience. These are many of the same organizations and entities that were described in Chapter 3. Businesses, NGOs, local and state government organizations, religious organizations, and many others can help you to communicate your message to the intended audience. While they may not be as willing as those individuals and groups described in the interpersonal and group channels to have at-length discussions about emergency preparedness, they may help communicate your message by posting signs, distributing fliers, playing videos on showroom monitors, making announcements, or referring audience members directly to you or your Website or social media page either in person or on their own Websites or social media pages. These organizations, groups, and other entities often operate on a much larger scale than do the individuals or groups mentioned in the previous two channels and can therefore have a much greater overall message reach. In addition, when they are recognized within the community, and enjoy a high level of respect among community

members, they can be very effective conduits, regardless of whether their mission relates to emergency preparedness. Their involvement in your campaign is, in essence, a sponsorship of your message.

4. *Mass media channels:* Communication methods included in these channels include those that broadcast a message out to large audiences. Mass media campaigns have been tried and tested in the public health field and have already found success in the emergency management field with emergency preparedness messages. The news media, which include television, radio, print, and Internet news outlets, are the most recognizable component of the mass media. However, the mass media is a much broader category that spans many other conduits, including:

- Magazines
- Billboards
- Theater
- Trade publications
- Cinema and television shows
- Talk shows
- Advertising
- Direct mail systems
- Entertainment programming

Until relatively recently, program messages were broadcast through mass media channels in a largely unidirectional manner. As traditional mass media channels have developed and expanded their online counterparts, and social media has become a standard element of a modern lifestyle, news and information consumption has increasingly become a more selective and social behavior (Napoli 2011). Sidebar 4.3 discusses characteristics of news stories that increase their likelihood of going viral, thereby increasing public exposure to the message.

5. *Interactive digital media channels*: Interactive digital media channels represent the most recent addition to the short list of communication channel categories. Communication methods included in these channels include those that exploit the Internet and other digital communication media to allow for direct interaction between communicator and recipient. Although this communication form shows incredible promise in terms of its expanding communicators' reach and success, it still carries inherent problems (see Sidebar 4.3). Sub-channels found within this category allow for greater matching of message to intended audience, but unlike the regular mass media

channels, these allow for audience feedback. The digital media are already recognized as one of the, if not *the*, fastest growing communication tools. With proper Webpage development and design, organizations can quickly and effectively reach large numbers of people with only a small investment in time and resources. Websites also allow for an immediate two-way interaction that is more difficult to attain through banners, fliers, and other message dissemination methods. A Website can be designed to simply communicate the developed message by including descriptions of planning initiatives with upcoming meeting dates, times, and minutes from meetings, or it can be highly complex and interactive with links to mitigation and hazard resources and sites and opportunities for questions and answers. Websites are also good venues for posting questionnaires for citizens to determine their perceptions of hazards and risks in the community or state, as well as to provide an additional outlet to generate feedback on issues. In many ways, this channel is a fusion of the previous four channel types.

6. *Mobile channels*: As of 2015, 64% of Americans owned a smartphone, up from 35% in the spring of 2011. Approximately one-in-five adult Americans (19%) own a smart phone and have limited or no high speed Internet access beyond their phone's data plan (Pew Research Center 2015). As such, cell phones have become a prominent-enough channel for campaign message distribution to warrant a separate discussion as a sub-category of interactive digital media channels. Many public health and emergency preparedness programs often now include a mobile communication component that provides information mostly through terse messages in the form of a short message service (SMS) or mobile version of a social networking service (e.g., text messages or tweets). Researchers have begun to examine how these types of messages are interpreted (Bean et al. 2016) and to identify content, style, and structural features associated with retransmission of terse emergency messages (Sutton et al. 2015). Early evidence suggests that messages that use imperative sentences and include a hashtag are retransmitted more often than those that don't. Inclusion of a URL for further information actually decreases retransmission rates (Sutton et al. 2015). Because this is a relatively new channel for message distribution, more research is needed to identify best practices for creating and distributing effective emergency preparedness messages through mobile devices.

SIDEBAR 4.3   CHARACTERISTICS THAT INCREASE VIRALITY OF MEDIA CONTENT

People currently have more channels and sources of news and other media content to choose from than ever before, and with the click of a button, they have the opportunity to share this content either privately (through email or personal messaging) or publicly (through their social media accounts or personal Webpages). An understanding of this selection and retransmission process can help program planners to craft messages for news outlets and online campaign materials that expand the campaign's reach beyond just the individuals who view any one particular news source or Webpage.

Research on the diffusion of media content has pinpointed the following characteristics of media content that increase the likelihood that they will be selected and shared:

1. *Emotionally evocative:* Media content that makes people feel high arousal emotions, regardless of whether they are positive (e.g., awe) or negative (e.g., anger, anxiety), is more likely to be selected (Knobloch-Westerwick 2015) and shared with others (Berger 2014; Kim 2015). Content that produces low arousal emotions (e.g., sadness) is less likely to be shared with others (Berger 2014).
2. *Novel:* People are more likely to select (Lee 2008) and share media content that is unusual, surprising, or that told them something new (Berger 2013, 2014; Berger and Milkman 2012; Kim et al. 2013). One study demonstrated that novel news stories were more likely to be shared through private channels (email) than public channels (social media posts), however (Kim 2015).
3. *Useful:* Media content that is practically useful to consumers is more likely to be selected (Knobloch-Westerwick 2015) and shared (Berger and Milkman 2012) as well. Some ways to make content more useful might be to provide resources (e.g., names of appropriate agencies or links to appropriate Websites), instructional information, and demonstrations.
4. *Prominent location:* When media content is displayed as one of several options on a Webpage (e.g., one of several news stories on a page), it is more likely to be selected when it appears on the upper left-hand corner of the page or other places of prominence, such as a "most popular stories" list (Kim 2015). Program planners may try to negotiate with smaller local media outlets for a place of prominence

(e.g., negotiating for emergency preparedness program information to appear in the upper left-hand corner of an office newsletter).

SIDEBAR 4.4   PROBLEMS ASSOCIATED WITH INTERACTIVE DIGITAL MEDIA CHANNELS

- *Credibility:* Most (but not all) Internet users are aware that anyone with Internet access can post information regardless of its accuracy. Communicators must therefore be able to demonstrate a high level of credibility if their message is to be taken at face value by target audience recipients—a requirement if they hope for their message to be believed. *Healthy People 2010*, a public health communication effort, recommends that communicators disclose the following information in order to build credibility among recipients (NIH, 2009):
  - The identity of the developers and sponsors of the site, how to contact them, and information about any potential conflicts of interest or biases
  - The explicit purpose of the site, including any commercial purposes and advertising
  - The original sources of the content on the site
  - How the privacy and confidentiality of any personal information collected from users is protected
  - How the site is evaluated
  - How content is updated
- *Recipient access:* The average computer user is affluent and well educated. Although Internet access is increasing, it is not universal like that of television and radio. First, there is the issue of physical access. Although the number of Americans with Internet access has increased exponentially over the last decade, the Pew Research Center estimated that about 16% of American adults still did not use the Internet in 2015. Second, there is the question of technical proficiency. Unlike passive learning as occurs on television, the Internet requires not only an active learning style but also an understanding about how to use the hardware and software required to find and access preparedness information. The gap between those with and those without Internet access is called the *digital divide* and tends to affect those living in poverty, the elderly, and other special needs populations.

Source: Adapted from the National Institutes of Health. (NIH). (2009). Healthy People 2010. NIH. http://www.healthypeople.gov/2010/.

Methods

The actual transfer of message content from communicator to recipient is performed through one or more message distribution methods. A message distribution method is an actual item, action, interface, or event that program planners use to draw the attention of the target audience member, and to inform him or her of the behavior change that is necessary (or how to access that information). As was true with the settings and the channels selecting, message distribution methods must fall within the access, interests, and learning styles of the recipient audience members. Several message distribution methods are specific to communication channels, including the following:

Methods unique to the interpersonal channel include discussions with:

- A teacher or professor
- A friend
- Family members
- An insurance agent or financial planner
- A building contractor
- A coach or counselor
- A religious figure (e.g., priest, pastor, rabbi, imam)
- A doctor

Methods unique to the group channel include:

- Classroom discussions
- Adult education
- Neighborhood association meetings
- Parent–teacher association meetings
- Municipal and civic club meetings
- Town hall meetings
- Office meetings (including brown bag lunches, for example)
- Religious gatherings
- Volunteer events

Methods unique to organizational and community channels include:

- Signs or free advertising in grocery stores, home improvement stores, hardware stores, or other businesses
- Information included in local utility bills or phone books
- Signs in subways, buses, or other forms of public transportation
- Signs or brochures offered in waiting rooms
- Information in hotel rooms or on tourist maps

- Message delivery by community advocacy groups
- "Bag stuffers" placed with purchases in stores
- Information printed on packaging (e.g., on a milk carton or cereal box)

Methods unique to the mass media channel include:

- Live broadcasts at preparedness events or recorded interviews
- Feature stories on preparedness events
- Mentions in news stories or programs
- Preparedness subject matter incorporated into TV shows or other television programs
- PSAs
- Magazine advertisements, articles, or messages
- Newspaper editorials
- Columns in newspapers and magazines
- Press releases
- Press kits
- Press conferences
- Call-in shows
- On-air announcements

Methods unique to the interactive digital media channel include:

- Emergency preparedness Websites
- Preparedness "Webinars" (online seminars)
- Online bulletin boards
- Online courses
- Online presentations
- Online videos
- Online forums
- Newsgroups
- Instant messaging services
- Email preparedness messages
- SMS (telephone messaging) messages
- Digital video conferencing (DVC)
- Web-based surveys
- Online preparedness games and activities
- Blogs
- Links from other Internet sites to your Website or links to preparedness information
- Informational kiosks

There are many other methods, which can be used on their own or combined, that apply to more than one communication channel.

These are limited only by the creativity of the planning team, and include (among many others):

- *Brochures, fliers, fact sheets, newsletters, and inserts*: These are relatively inexpensive to produce and can be useful in reaching a wide audience. The materials can be created either internally or externally, and may be something that a business with printing capacity could donate to the campaign in kind. If created electronically, these materials can be generated and distributed for little or no cost. As with all publications, all materials should be reviewed for accuracy and message, approved by appropriate staff, and tested with members of the target audience before they are distributed. The materials should be clear and easy to read and understand. The message should include a designated department or contact name and phone number in case a reader is interested in learning more. One way to quickly reach a wide audience is to work with a partner, such as a utility, to include the materials as an insert in a bill. Alternatively, partners may agree to distribute the materials to their clients or customers. Examples include electricity or phone bills, the Yellow Pages or phone book, at grocery or department stores, in government buildings, and at libraries.
- *Festivals, fairs, and other public events*: Public events provide unique opportunities for program personnel to reach large numbers of their intended audience in a relaxed and informal atmosphere. The events may be initiated and managed by the organization for the purposes of communicating with the public, or the organization may simply decide to participate in an event being managed by another organization for a related or unrelated purpose (such as would be the case with an annual county fair). The communication opportunities at a large public event are diverse and may range from an informational booth to performances and demonstrations. Often, even if the event organizers are charging a set fee for booth space or other involvement, it is possible to garner donated time or space because of the public-service nature of the communication effort. These events allow for the use of several of the different available communication channels. In addition, they allow organizations conducting public education efforts to talk to their audience about their experience with hazards and try to use this information to better tailor their education efforts in the future. A particularly beneficial aspect of this form of communication is that the event provides people with an opportunity to ask questions face-to-face.

- *Advertisements*: Organizations of all types are often willing to donate or otherwise provide advertising and other communication means to disaster preparedness programs. Businesses can be tapped to assist in educational efforts both within and outside of the realm of their offices. Internally, efforts could include employee preparedness campaigns or materials distributed to employees to take home to share with friends and family. Externally, businesses may help by providing advertising time or space, materials and equipment, endorsement of the campaign, inserts in bills or newsletters, mailings, giveaway items for events, and other things as appropriate for each business type. Religious groups and churches can distribute pamphlets or have speakers at their many events, and may even sponsor special events focusing on disaster preparedness topics. Social organizations operate in a similar fashion and would likewise have the capacity to foster public education of its members or the public in general. Using guest speakers and experts, public education teams can reach these captive or interested audiences.
- *Formal education (in schools)*: Schools are natural places of learning, and as such they can foster effective disaster-specific education among students. Schools are very often receptive to education efforts aimed at decreasing the vulnerability of students. In-school programs often involve disaster safety mascots (such as Sparky the firedog), representatives from the emergency services (a firefighter or police officer), or other public officials. In school, education is either classroom-based or performed in large auditoria. Some schools may allow posters to be hung on classroom and hallway walls or to have representatives from the organization present at large events where a table or other educational venue can be set up. Educational materials that target student populations could include special disaster-specific courses (long or short), distributed materials and fact sheets, information integrated into regular coursework, games, coloring books, and contests, among others. When designing a school-based emergency preparedness program, it is important for program planners to remain cognizant of the difficult balance between preparing students for scary events and scaring them. Sidebar 4.5 discusses a situation in which the needs of the emotional well-being of school children were neglected in the name of preparedness education.
- *Adult and other "out-of-class" education*: Special courses can be designed to teach adults or out-of-class students about disaster preparedness in much greater detail than is possible in

distributed documents or media announcements. Programs such as CERT have been widely successful in creating local cadres of citizens prepared to respond to disaster events. Organizations could create CERT-type courses that are tailored to the specific needs and abilities of their audience (see Figure 4.3).

- DVDs and books
- *Emergency drills and exercises*: Emergency drills and exercises test one or more aspects of disaster response by exposing participants to an imagined or recreated disaster scenario. Tabletop exercises involve the reading of a disaster narrative followed by questions and discussions. Functional and full-scale exercises involve action that is more realistic, oftentimes with actors playing the various roles involved in an actual response. Drills and exercises are effective on several levels, including their ability to raise awareness to a disaster, their ability to highlight deficiencies in preparedness, and the reinforcement of effective practices that save lives and property. In addition, they tend to garner media attention. The greatest detriments to this communication method are the cost and planning difficulties it involves.

FIGURE 4.3 Emmitsburg, Maryland, March 10, 2003—FEMA's National Emergency Training Center is the site for dozens of classes, including sessions that train CERT leaders from across the country. (Courtesy of Jocelyn Augustino/FEMA News Photo.)

- *Alternative media*: For most audiences, and most common messages, television, radio, and print are the conventional methods of delivery. However, special media is required for some special needs audiences, such as Braille for the blind.

Other examples of transmission methods include:

- Posters
- Bookmarks
- Handbooks or manuals
- Checklists, to-do lists, and shopping lists
- Disaster preparedness–themed game boards
- Cartoons and comic books
- Photographs
- Theatrical performances
- Informational pages in telephone books or other directories
- Information printed inside matchbox covers
- Disaster information displays or kiosks
- Markers or signposts established to remind residents of past disaster incidents
- Tours containing hazard and preparedness information
- The creation of a speaker's bureau (to guarantee that any service organization, parent–teacher group, or church group can learn about emergency planning)
- Disaster preparedness camps or workshops
- Pre-assembled do-it-yourself preparedness kits
- Public service announcements
- Exhibits
- Conferences
- Disaster simulations
- Disaster awareness events
- Branded merchandise
- Communication programs internal to organizations (such as with employees, members, parishioners, etc.)

SIDEBAR 4.5   UNANNOUNCED ACTIVE SHOOTER DRILLS IN SCHOOLS

According to a 2016 report from the United States Government Accountability Office, two-thirds of U.S. schools engage in some form of active shooter drills. Across the country, for the past two years, news outlets have been peppered with stories about students and teachers being terrified when these types of drills were held in their school with no warning that it was a drill. The rationale behind an unannounced drill is that nothing will prepare students and teachers better for an emergency event than the real thing. These types of drills, however, have reportedly caused severe emotional distress for teachers and students who were led to believe their lives were in jeopardy. Students, teachers, and parents were furious when they were informed that the event that brought Winter Haven middle school into lockdown as armed police officers burst into classrooms with their weapons drawn was simply a drill. Students reported fearing for their lives (Grider 2014). An Oregon teacher brought a lawsuit citing civil assault, emotional distress, false imprisonment, failing to protect her and supervise the staff, and depriving her of her liberty without due process after a man dressed in a black hoodie and goggles burst through her classroom door, leveled a gun at her face, and pulled the trigger, which produced the sound and smell of gunfire, during a surprise active shooter drill at her school in Halfway, Oregon (Denson 2015). When working with human participants, it is of utmost importance for program planners to weigh the risks of any exercise versus the anticipated benefits. Although unannounced drills are thought to prepare teachers and students better for real-life active shooter situations, is the difference in the levels of preparedness among teachers and students who underwent active shooter training surprise drills and those who underwent active shooter training without surprise drills great enough to offset potential risks such as post-traumatic stress, delays in taking protective action in a real active shooter situation because students and teachers assume it is a drill, and other health complications due to the hectic nature of the drill (e.g., a teacher having a heart attack)?

Source: US Government Accountability Office, 2016.

SELECTING COMMUNICATION CHANNELS AND METHODS

Communication channels and methods are selected according to how the audience is most likely to receive the information being communicated, and the resources and abilities of the program. Communicators can use a single channel, or even a single method, but they are more likely to see a desired change in target audience behavior if they employ a combination of channels and methods to broadcast their message. In addition, when resources allow, the format of the message can be varied and communicated to the audience in many different ways, as often as is possible and practicable. The generally accepted belief is that more channels and more methods translate to wider exposure.

To maximize exposure, planners should focus on channels with which the target audience has regular contact, and that they perceive as credible. Familiarity with the channel and with the communicators themselves helps to build message acceptance. For example, projects that use popular entertainment media (e.g., movies, soap operas, radio plays, music, theater, comics, and so on) have been found to be particularly successful because target audience members can identify with the heroine or hero, or a well-known idol, giving them a motivational push in the desired direction of change.

Because the impact of a single interaction can be short-lived, repetition of the message helps to ensure that learning occurs. Static images and messages, such as those on posters or PSAs, eventually become monotonous, and target audiences may stop paying attention to them completely. For this reason, it may be necessary to change channels, materials, and messages from time to time.

Interpersonal contact is ideal for an education effort, regardless of the channel or combination of channels selected. The mass media is adept at building interest in a topic, but personal consultation or motivation by a trusted caregiver can make all the difference between mere awareness of a topic, having a positive attitude toward it, and actually adopting the new behavior. Personal communication can strengthen the lessons learned through all other channels and can fill in the gaps where mass media and other less personal channels fail to penetrate. It is always wise to include some avenue that allows for interpersonal contact between the target audience and communicators.

For each channel and method under consideration, program planners should measure the pros and cons. This can be done by considering the following questions:

- What access does your organization have to the channel or method?
- How many people will be exposed to the message transmitted by the channel or method?
- Will target audience members pay attention to the method transmitted by the channel?
- Does the intended audience accept and trust the channel or method?
- Can the target audience be influenced by the channel or method?
- Is the channel or method appropriate for conveying information at the desired level of simplicity or complexity?
- If skills need to be modeled, can the channel or method be used to model and demonstrate specific behaviors?
- Can the channel or method provide interactivity between the target audience and communicators?
- Using the channel or method, how long will the message last (i.e., will it be transmitted once, lasting seconds, or will it last for weeks or months as with signs or print materials)?

- Can the channel or method allow the intended audience to control the pace of information delivery?
- Can the target audience control the pace at which information is delivered?
- Are there any opportunities for repetition with the channel or method?
- Does the channel or method increase the likelihood that the target audience members will retain the message?
- Does your program have the resources to use the channel or method?
- Is the channel or method appropriate for the activity or material you plan to produce (see Figure 4.4)?
- Will the channel or method reinforce messages and activities you will develop through other routes (in order to increase overall exposure among the intended audiences)?

Once channels are identified, the basic principles of advertisement should be observed. The following formula has been time-tested for use in determining the likelihood of success when exposing a message to the public:

$$\text{Reach} \times \text{Frequency} = \text{Success}$$

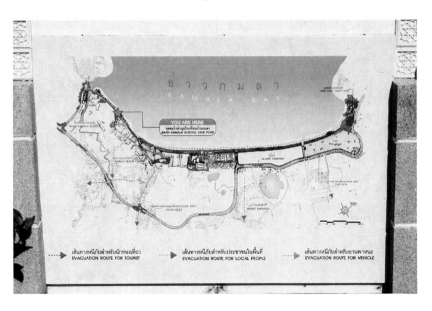

FIGURE 4.4   Tsunami evacuation sign, Phuket, Thailand. This evacuation sign is intended to provide a preparedness message to an audience that generally has a very short attention span to such matters—tourists on vacation (Author photo).

where Reach is the percent of the target population in a geographically defined area exposed at least once to the message during a specific time frame, and Frequency is the number of times a message has been broadcast to a target audience.

A Canadian public health communication program that promotes healthy living, Active2010, has identified the following strengths and weaknesses of several of the methods listed previously:

Strengths	Weaknesses
Print Media (newspapers, journals, and magazines)	
Large reach	Literacy implications
Can be free or low cost	Message must be newsworthy
Information can be kept and shared	Exposure can be limited to one day
Information covered more thoroughly than other mass media channels	Possibly low emotional appeal
Works well with complex messages	Can be expensive
Newsletters	
Reaches opinion leaders	Labor intensive
Low cost	Tends to preach to the converted
High message preservation	Literacy implications
Responsive	
Radio	
Large reach	Can be expensive
Range of formats	No visuals
Can be low cost or free	Little or no placement control
Can be interactive with call-ins	PSAs tend to be played during off-hours
Use of scripts can give the impression that messages are live and from the radio hosts	May only reach a specific audience
Timely and repetitive	Limited to radio reception area
Possible use of celebrities	Limited audience retention
Literacy not an issue	
Television	
Extensive reach	Can be very expensive
Can be free	High level of complexity is possible
Different target groups reached	May be a limited reach
Visual impact	PSAs run infrequently and at low viewing times
	Messages may be obscured by commercial clutter
	Retention can be difficult

Continued

Strengths	Weaknesses

Posters, Signs, and Billboards

Attract attention	Can be expensive
Wide reach	Low audience specificity
Captive audience	Limited to short, simple messages
High message repetition	
Geographically focused	
Visuals can have great impact	

Telephone

Confidential, personal, and private	Cost can be high
Interactive	Intrusive
Follow-up is possible	Labor intensive
Efforts can be directed to specific audiences	
Can be inexpensive	

Electronic (including CD-ROM or DVD)

Large reach (but select audience)	Literacy barrier
Interactivity is possible	High cost for equipment
More youth-friendly	Requires skills and training
Easily updated	

Internet

Can reach large numbers of people quickly	Can be expensive
Can instantaneously update and disseminate information	Many target audiences do not have Internet access
Control over information is possible	Audience must be proactive (they must find and access the Internet themselves)
Information can be tailored to specific audiences	Newsgroups and chat rooms may require monitoring
Can be interactive	Can require maintenance over time
Information can be presented in a graphically appealing way	
Can combine the audio/visual benefits of TV or radio with the self-paced benefits of print media	

Mail

Reaches specific area (e.g., zip code)	Cost can be high
Information can be retained	Can get lost or seen as junk mail
Follow-up is possible	Literacy can be an issue
Appeals to visual learners	Can create negative associations
Can be directed (named individually)	

Continued

Strengths	Weaknesses
Point of purchase (such as in a hardware store)	
Timely	Relatively small reach
Immediate reinforcement	Loses effectiveness over time
Can be interactive (e.g., demonstrations)	Can discriminate against low-income people
Information is targeted where it is needed	Difficult to partner if controversial
Good opportunities for partnerships	Depends on others to get the message out
Presentations	
Interactive	Relatively small reach
Specific and captive audience	Can be costly in time and resources
Timely information	Poor retention
Control of content	Presenter's beliefs and biases may affect message
Training	
Reaches specific audience	Low motivation if attendance is not voluntary
Strong multiplicative power	Different learning styles may not be accommodated
Builds skills	
Peer-to-peer support	Limited one-on-one consultation
Interactive	Commitment to follow-through not guaranteed
Informal networks	
Interactive	Information may be biased or unreliable
Comfort of cultural similarities	Focus on experience may be narrow
Familiar and safe	Requires a certain personality
Provides access to other networks	Can be exclusive to some
Social support provided	Limited, homogenous group
Contests, Fairs, Fundraisers, and Festivals	
Large reach	Difficult to follow-up on and evaluate
Interactive and fun	Difficult to tailor to a specific audience
High visibility and interest	Labor- and resource-intensive
Opportunity for media coverage	Short lifespan and narrow focus
Captive audience	
Interpersonal Channels	
Most effective for teaching and helping	Can be expensive and time consuming
More credible	Can have limited target audience reach
Permits two-way discussion	Can be difficult to access these channels
Can be motivational, influential, and supportive	Sources need to be convinced and taught about the message themselves

Continued

Strengths	Weaknesses
Organizational and Community Channels	
May be familiar, trusted, and influential	Can be costly and time consuming to establish
May provide more motivation/ support than media alone	May not provide personalized attention
Can be inexpensive	Organizational constraints may require message approval
Can offer shared experiences	
Can reach larger intended audience in one place	May lose control of the message if adapted to fit organizational need

SELECTING SPOKESPEOPLE

For many (although not all) of the communication channels and methods listed previously, the planning team must select and train spokespeople to transmit their messages to the intended audience. The task of selecting spokespeople is one that deserves careful consideration of the planning team because he or she may be as important as the message itself. Risk communication messages are so diverse that almost everyone, including children, parents, the elderly, educators, the illiterate, and employers, is capable of communicating them. It is the variance between and particulars of message settings, channels, and target audience members that determine which of these various spokespeople is likely to be the most effective at bringing about actual behavioral change. These different spokesperson characteristics must be identified and exploited in order to increase the likelihood of message reception *and* acceptance among different target audiences. While some spokespeople may be great public speakers and have the ability to sway the opinions of large audiences, others may be similarly effective working with individuals through interpersonal interactions. The goal is to make target audience members feel personally addressed and, likewise, taken seriously by the spokesperson. When assessing and selecting communicators, the following measures may be used:

1. *Speaking ability*: Not all people can communicate a message in an effective manner in such a way as to convince the recipient of their message. One of the most common fears, in fact, is that of public speaking. Others may fail to present arguments coherently, losing the point of their message in transmission. Speaking ability, whether in one-on-one situations or to large audiences, is central to communication and is easy to assess by looking at experience and successes.

2. *Reputation among audience members (trustworthiness and credibility)*: Message recipients will judge a message not only

by its words but also according to any preconceptions they have about the spokesperson. The changes in behavior that audience members are expected to make are changes that will likely affect their thinking, their finances, and possibly their way of life. Understandably, people will only be willing to take the prescribed advice if they hold a great amount of trust in the spokesperson—and for each spokesperson, trust and credibility will differ according to the audience. Clearly, anyone who has previously betrayed the trust of their audience, or has even been accused of doing such, would have difficulty finding receptive ears. Credibility, or the ability to be convincing, is related to trust and varies by audience for each communicator. For instance, while citizens with legal residency status may find a high-ranking government official to be credible, illegal immigrants who are more likely to be evasive of the government will likely disregard the message entirely.

3. *Subject matter knowledge*: Spokespeople must have a strong understanding of the topic, or at least of the information contained in the message they are communicating. If they appear to waver at all in their understanding, or if they make a factual error, the audience will negate their message entirely. Even one small factual error, if discovered by the audience, will likely result in complete message failure.

4. *Image of authority*: In certain situations, audience members will listen to a spokesperson's message only when they believe that the spokesperson is more knowledgeable about the topic than they are. For this reason, the spokesperson's credentials become as important as the knowledge he or she is imparting. With children, for instance, almost any adult will seem convincing. For an educated adult, however, information about the spokesperson's background will play into the believability of the message.

5. *Obvious lack of vested interest*: Spokespeople must convince their audience that they are providing risk reduction information simply out of care or concern. If the audience feels that the spokesperson has anything personal to gain from changes in audience behavior (such as a financial gain resulting from the sale of some product like pre-assembled emergency kits), or that his or her intentions are politically self-serving, then they will not be likely to change their ways.

6. *Ability to connect, sympathize, or empathize with the audience*: Finally, the audience must be able to relate to the spokesperson. The spokesperson can often achieve this through the exploitation of personality, common traits, or characteristics shared with the audience, or through relating common experiences.

No spokesperson will suit every audience's needs. Therefore, planners will have to have an open mind when considering the ideal candidates. The following categories of communicators illustrate the wide range of possibilities available to the planning team:

- Peers (friends, people of the same age or gender, people of the same financial status, people of the same demographic, etc.)
- Family members (parents, children, brothers, sisters, etc.)
- Teachers
- Employers (managers, business owners)
- Caregivers
- Advocates (union leaders, representatives)
- Retailers (local or national)
- Authority figures (community leaders, elected officials, police officers, firefighters, EMS technicians, etc.)
- Religious leaders
- Community groups (Boy Scouts/Girl Scouts, 4H, Jaycees, etc.)
- Celebrities (athletes, musicians, actors; see Sidebar 4.4)
- Cartoons, puppets, or mascots
- Actual disaster victims

SIDEBAR 4.6   SMOKEY BEAR

One of the most effective emergency preparedness communicators of all time, and clearly one of the most recognized in the United States, is Smokey Bear. The Smokey Bear campaign was created by the Ad Council in 1944 to serve as the face of forest fire prevention in the United States, educating and urging citizens to take the necessary precautions to both prevent and respond to forest fire emergencies. Over the years, in what has become the longest running public service campaign, Smokey has been depicted in cartoons, animations, posters, radio ads, books, as a costume-wearing mascot, as stuffed animals, and much more. Smokey's message, "Only you can prevent forest fires," is credited with decreasing the acreage of land lost annually to forest fires from 22 million to 4 million. As a testament to the campaign's reach, a 1989 survey found that 71% of American children ranging in age from 5 to 13 recognized the image of Smokey Bear and could recount his fire prevention message (Fuller 1991). The U.S. Forest Service, the Ad Council, and the National Association of State Foresters administer Smokey Bear, and his image is protected by federal law. Communicators can arrange through their state forester to have Smokey Bear appear at certain events, given that they are large and open to the public.

DESIGN AND DEVELOP MESSAGE CONTENT

Upon completing the formative research behind the campaign, planners can begin to develop messages that are based on their findings. By ensuring that they consider the basic tenets of communication science, practitioners can maximize their likelihood of message effectiveness. This section provides an overview of some such considerations.

Message appeal is one of the first and most critical decisions program planners make when designing their messages. Three of the most common appeals used in persuasion attempts are humor, guilt, and fear. Each is described in the following:

1. *Humor*: Humorous appeals have enjoyed modest success in motivating people to engage in particular behaviors in the past. Generally, when people find themselves entertained by a humorous message, they are unable to carefully process the most important points that the message is trying to transmit. Because of these inherent problems, humorous appeals work best in simple campaigns such as advertising because they are able to increase brand recognition without having to make a compelling case for product use. Brand recognition is not guaranteed with humor appeals, however, because oftentimes people become so wrapped up in enjoying the joke that they fail to pay attention to the brand or behavior being promoted by the message.

2. *Guilt*: Messages that use guilt appeals are relatively easy to design because it is rather easy to invoke feelings of guilt in people who have failed to engage in a particular behavior. Guilt appeals often grasp upon message recipients' care and concern for loved ones. Research suggests that guilt appeals are highly effective when messages are exchanged in face-to-face encounters. However, target audience members do tend to downplay the importance of, and even avoid, people who make them feel guilty. For this reason, guilt appeals are not recommended for campaigns that are mostly using mass media to spread the message.

3. *Fear*: Fear appeals, which convince target audience members that something bad will happen to them or people close to them if they fail to engage in a promoted behavior, can be a highly effective persuasion method (see Figure 4.5). Fear appeals are most common in the field of emergency management preparedness campaigns. Planners seeking to use fear appeals must be very careful, however, as these messages can and often do backfire.

By this point in the campaign design process, program planners have a good understanding of the target population's risk and the

FIGURE 4.5 Public health education has long used fear appeals to encourage smokers to quit their habit. This series of anti-smoking packaging in Singapore uses an extreme form of fear appeal (Author photo).

protective behaviors they may take to mitigate this risk, so now the question program planners must answer is "Why are members of the target audience not already engaging in this protective behavior to reduce their risks?" Perhaps, the most important reality to keep in mind when designing campaign messages to motivate behavior and behavior change is that simple awareness is rarely, if ever, enough to motivate members of a target audience to engage in the recommended protective behavior. It is not uncommon for people to be fully aware of their own risk and how they may mitigate it, and yet still fail to take action. For any given population, there are countless unforeseen barriers preventing individuals from engaging in protective behaviors to lower their risk.

Fortunately, decades of social science research has produced a number of theories that identify these barriers and messages designed to address these barriers. Theory-based messages have been shown to motivate individuals to take action when simple messages about awareness do not. The following sections will describe several such theories and their constructs. Each theoretical construct may be viewed as a barrier to behavior change. Program planners may be best served by selecting an appropriate theory to guide in message design and use the lists of theoretical constructs provided as a checklist of considerations when making decisions about campaign slogans, activities, and takeaway messages (i.e., the message design process).

The Extended Parallel Process Model

As mentioned previously, fear appeals are most common in the field of emergency management preparedness campaigns. Witte's (1994) Extended Parallel Processing Model (EPPM) provides a set of guidelines for constructing effective fear appeal messages.

The theory lists four main constructs to consider when designing messages meant to scare people into taking protective action. The first two constructs have to do with the threat itself:

1. *Perceived susceptibility:* Messages designed to scare people into taking action to protect themselves make people feel as though they are personally vulnerable to the threat being discussed. If people do not feel that they and their loved ones are particularly vulnerable to a threat at the moment, they will not be motivated to take action to mitigate that threat. One example of failure to take emergency preparation action due to low perceptions of susceptibility is people who refuse to evacuate their homes before a killer storm hits the area. This group of people may not feel susceptible because past storms have hit the area and didn't cause as much damage as was predicted, or they may just have trouble psychologically accepting the idea that such a dramatic and unlikely event would happen in their lives. And so, they choose to take their chances and try to wait out the storm in their own homes. Emergency preparedness messages designed to raise target audience members' perceptions of susceptibility to the threat may provide statistics about the likelihood of experiencing a negative outcome for failing to comply with the recommended behavior. Sometimes, it helps to include stories of people who are similar to members of the target audience who suffered the consequences of failure to take action. These messages are meant to make members of the audience think "That could have been me."

2. *Perceived severity*: Members of a target audience who already feel susceptible to the threat at hand are still unlikely to take protective

The additional two constructs of the HBM are:

1. *Perceived benefits and perceived barriers*: Perceived benefits and perceived barriers to engaging in the recommended behavior are listed together because the HBM specifies that an individual will only engage in the promoted health behavior if the perceived benefits associated with the behavior outweigh the perceived barriers to engaging in that behavior. Before designing campaign messages, program planners should do formative research with members of the target audience to compile an exhaustive list of all of the perceived benefits and barriers. If the benefits outweigh the barriers, and individuals are still not engaging in the recommended behavior, it is likely that their failure to act is attributable to one or more of the other HBM constructs. If, however, the barriers outweigh the benefits, program planners should design messages that promote additional benefits to engaging in the behavior (that are not already on the list of people's current perceptions of benefits) and/or eliminate some of the perceived barriers to engaging in the recommended behavior. For example, members of a target audience may fail to compile a basic disaster supplies kit because they only perceive one benefit—something in the kit may be of use at some point in their lives, but they perceive two barriers—the cost of the supplies is prohibitive and they do not have enough space in their small apartment to store gallons of water and other supplies. Based on this information, program planners might design some messages to eliminate some of the barriers, such as providing tips on where and how members of the target population might acquire their kit materials at low cost and demonstrating creative ways for storing such items in small spaces.

2. *Cues to action*: Sometimes members of a target audience are completely on board with engaging in preparedness behaviors, but because it is not first and foremost in their minds at all times, they just need a nudge or reminder to take action. For example, parents may make emergency plans with their children that need to be adjusted from time to time with updated optimal meeting spots, contact information, etc. Program planners may build in periodic email or text message prompts, or hold annual fairs or events to serve as a reminder to update family plans.

THEORY OF PLANNED BEHAVIOR

Not all emergency preparedness messages are framed as a public health issue. A more general theory that has been used for understanding, predicting, and changing human social behavior is Ajzen and

Fishbein's (1980). Theory of Planned Behavior (TPB). Program planners using the TPB to guide their message design should consider three main theoretical constructs that are predictive of behavioral intentions, which ultimately lead to engaging in the behavior itself:

1. *Attitudes*: For any given behavior, individuals are thought to hold a variety of different behavioral beliefs, which are perceptions that a given outcome is likely if they engage in the behavior at hand. Some of these behavioral beliefs may be positive (e.g., If I enroll in the active shooter workshop that is being offered at my workplace, I will learn the skills that are necessary to survive in the event of this type of situation in my office), and some may be negative (If I enroll in the active shooter workshop that is being offered at my workplace, I have to take time from my busy day to attend; If I enroll in the active shooter workshop that is being offered at my workplace, I will be forced to think through a situation that I'd rather avoid thinking about). The composite of all behavioral beliefs, weighted by how positive or negative as well as how likely the outcome is, makes up an individual's attitude toward the recommended behavior. If the positive, behavioral beliefs outweigh the negative behavioral beliefs, members of the target audience will have a positive attitude toward the behavior, so a lack of action is likely due to one of the other TPB constructs described later. If the negative behavioral beliefs outweigh the positives, members of the target audience have a negative attitude toward the behavior, which may be why they are not engaging in the recommended protective behavior. If this is the case, campaign messages may be designed to change people's attitudes toward the behavior by promoting additional positive behavioral beliefs (e.g., enrolling in the active shooter workshop that is being offered at the workplace will give participants peace of mind that they know what to do in such a situation) and downplaying or eliminating prominent negative behavioral beliefs (e.g., Lunch is provided at the workshop, so the time spent at the workshop is just the time participants are usually away from their offices for lunch anyway).

2. *Norms*: Although the theory generally only considers one type of norms (i.e., social norms) in predicting behavioral intention, researchers have found that consideration of two other types of norms, descriptive norms and injunctive norms (Cialdini, Reno and Kallgren 1990), may offer further insights into behavioral intentions.

   2A. *Subjective norms*: Subjective norms refer to a person's perception of what others who are important to the person expect him or her to do. A message used in an attempt to persuade with a subjective norm should seek to remind or reveal to the target audience that the people closest to them, such as family and friends, expect them to engage in the behavior being promoted. For example, an emergency preparedness campaign might include messages reminding the target audience of their children's expectations for them to have a plan to keep them safe in the event of an emergency.

2B. *Injunctive norms*: Rather than just considering what important others expect, injunctive norms involve the types of behavior of which important others approve and disapprove. It is generally expected that behaviors that are in line with the injunctive norm will be socially rewarded and behaviors that go against the injunctive norm will be socially punished. A message used in an attempt to persuade with an injunctive norm should seek to remind or reveal to the target audience that the people who are most important to them approve of or disapprove of the behavior in discussion. For example, an emergency preparedness campaign might include messages revealing to the target audience the percentage of their peers who think that they ought to talk to their children about the plan of action in the event of an emergency.

2C. *Descriptive norms*: Descriptive norms refer to the prevalence of a behavior within a population. It has been shown that people tend to perceive that certain unhealthy behaviors are far more common in a population than they actually are. In terms of emergency preparedness, people may feel that their failure to take proper actions to prepare themselves and their families for a disaster is excusable because most other people have not prepared themselves or their families either. If people were informed that most other people have, in fact, taken the proper emergency preparedness actions, they are likely to feel pressurized to take these behaviors themselves in order to be normal.

Program planners who are interested in using the TPB to guide in campaign design may visit Dr. Icek Ajzen's Webpage, which provides sample questionnaires and specific instructions for TPB campaign design and evaluation (Ajzen 2017).

PILOT TEST AND ADJUST MATERIALS

Program planners use the insight provided by theory as well as results of formative research that was conducted in the early stages of campaign development to create targeted campaign messages. It is important to remember, however, that sometimes campaigns even with the most carefully developed materials that take all theoretical and formative research into account end up missing the mark with the target audience. Therefore, once campaign materials have been generated, it is necessary to conduct additional focus groups to pilot test them all before making any decisions about their use in the campaign. These focus groups should be conducted in a fashion similar to those conducted before the start of the campaign development process. This time, however, rather than asking questions about group members themselves, group moderators should probe for group members' thoughts about each of the potential campaign messages, often presented through mock-up campaign materials. Some salient questions to ask may include:

1. What do you think about when you see/hear/read this message?
2. Which message do you like best, and why?
3. Which message do you like least, and why?
4. Which font/color scheme do you like best, and why?
5. Which font/color scheme do you like least, and why?
6. Would you be motivated by this message to engage in the prescribed behavior?

Pilot tests can provide the insight necessary to weed out messages that are generally despised, despite being guided by theory and derived from the formative research on target audience members. Moreover, even messages that are highly regarded by focus group members can still be improved upon. The purpose of the pilot test meeting is to identify which of the messages would be most effective among group members and what changes can be made to the message to make it even more effective. Based on the results of this exercise, campaign designers should select a single message design, make any final adjustments that may have been suggested within the group, and prepare for message distribution.

ACTIVITIES AND EVENTS PLANNING

Many of the communication channels described in this chapter involve participatory activities or events for campaign message distribution. Events and activities are beneficial in that they allow program planners the opportunity to extend the reach of their campaign across many audience members at once. However, this adds a certain level of complexity because of the planning that must be conducted in advance of the activity or event to ensure that it achieves the desired outcome. Event planning is a distinct skill set that should be considered when forming the planning team. As was true with the selection of communicators, planners should consider the preferences and needs of the audience in the planning for risk communication events and activities.

The following list provides a brief overview of the issues that must be considered when planning events or activities:

- Should the event or activity be stand-alone (e.g., a demonstration at a local elementary school), co-hosted by other organizations with similar interests (e.g., a public safety fair), or should the organization piggyback a larger event that is being planned and conducted by another organization (e.g., a county fair)?
- When should the event be held, at what time of day, and for what duration?
- What budget exists or should be allocated for the event?
- How many participants or attendees are expected to come, what is their demographic makeup, and what are their expectations and reasons for attending?
- How will the event be advertised (press releases, or print, television, and radio ads), or will invitations be used?
- How will you ensure publicity for the event? Will the press be invited and what information will you provide them (e.g., press kits)?
- What type of venue is required to host the event (including size, accessibility, services, equipment, etc.), and what options exist in the community?
- How will the event be managed?
- What will the staffing needs be (workers and volunteers), what skills will be required, how will schedules be managed, and what will be the standard operating procedure for staff and volunteers interacting with the public?
- Which speakers will be invited and what will they talk about?
- What activities will take place and how will they be conducted?
- What risk reduction educational materials will be created and distributed and how many are needed?
- Will food and refreshments be served?
- What supplies (e.g., giveaways, paper and pens) and equipment (e.g., audio/visual, communications) are needed to conduct the event or activity?
- What liability coverage is required, and what exists or is being done to ensure the safety of all in attendance (emergency exits, law enforcement, and emergency medical care)?

- Is access to all participants with special needs ensured (see http://www.health.state.ny.us/nysdoh/promo/events.htm   for more information)?
- How can participants be tracked after the event?
- What are the expected outcomes of the event or activity, and what methods for evaluation exist?
- What follow-up will be conducted?

ESTABLISHING A PROJECT TIMETABLE

One of the last project management tools created before campaign implementation begins is the project timetable, which details both implementation and evaluation of the campaign. Communication campaigns involve dozens, if not hundreds, of individual tasks that must be carried out. Timelines allow for the priority ranking of tasks and help to illustrate tasks across the life of the project (making other management problems such as staffing and funding easier to assign). The timeline is most effective if it includes every task that will be carried out, no matter how small. By including all tasks, project managers help to ensure that they are able to carry out all tasks at the time they are needed, to assign workers or volunteers and resources to only one task at a time, and to make sure that the project is kept on its intended schedule. Timetables should be created in a way that allows for mid-campaign changes, and additions or deletions of individual tasks that become irrelevant as the project is implemented. In addition, because timelines are fluid in nature, they should be reviewed periodically and adjusted to account for any changes that have occurred since the last review.

CREATING THE COMPREHENSIVE COMMUNICATION PLAN

The culmination of project planning is marked by the creation of a comprehensive communication plan. The communication plan provides those working on the campaign with an accurate blueprint of how the intended communication will play out, and provides for all partners a tangible and established record of what will be taking place and what is expected to occur as a result. This document presents and explains the project's budget, and justifies spending where required. Finally, it illustrates the lifecycle of the campaign. There are several components normally included in a comprehensive communication plan, as follows:

- The campaign strategy (described at the beginning of this chapter)
- A program logic model partnering plans

- Message and materials development and testing plans
- Implementation plans (including standard operating procedures and plans for distribution, promotion, and process evaluation [described in Chapter 5], for example)
- Outcome evaluation plans
- Task lists and timelines

CONCLUSION

The development of a campaign strategy and a communication plan requires as much creativity as is required for the theory and the application of tested methodologies. At the completion of this step, the planning team will have determined how they will communicate with their audience, including the settings, channels, and methods. Their campaign strategy will be set, as dictated by the market research they conducted in preparation for the risk communication efforts to follow. Chapter 5 describes the process by which all of this preparation becomes actual communication, and the ways in which communicators measure their effectiveness.

REFERENCES

Ajzen, I. (2017). *Theory of Planned Behavior.* Accessed January 2017 http://people.umass.edu/aizen/tpb.html

Ajzen, I., and Fishbein, M. (1980). *Understanding Attitudes and Predicting Social Behavior.* Englewood Cliff, NJ: Prentice Hall.

Bean, H., Liu, B. F., Madden, S., Sutton, J., Wood, M. M., and Mileti, D. S. (2016). Disaster warnings in your pocket: How audiences interpret mobile alerts for an unfamiliar hazards. *Journal of Contingencies and Crisis Management, 24*(3), 136–147. doi: 10.1111/1468-5973.12108.

Berger, J. (2013). *Contagious: Why Things Catch On.* New York: Social Dynamics Group, LLC.

Berger, J. (2014). Word-of-mouth and interpersonal communication: Review and directions for future research. *Journal of Consumer Psychology, 24*(4), 586–607.

Berger, J., and Milkman, K. (2012). What makes online content viral? *Journal of Marketing Research, 49,* 192–205.

Cialdini, C. A., Reno, R. R., and Kallgren, C. A. (1990). A focus theory of normative conduct: Recycling the concept of norms to reduce littering in public places. *Journal of Personality and Social Psychology, 58,* 1015–1026.

Cockerham, W., Lueschen, G., Kunz, G., and Spaeth, J. (1986). Social stratification and self-management of health. *Journal of Health and Social Behavior, 27*, 1–14.

Covello, V., and Sandman, P. M. (2001). Risk communication: Evolution and revolution. In *Solutions to an Environment in Peril*. A. Wolbarst, Ed. Baltimore, MD: Johns Hopkins University Press, pp. 164–178.

Denson, B. (2015, April 20). Teacher terrified by surprise "active shooter" drill in eastern Oregon schoolhouse files federal lawsuit. *The Oregonian*. http://www.oregonlive.com/pacific-northwest-news/index. ssf/2015/04/teacher_terrified_by_surprise.html

Fuller, M. (1991). *Forest Fires*. New York: Wiley.

Grider, G. (2014, November 16). Florida students terrified as Police hold unannounced active shooter drill in elementary school. *Now The End Begins*. http://www.nowtheendbegins.com/florida-students-terrified-police-hold-unannounced-active-shooter-drill-elementary-school-video/

Kim, H. S. (2015). Attracting views and going viral: How message features and new-sharing channels affect health news diffusion. *Journal of Communication, 65*, 512–534. doi: 10.1111/jcom12160.

Kim, H. S., Lee, S., Cappella, J. N., Vera, L., and Emery, S. (2013). Content characteristics driving the diffusion of antismoking messages: Implications for cancer prevention in the emerging public environment. *JNCI Monographs, 2013*(47), 182–187.

Knobloch-Westerwick, S. (2015). *Choice and Preference in Media Use: Advances in Selective Exposure Research*. New York, NY: Routledge.

Lee, J. H. (2008). Effects of news deviance and personal involvement on audience story selection: A web-tracking analysis. *Journalism & Mass Communication Quarterly, 85*, 41–60. doi: 10.1177/107769 900808500104.

Matthews, K. (2008). *Survey Finds Holes in U.S. Disaster Preparedness*. The Associated Press. September 21. http://bit.ly/2jq1JgV.

Morgan, M. G., Fischoff, B., Bostrom, A., and Atman, C. J. (2002). *Risk Communication: A Mental Models Approach*. Cambridge: Cambridge University Press.

Napoli, Philip M. 2007. Media policy: An overview of the field. McGannon Center Working Paper 19. Bronx, NY: Fordham Univ.

NIH. (2009). *Healthy People 2010*. NIH. http://www.healthypeople. gov/2010/

NRC (National Research Council). (1989). *Improving Risk Communication*. Washington, DC: National Research Council, National Academies Press.

Pew Research Center. (2015). *U.S. Smartphone Use in 2015*. http://www. pewinternet.org/2015/04/01/us-smartphone-use-in-2015/

Rosenstock, I. M. (1966). Why people use health services. *Milbank Memorial Fund Quarterly, 44*, 94–124.

Sutton, J., Gibson, C. B., Phillips, N. E., Spiro, E. S., League, C., Johnson, B., Fitzhugh, S. M., and Butts, C. T. (2015). A cross-hazard analysis of terse message retransmission on Twitter. *Proceedings of the National Academy of Sciences of the United States of America, 112*(48), 14793–14798. doi: 10.1073/pnas.1508916112

Swanson, J. (2000). Unnatural disasters. *Harvard International Review, 22*(1), 32–35.

United Nations. (2015). *The World's Women Chapter 3: Education.* http://unstats.un.org/unsd/gender/chapter3/chapter3.html

United States Government Accountability Office. (2016). *Emergency Management: Improved Federal Coordination Could Better Assist K-12 Schools Prepare for Emergencies.* http://www.gao.gov/assets/680/675737.pdf

Witte, K. (1994). Fear control and danger control: A test of the extended parallel process model (EPPM). *Communication Monographs, 61,* 113–134.

Witte, K. (2017). *Research Support Information* (Survey Items, Focus Group Protocol). https://msu.edu/~wittek/#anchor2

World Bank. (2002). *Natural Hazard Risk Management in the Caribbean.* Latin American and the Caribbean Region: World Bank.

CHAPTER **5**

Campaign Implementation and Evaluation

INTRODUCTION

Upon completing all of the background research, design, and planning, it is finally time for the project team to begin implementing its campaign. In Chapter 3, the importance of setting measurable goals and objectives was stressed. Meeting those objectives is the entire purpose of the campaign, and by assessing them directly, the campaign team is able to determine whether those goals have been met or whether the campaign was a success. One should never use arbitrary or anecdotal evidence to assume campaign objectives were met; only properly planned and conducted evaluation can measure the impact a campaign has had on an audience. This chapter examines the launch, management, and evaluation of an emergency preparedness public education campaign.

CAMPAIGN LAUNCH

A program's launch sets the stage for the rest of the campaign to follow. It is therefore crucial that planning teams have previously taken the time to consider as many of the roadblocks the campaign may face and have already formulated plans of action to avoid what is preventable (see Sidebar 5.1). While in-process changes are possible, the campaign team should always set out to achieve its goals with the campaign it launches.

Many programs begin with a *kickoff event*. Like the kickoff meeting described in Chapter 4, a kickoff event is designed to draw attention—in this case to the launch of the campaign. A campaign cannot successfully persuade its audience if the members of that audience are not exposed to its messages. Therefore, the kickoff event is sometimes used to garner media coverage of the campaign, which in turn creates exposure. Campaign planners must keep in mind that as significant as they believe the message of their campaign to be, it will be but one of thousands of critical issues competing for news coverage every day. Therefore, it is vital that they create something exciting and new that grabs people's attention (see Figure 5.1). Whatever the event, it should always be closely tied to the campaign's issue and allow ample opportunity to expose people to the campaign's message.

A well-run kickoff event produces what is referred to as *brand recognition*. Brand recognition helps audience members to pay attention to and later recall campaign messages when they encounter spokespeople and their methods. A kickoff event can also generate increased community involvement in the espoused cause, which in turn may lead to an increase in interpersonal conversations about the issue being promoted. All of these generally lead to a positive change in behavior.

FIGURE 5.1   New Orleans, Louisiana, May 21, 2006—Wali Armstead, FEMA Public Affairs Officer, hands a preparedness kit to raffle winner Mary Rogers at the "FEMA Family Preparedness Day" in New Orleans. FEMA brought together many organizations to present emergency preparedness information to allow parents and children to gather emergency supplies and decide where they will find safe shelter for themselves and pets during dangerous storms. Many of the items that go into an emergency supply kit were provided free at the event during raffles, activities, and games. (Courtesy of Marvin Nauman/FEMA Photo.)

THE MEDIA

In order to inform the press about a kickoff or other event, or about the campaign in general, campaign designers create media kits that are distributed to various local and national media outlets. A media kit is a collection of information about the campaign that generally includes things such as:

- A press release about what is being promoted
- Research and statistical information about the issue as it pertains to the target audience of the media outlet, complete with charts, graphs, and other visuals that can be used in a news story
- Background information about the problem and the proposed solutions
- Credibility-enhancing background information about those associated with the campaign

Media kits are relatively simple to make, but it can quickly become expensive if they are developed for every outlet. Therefore, it is highly cost-effective to research local media outlets before considering which to approach. It would be wasteful, for instance, to send a media kit to a newspaper that clearly never covers any issues that are similar to the one promoted by your campaign. Among the outlets that are decidedly viable options to receive media kits, it is also important to consider that it is not a guarantee that your media kit will be read. If possible, it is a good idea for a spokesperson from the campaign to hand-deliver all media kits directly to people working at the media outlet.

SIDEBAR 5.1 LAUNCH CHECKLIST

It is always important to consider all possibilities and to be prepared for things that may not work according to plan. This is particularly important when the campaign launch includes a kickoff event that is going to be covered by media outlets. The NIH's *Planner's Guide to Making Health Communication Programs Work* provides a checklist, in the form of questions, which can be used before launching a campaign to ensure that everything about the campaign's launch has been considered. Items on this checklist include:

- Are our partners prepared for the launch?
- Have we invited all the necessary partners and stakeholders who have been involved in program development?
- Have we prepared (or trained, if necessary) our staff and spokespeople?

- Are program-related services (e.g., a hotline, inspection service) in place?
- Do we have a list of media outlets we need to contact?
- Are all of our promotional materials ready?
- Do we have enough materials to start the program (e.g., PSAs and media kits) and respond to inquiries (e.g., leaflets for the public)?
- Are reordering mechanisms in place?
- Do we have mechanisms in place to track and identify potential problems?
- Are emergency managers and other emergency service providers in the community aware of our program and prepared to respond if their constituents ask about it?

Source: National Cancer Institute. 2004. *Making Health Communication Programs Work.* Department of Health and Human Services. National Institutes of Health. http://bit.ly/1KZAQHb.

EVALUATION

In their chapter, "Communication Campaign Effectiveness: Critical Distinctions" in Rice and Atkin's (2001) widely cited book, *Public Communication Campaigns,* Salmon and Murray-Johnson drew a distinction between campaign *effectiveness* and campaign *effects.* An *effective* campaign is one in which the goals and objectives set during the preliminary stages of campaign design are met. Campaign *effects,* on the contrary, are any outcomes produced by the campaign. Not all campaign effects contribute to campaign effectiveness. In fact, in some cases, campaign effects can be contrary to the campaign's purpose. For example, in the public health sector, a systematic review of published studies evaluating substance abuse prevention programs found that, although some programs resulted in reduced levels of drug and alcohol consumption, and some had no impact on substance use at all, others appeared to *increase* drug and alcohol use among target audience members (Werch and Owen 2002). There are various reasons that explain why this might occur, but it is suggested a primary cause is criticism of the campaign and its efforts by people influential to the target audience members. In such cases, a campaign may be highly effective in generating message exposure but is considered *ineffective* because it produces an *effect* that is opposite its intended objective. Proper evaluation needs to detect contradictory effects and stop them from spreading.

In addition to preventing further harm, evaluation improves the odds that a program will be successful. Using evaluation methodologies, campaign designers are forced to set measurable objectives that the campaign will attempt to achieve. Once established, these decisions may be used to guide all factors relevant to the design process. Materials, events, and messages are each created and designed according to the goal of meeting these predefined objectives.

OBJECTIVITY IN EVALUATION

After spending large amounts of time and energy creating campaign materials, it can be impossible to provide a truly objective viewpoint on the project using one's own personal assessment of success. Even the most unbiased individual is unlikely to succeed in observing a strictly representative sample of the target audience in order to ensure that observed effects are uniform throughout the target population. Therefore, the final campaign assessment should ideally be based on trying to achieve pre-set effects that are objectively measurable.

Based upon the three primary public disaster preparedness education goals, namely (1) raising awareness of the hazard or risk(s); (2) guiding public behavior, including pre-disaster risk reduction behavior, pre-disaster preparedness behavior, post-disaster response behavior, and post-disaster recovery behavior; and (3) warning the public, some examples of measurable effects may be:

1. Increasing the total number of visits to a Website
2. Increasing scores on a knowledge test distributed among the target audience
3. Increasing sales of safety or preparedness equipment being promoted
4. A count of the number of people engaging in the promoted behavior obtained through some type of random selection such as random digit telephone calling

Objectives based on these goals could include, for example:

1. Increase by 20% the number of hits on the campaign's Website within two months of program launch
2. Increase the average score on a knowledge test administered to high school students by five points within two years of program launch
3. Increase the total number of people using tornado-resistant safe rooms in the target area by 10% within three years of program launch

THE JUSTIFICATION FOR EVALUATION

In the end, campaign success is determined not by the number of people who merely were exposed to the message, nor by the degree to which people "like" or "enjoy" the campaign materials or messages, but rather by the degree to which it meets the objectives set at the beginning of the campaign design process.

Campaign assessment is not a simple task. Most of the statistical techniques required to achieve a useful evaluation of campaign effect sizes are well beyond the scope of this book. For this reason, it is highly recommended that campaign evaluation be left to professionals with statistical expertise and training relevant to public education campaign design. Hiring a professional with such knowledge can cut heavily into the overall campaign budget, which is the primary reason why project planners often neglect evaluation. Campaign planning teams may reason that it is senseless to spend money on evaluation that could have otherwise gone toward extending the campaign's reach and increasing exposure among the target audience. The response to such accusations is that campaign evaluation is the *only way* to ensure that the campaign is effective in meeting its objectives. Perhaps, more importantly, without evaluation there would be no way to ensure that the campaign is not producing any effects that run *counter* to its objectives. Finally, if campaign evaluation indicates that the messages have been highly effective, the results can be used to garner more funding to continue with the campaign to extend far beyond its initial reach.

Launching a campaign is generally both an exciting and a stressful event. It can be fun to see a vision, created through much research and hard work, transformed into reality. Still, it is crucial to recognize that no matter how well prepared, organized, and straightforward the implementation plan may be, and no matter how responsible and well-trained campaign staff is, it is almost certain that not everything will go according to plan when it is time for implementation. For this reason, it is vital to monitor the ongoing campaign through process evaluation.

PROCESS EVALUATION

Process evaluation is a procedure through which researchers assess the degree to which campaign implementation is being conducted as planned. Process evaluation is conducted at specified points throughout the campaign. For instance, it would be impossible for brochures that were designed to provide the public with information about local natural hazards to do so if they were never actually distributed to the target audience. Likewise, promotional events would be unlikely to have the intended impact if the target audience was not made aware of them through proper advertising methods. Throughout the course of a campaign, countless details can be forgotten, misunderstood, or misinterpreted by campaign staff or audiences. A proper process evaluation helps to measure these effectiveness issues by answering the following three questions:

1. *Is the target audience being exposed to the message?* As was previously noted, a campaign cannot effectively meet its objectives if the target audience does not see or hear its messages. The process evaluation effort should therefore include a measurement of campaign exposure among members of the intended audience.
2. *Is the campaign producing any unanticipated adverse effects?* No matter how much formative research or theory is used to guide campaign design, there is no way to predict how an audience will interpret a message. Even the most well-intentioned message can be misinterpreted or disliked by the audience for reasons not understood by the program planners. Sometimes, focus groups that are used in formative research fail to form a representative sample of target population members, which in turn increases the likelihood that opinions and tastes of the general target populations will be misjudged. Process evaluation assesses overall reactions among the intended audience. For instance, process evaluation results may suggest that campaign messages are offensive, misunderstood, disliked, or simply ignored, giving communicators a chance to adjust mid-stream and avoid outright campaign failure.
3. *Is the campaign being conducted exactly as planned?* Unforeseen roadblocks undoubtedly appear during the course of campaign implementation. Process evaluation helps to correct that which can be fixed and documents that which cannot. This information provides program planners with an opportunity to assess their outcomes in response to what *is being done*, as opposed to what *was planned to be done*, giving them the chance to make more knowledgeable process adjustments.

Program planners should consider how a campaign is conducted when making assertions about the campaign's effectiveness at its conclusion. It is crucial to remember that all of the effects that are detected in campaign evaluation should be attributed to the actual campaign that was carried out rather than the campaign that was planned. Information about these effects comes from the campaign's *summative evaluation*. Although summative evaluation is not actually conducted until the conclusion of the campaign, it plays a large role in decisions made throughout the entire process. The following sections detail various campaign design decisions to be made and the implications they have for final campaign evaluation.

EXPERIMENTAL AND QUASI-EXPERIMENTAL DESIGN

In a perfect world, all campaign summative evaluations would stem from perfectly executed *true experimental designs*. True experimental designs are the only way to rule out all other explanations for the effects produced by the campaign effort. The following section defines experimental design and distinguishes it from simpler designs called quasi-experiments. The most common types of experiments are listed. In addition, suggestions are made about the practicality of each as it pertains to your own campaign.

True Experimental Designs

A true experimental design is the only way to determine conclusively that the effects produced are due to the campaign and the campaign alone. All other designs open themselves up to a variety of criticisms and alternate explanations for the effects produced. True experimental designs necessitate three conditions:

1. *Treatment group:* The treatment group is the segment of the population that receives the campaign that has been designed to produce changes in knowledge, attitudes, and behavior.
2. *Control group:* The control group is the segment of the population that is the same as the treatment group in all ways except for the fact that it does not receive the campaign messages that were designed to produce changes in knowledge, attitudes, and behavior. The control group provides a marker of what would be happening throughout the entire population had it not been for the campaign. Keeping all things (i.e., demographics, living conditions, location, etc.) except for the campaign constant allows for the attribution of all differences between the treatment and the control group at the conclusion of the campaign to the campaign itself.
3. *Random assignment to conditions:* Random assignment to conditions means that every person to be assessed in the final evaluation has an equal chance of being assigned to either the treatment or the control group. Statistically speaking, use of random assignment provides the greatest probability that all things, including demographics, living conditions, location, and others, are evenly distributed across the treatment and control conditions. Random assignment to conditions is the only method that allows researchers to assume that all things besides the campaign itself were held constant between the treatment and control groups and therefore any differences between the treatment and control groups can be attributed to the campaign.

When using random assignment, it is important to remember that "random" does not mean "chaotic." A legitimately random assignment technique gives everyone involved an equal probability of being assigned to either the control group or the treatment group. Evaluators can do this using traditional or computerized randomization models that range from picking slips of paper out of a hat to highly complex number-generating software.

Random assignment is what differentiates true experimental designs from quasi-experiments (a term introduced by Campbell and Stanley [1963]), which are discussed later in this chapter. There are three types of true experimental designs, the benefits and drawbacks of which are described. Program planners should be aware, however, that these methods and examples are presented in a simplistic manner, and that the results they generate do not offer as clear effects as could be claimed by experimenters who apply rigorous experimental design and statistical data testing. Moreover, while it is not always feasible, trained professionals should evaluate campaigns for this reason. The three types of true experimental designs are:

1. *Post-test only control group design:* This method is the simplest of true experimental designs. This design assesses all participants in both the treatment and the control groups in terms of the independent variable at a single point in time after the campaign has completed. Randomly assigning all participants to either the control group or the treatment group allows researchers to assume that their scores on the outcome variable before campaign implementation are roughly even. Because the control group is not exposed to the campaign, it is expected that its outcome scores will remain constant throughout the campaign. Those in the treatment group, however, should change outcome scores as a factor of campaign exposure such that they meet the objective set in the campaign's early design. The post-test scores of those in the control condition can be used as an indicator of what the scores would be for the treatment condition before the campaign, and any difference between the treatment and control group in terms of scores on the outcome variable can be attributed to the campaign. Therefore, for example, if campaign planners set out to measure their success in increasing emergency preparedness knowledge among high school students by 20%, they might use the following steps:
   a. Recruit several high schools that agree to participate in the study.
   b. Use random assignment to create control and treatment groups. Because the campaign would likely be conducted

within the schools themselves, preventing those in the control group from being exposed to the campaign would be difficult. Therefore, changing the *unit of analysis* from the individual (student)-level to the group (school)-level would yield results that are more accurate. This change would mean that each *school*, rather than each *student*, would be assigned a unique number, and all students in the schools whose numbers were randomly selected would be considered part of the treatment group.

c. Administer the campaign within all schools in the treatment condition and not in the schools in the control condition.

d. After the conclusion of the campaign, assess all students in both conditions in terms of the outcome variable. In this case, the objective is to increase knowledge about emergency preparedness among high school students. Knowledge may be assessed through a test that may be administered to all students in both the treatment and the control conditions. The resulting scores from this test serve as the post-test measure of the outcome variable of importance. It is important to remember that if the unit of analysis is at the school level, the post-test score of the treatment group will be calculated by averaging together *the average test score of each school* in the treatment condition, and the post-test score of the control group will be calculated by taking the average of the *average scores of each school* in the control condition. If the unit of analysis had been at the *individual* level, then the post-test scores could be obtained by taking the average of individual scores of people in each condition. However, because it was schools that were randomly assigned to conditions rather than individuals, the average score from each school is the lowest unit of analysis permitted.

e. Compare the average post-test scores of those in the treatment group with the average post-test scores of those in the control group. As noted previously, because random assignment was used, it can be assumed that before the campaign the two groups were equivalent in their emergency preparedness knowledge. Then, the treatment group received the campaign and the control group received nothing. Therefore, any differences between the groups in terms of emergency preparedness knowledge can be attributed to the campaign itself.

If the average test scores of schools in the treatment condition are 20% higher than the average test scores of the schools in the control condition, then we can assume that the campaign was successful in achieving the objective to increase emergency preparedness knowledge by 20%. In this case, it would then be wise to conduct the same campaign in the schools that served as the control group during the experiment. If the average test scores of schools in the treatment condition are not 20% higher than the average test scores of those in the control condition, then it can be concluded that the campaign did not meet its objective and should therefore not be implemented elsewhere until campaign adjustments have been made.

All true experimental designs allow researchers to determine whether the campaign had an adverse effect on the outcome variable, as was the case in some of the public health campaigns discussed at the beginning of this chapter. If the average post-campaign test scores of schools in the treatment condition are actually lower than average test scores of schools in the control condition, researchers may conclude that the campaign in fact moved the population of interest further away from the campaign's goals and that they would have been better off if no campaign had been conducted at all. Obviously, under such conditions, it would be irresponsible and unethical to continue with the campaign or to implement the same campaign in any additional communities in the future.

The post-test only design is the simplest of all true experimental designs. It is more efficient and less costly than other experimental designs because it requires data collection at only one single point in time. However, equalization through randomization is only a statistical probability—not a guarantee. Therefore, there is always a possibility that even after randomization, starting scores on the outcome variable differ across conditions. If this was the case, it would not have been appropriate to attribute to the campaign all differences in scores on the outcome variable after the campaign has concluded. Doing such could result in incorrect inferences about the campaign's effectiveness. For example, if after randomization, the average emergency preparedness knowledge score in the treatment group was 20% higher than the average emergency preparedness knowledge score in the control condition before the campaign, then after the conclusion of the campaign, if the difference in knowledge scores between the two groups is still only 20%, the campaign would actually have had no effect on the outcome variable. If we had assumed the two groups' scores to be equal to begin with, we would have hailed the campaign's success and recommended investing time and money into continuing with an ineffective campaign and implementing it in new areas beyond the study. These concerns often drive planners to choose more complicated designs, such as the pre-test post-test control group design discussed next.

2. *Pre-test post-test control group design:* As suggested by its name, a pre-test post-test control group design is an experimental design involving a randomly assigned control group and a randomly assigned experimental group, both of which are assessed in terms of the outcome variable before the campaign starts as well as at the conclusion of the campaign. If we choose to use a pre-test post-test control group design instead of a post-test only control group design, for example, about increasing emergency preparedness knowledge among high school students provided previously, much of the process would remain the same:

a. Recruit a number of high schools to agree to participate in the study.

b. Use random assignment techniques to create control and treatment groups. It would still make sense to use schools as the unit of analysis, rather than individual students.

c. Rather than making the assumption that random assignment equalized emergency preparedness knowledge scores across treatment and control conditions as was done with the post-test only design, the pre-test post-test control group design allows planners to ensure that scores are comparable before the start of the campaign by taking a measure of knowledge across both conditions before campaign implementation. In order to do this, one would assess all students in both conditions in terms of the outcome variable using the same test that will be used for the post-test after the campaign's completion. The resulting scores from this test serve as a pre-test measure of the outcome variable of importance. As noted, because schools have been randomly assigned to condition, the difference between scores produced by schools in the treatment condition compared with those produced by schools in the control condition should be negligible in the pre-test measurement. If this is not the case, it will be inappropriate to attribute all differences in knowledge scores between the treatment group and the control group to the campaign.

d. Once pre-test measures have been taken, planners administer the campaign in the treatment group schools and do nothing in the control group schools, just as occurred in the post-test only design.

e. At the campaign's conclusion, Step c is repeated to calculate post-test scores for both conditions. By comparing the pre-test score of the treatment condition with the post-test score of the control condition, researchers can determine whether the campaign has met its objective of increasing emergency preparedness knowledge by 20%. The pre-test post-test control group design also allows us to determine whether increases or decreases in knowledge are, in fact, due to the campaign, or whether they are due to some other external factor by comparing changes in knowledge over time in the treatment condition to changes in knowledge over time in the control condition. Even if knowledge increases in the treatment condition from pre-test to post-test, if the post-test knowledge scores in the control condition are comparable with the post-test knowledge scores in the treatment condition, then the knowledge gain cannot be attributed to the campaign. In addition, if the post-test knowledge scores in the control condition are higher than those in the treatment condition, researchers must consider the possibility that the campaign may have had a negative impact. This result suggests that students would have been more knowledgeable about emergency preparedness if they had not been exposed to the campaign.

Although pre-test post-test control group designs are better able to confirm that differences between the treatment and control groups at post-test are completely attributable to the campaign itself, and the pre-test function allows for a determination of exactly how much knowledge was gained or lost over the course of the campaign, this particular design also has drawbacks. First, because this design requires data collection at two points in time rather than one, it is less economical and less efficient than the post-test only control group design. The process of giving participants the same test twice also raises concerns about the validity of results. It may be argued that scores may differ from time one to time two simply because participants have taken the test before and they may have discussed some answers or even looked up the answers to some of the questions they did not know. This effect should hold constant across treatment and control conditions, so increases in scores due to this effect should occur equally in both conditions, making any further differences attributable to the campaign.

Another concern may be that giving students the pre-test will prime them to pay closer attention to the campaign being conducted around them than they would have if they had not been tested on the material. For example, a student who did not know the answer to a particular test question, who then one week later sees a bulletin board with the answer to the question posted on it, may be more likely to retain that information from the bulletin board than he or she would have had it not been a test question previously missed. If this is the case, then the results of the post-test may make the campaign messages appear more effective than they actually would be for high school students who had not been pre-tested.

3. *Solomon four group design:* The final true experimental design eliminates both concerns from the post-test only control group design about the limitations of random assignment in equalizing scores across conditions, as well as the possibility of the previously discussed priming effect in the pre-test post-test control group. As suggested by its name, the Solomon Four group design divides participants into four groups, two of which are used to conduct a post-test only control group design, and two of which are used to conduct a pre-test post-test control group design. Thus, the four groups composing the Solomon Four are the control group for the post-test only control group design, the treatment group for the post-test only control group design, the control group for the pre-test post-test control group design, and the treatment group for the pre-test post-test control group design.

Theoretically, a Solomon Four group design may be considered "the best of both worlds." Comparing the results from the pre-test post-test control group design with the post-test only control group design can eliminate concerns about trusting too much in random assignment to equalize groups as well as concerns about testing effects from pre-test to post-test. However, because this design involves twice as many groups, it is more costly and complicated than other true experimental designs. For this reason, a Solomon Four group design is rarely used in experimental research.

While the post-test only control group design and the pre-test post-test control group design are less costly and less complex than the Solomon Four group design, they are still often an unrealistic expectation for practitioners with limited time and resources. In the field of emergency management, it is also often true that practitioners cannot withhold information from a certain segment of the population, such as those who are selected to serve as an experimental control group. Therefore, many communication campaigns choose to use a *quasi-experimental* design instead. Quasi-experiments are similar to true experiments in most respects, other than that they do not fulfill all true experiment design requirements (usually because they do not assume random assignment to treatment and control conditions). Only true experimental designs allow for the attribution of effects to the campaign and not some other variable. However, under those conditions in which true experiments are not possible, quasi-experiments can still provide information about the target audience regarding the campaign's dependent variable.

Three types of commonly used quasi-experimental designs are as follows:

1. *One-shot case study:* A one-shot case study involves a single group of people who receive a treatment and are assessed in terms of the outcome variable only after the conclusion of the campaign. Because this design provides a treatment to only one group at a single point in time, there is no point of comparison to detect what types of effects were produced by the campaign. For example, even if, at the conclusion of the campaign, the target audience appears to be taking the actions recommended by the campaign, practitioners cannot be sure that they are doing so in response to the campaign or if they had already engaged in the behavior prior to the campaign. For this reason, the one-shot case study is not recommended as a proper evaluation of campaign effects.

2. *Non-equivalent groups design:* The non-equivalent groups design is similar to the post-test only control group design except that rather than randomly assigning all participants to either a treatment or control group, the practitioner uses two intact groups to serve as the experimental and control groups. For example, in the previous scenario involving educating high school students about emergency preparedness, a non-equivalent groups design might simply designate two schools that had similar characteristics (e.g., private schools from small rural towns) to serve as the control group and the treatment group and then analyze the data at the individual level. Because this process did not involve random assignment to conditions, and there was no pre-test provided, practitioners cannot know how the groups differed in terms of the dependent variable before the treatment was provided. Therefore, it would be inappropriate to interpret the difference between knowledge scores in the treatment group and the control group as campaign effect size. However, because there is no theoretical reason to suspect that the groups may differ in scores, an outcome assessment indicating that knowledge scores in the group that received the treatment were considerably higher than knowledge scores in the group that received no treatment may reassure researchers that the campaign produced the intended effect better than any outcome that may be provided by the one-shot case study.

3. *One-group pre-test post-test design:* The one-group pre-test post-test design is similar to the pre-test post-test control group design, except it does not involve a control group. If practitioners are forced to use a quasi-experimental design due to time, monetary, or logistic constraints, this design is probably the best option for gaining insight into campaign effectiveness. However, because there is no control group for comparison, it is not appropriate to attribute changes from pre-test to post-test to the campaign, as one cannot be sure that changes were not due to testing effects or some other incidental effect that occurred at the same time as the campaign.

When drawing conclusions about campaign effects, it is important to remember to associate the effects achieved or lack thereof with the campaign that actually took place, as opposed to the campaign that was planned. This is another reason why process evaluation is essential. If a major channel of message dissemination is in brochures that never actually are distributed to the population of interest, and the final assessment of the campaign indicates no change from pre-test to post-test in terms of the outcome variable, then it would be incorrect to conclude that the brochures themselves were ineffective. If people are not exposed to the message, researchers cannot use post-test measurements to make judgments about the effectiveness of the message.

The point of evaluating the effectiveness of a campaign is to provide insight into what has worked and what has not worked in meeting the pre-set campaign objectives so that future attempts may use this information in guiding campaign design. Thus, it is important to keep records of all aspects of the campaign, including all background research, focus group and other formative research information, materials that were pre-tested and those that were distributed, pre-test measures, process evaluation information, and post-test measures. There is no guarantee that even the most carefully designed campaign will meet its intended objectives. Keeping clean records of all campaign materials ensures that something can be learned from the process, regardless of the outcome. Documenting all procedures and their impact will also help to save money in future campaigns by providing insight into what has and has not worked with regard to the population or the behavior of interest in the past. If program planners hired professionals to conduct evaluations, they may want to share their results with others, which could include publishing them. Publishing results helps to increase campaign success and decrease setbacks in emergency preparedness knowledge and behavior by contributing to the knowledge base about how to effectively communicate risks and promote behavior change among different segments of the lay population.

CONCLUSION

The purpose of this chapter was to provide guidance for campaign implementation and evaluation. In the initial planning stages, campaign planners must set specific goals and objectives for the campaign to meet. Meeting these pre-set objectives is the entire purpose of the campaign. Therefore, it is crucial that these objectives be measurable in order to determine objectively whether the campaign had its intended effect.

There is always the possibility that a campaign produces *effects* but is not considered *effective* in meeting its intended goals. Sometimes, campaigns may even bring about effects that move the target audience further *away* from campaign designers' goals. Process evaluations help to recognize these unintended effects and allow researchers to end or reverse them as quickly as possible.

In addition to preventing future harm, campaign evaluation also forces campaign planners to set measurable objectives that the campaign seeks to achieve. Public disaster preparedness education campaigns generally have three overarching goals:

1. Raising public awareness
2. Guiding public behavior
3. Warning the public

Objectives are specific measurable outcomes derived from these goals. Campaign success is determined solely by the degree to which it meets the pre-set objectives, rather than sheer exposure or the degree to which people "like" or "enjoy" the materials.

The authors of this book strongly recommend that campaign planners hire professionals to assess the true outcomes of their campaign. This requires funding that will draw from limited budgets, but it can result in significant positive dividends by preventing counterproductive effects or by providing a template for future campaigns.

Using a true experimental design is the only way to determine conclusively that the effects observed in evaluation are due to the campaign and not some outside factor. This type of design requires a treatment group, a control group, and random assignment to conditions. This chapter discussed three types of true experimental designs:

1. Post-test only control group design
2. Pre-test post-test control group design
3. Solomon Four group design

Sometimes resources do not allow for true experimental designs. In this case, quasi-experimental designs can provide information about the target audience. Quasi-experiments are similar to experiments in most respects, but they fall short of fulfilling the requirements of true experimental designs, usually because they do not involve random assignment to treatment and control conditions. This chapter discussed three different types of quasi-experimental designs:

1. One-shot case study
2. Non-equivalent groups design
3. One-group pre-test, post-test design

It also issued caution regarding the drawing of conclusions from each.

When drawing conclusions about a campaign, it is also important to attribute effects to the campaign that took place, rather than the campaign that was planned. The point of evaluating the effectiveness of a campaign is to provide insight into what has worked and what has not worked in meeting pre-set campaign objectives, so that campaign designers can learn from and apply this information in future campaign designs.

REFERENCES

Campbell, D. T. and J. C. Stanley. 1963. Experimental and quasi-experimental designs for research on teaching. In N. L. Gage (Ed.), *Handbook of Research on Teaching*, 171–246. Chicago, IL: Rand McNally.

Salmon, C. T. and L. Murray-Johnson. 2001. Communication campaign effectiveness: Critical distinctions. In R. E. Rice and C. K. Atkin (Eds.), *Public Communication Campaigns*, 168–180, 3rd ed. Thousand Oaks, CA: Sage.

Werch, C. E. and D. M. Owen. 2002. Iatrogenic effects of alcohol and drug prevention programs. *Journal of Studies on Alcohol, 63,* 581–590.

CHAPTER 6

Program Support

INTRODUCTION

All disaster preparedness campaign endeavors require adequate financial, human, and other resource support. Support must be appropriate for the degree of effort required and for the levels of exposure desired. And if plans call for the campaign to be ongoing, support must also be sustainable. Organizations of any type, whether public or private, or for-profit or nonprofit, often find securing such resources to be their greatest challenge. For businesses, this often boils down to convincing leadership of the resilience value of preparedness in order to justify the investment. But for public-sector and nongovernmental organizations, fundraising may require significant grant-writing, partnership-building, and other fundraising activities.

By the time most project planners with small or insufficient coffers have begun thinking about funding shortfalls and budgetary constraints, they have likely completed the first step in the budgeting process— namely *recognizing and accepting that the project requires additional funds to get started.*

Most projects, even those that are based upon well-established ideas and impressions, or which have a fully developed project plan, must raise or locate additional support in the form of money, in-kind assistance (e.g., supplies, raw materials, or services), or labor. The solution to this problem comes with knowing how and where to acquire such resources. A fundraising plan is an effective tool to guide that effort.

In order to design and run a fundraising campaign, it is first necessary to determine exactly how much money and what resources are needed. These figures are known as the fundraising goal, or *the amount upon which all components of the fundraising campaign are based.* Accuracy in determining this number is vital, as it immediately becomes the motivating factor for the fundraising team and the primary performance measure in determining whether your organization is successful in its efforts.

In determining the fundraising goal, it is important that you do not set your organization up for failure. The goal should be based upon two determining factors:

1. How much money is actually needed?
2. How much money can realistically be raised? (See Sidebar 6.1)

The amount of money that is actually needed is generally easy to calculate or estimate. Planners should have an accurate impression or assessment of the organization supporting the project, including its needs and expenses. Planners should consider at length the specific needs of their project. If a project budget has not been developed already, it is a good time to do so. Project budgets should include all possible costs that may be incurred across the life of the project, including equipment, rental space, technology, utilities (new phone lines, for instance), services, and any other fees. The fundraising process itself should be included if there are associated expenses. If this project is to be ongoing, planners must be sure to calculate ongoing/recurrent fees and costs. Planners do not want to reach their fundraising goal only to find that they are still unable to implement their project because some unforeseen or ill-considered expenses were omitted from the initial analysis. For this reason, it is good to include some leeway in the budget that accommodates most unknown expenses when such uncertainty exists. A budget is considered the "road map" to the fundraising goal, so details count.

For planners embarking upon a fundraising effort for the first time, it may be difficult to gauge the potential of the fundraising effort, and forecasts are based upon assumptions rather than experience. When grants or program funds are the target of the fundraising effort, there usually exists a general range of funding that can be expected. However, when planners approach the community or beyond in order to acquire resources, they may need to consider the abilities of residents, businesses, and other stakeholders to provide such funding or other resources, and the salience of the issue being addressed by the preparedness effort. Most disaster preparedness projects appeal to a wide range of audiences, as the products of such efforts ultimately build tangible community strength.

SIDEBAR 6.1   SETTING FUNDRAISING GOALS

If possible, fundraising potential can be measured by assessing previous community support for other efforts or organizations. This can be done by contacting partner organizations or other network contacts. Tony Poderis, a successful fundraising expert who has developed several successful fundraising tools, provides those tools to groups new to fundraising to help them determine their fundraising goals. The highlights of his findings are listed in the following:

1. A goal must be based upon the ability to raise the money to pay for it, not by deciding how much money is needed to be raised based on the expense. It is vitally important not to let "the tail wag the dog."
2. The amount of money to be raised must meet with the consensus of the organization's volunteer and professional leadership. You cannot have "It's too much" or "It's not enough" divisive arguments within the organization at the time prospects are being solicited.
3. The goal should be enlarged, if at all possible, with foresight and planning to meet future capital needs. This will help to avoid subsequent closely recurring additional capital campaigns, which could stretch the resources of an organization, antagonize prospects, and possibly have a negative effect on annual fund campaigns.
4. The final goal amount must be related to viable potential prospects identified and individually rated for their maximum giving potential and by factoring the leadership's commitment to personally give to the project and raise money for it.
5. The total goal is composed of trustee, individual, corporate, and foundation divisional goals as determined by realistic and appropriate evaluations of their respective potential. Those divisional goals must never be arbitrarily set.
6. The fundraising goal is more than just establishing the final number. The organization should determine other goals in order to have certain amounts of cash at various stages of the project's development to pay ongoing expenses. It is important to solicit prospects capable of providing early and up-front cash to help meet those developing money needs.
7. The amount to be raised should be influenced by advance leadership pledges, suggested to represent approximately one-quarter of the goal as determined by some form of a pre-campaign feasibility effort. As much as possible, the board of trustees' aggregate contribution should represent at least one-third of the total goal.
8. The goal should be related to the fewest number of gifts in the largest possible amounts: one-third of the money should be raised from about 15 gifts, the next one-third from an additional 75 to 100 gifts, and the last one-third from all other gifts.

9. Noncash contributions, such as in-kind goods, products, and services, should be factored into the goal as much as possible to help lessen the need for actual cash.
10. Major benefactors recognize that it costs money to raise money. They will support a capital campaign goal that incorporates all reasonable campaign fundraising expenditures, including professional fundraising consultants' fees. While such campaigns are not conducted by employing professional consultants whose fees are initially based upon a percentage of the goal or actual funds raised, it generally works out that total expenses will be in the 5 to 8% range relative to the goal.

Source: Poderis, T., *12 Things You Should Know about Setting a Capital Campaign Goal.* Fund Raising Forum, 1997. http://bit.ly/1ToavZO.

Your available fundraising resources are the reality against which your goal should be measured for feasibility. These resources consist of fundraising campaign leadership and solicitors available to work a campaign, and a realistic, evaluated list of prospective donors. If the resources are insufficient to raise the money you have targeted in your goal, there are only two available options:

1. The resources must be enlarged to meet a goal equal to the need.
2. The capital project's expense budget must be reduced to allow the goal to be set lower, at a level consistent with available resources.

Your fundraising campaign must not be set in motion until one or the other of these two options is established.

TYPES OF PROGRAM SUPPORT

There are three major categories of program support that may be acquired:

1. Cash
2. In-kind donations
3. Volunteer resources

Each of these serves a different purpose, and in the case of most projects, all three are needed to some degree.

Cash is the most versatile, as it generally presents few restrictions with regard to when it must be used and for what. Of course, it must be used in support of the project, as dictated in the budget that was used

FIGURE 6.1   In-kind donations can reduce project costs significantly. In this community preparedness day fair, Arlington County, Virginia, firefighters demonstrate victim extraction on a donated automobile (Author photo).

to raise the cash in the first place, but this gives planners a considerable amount of leeway.

In-kind resources, which can come in the form of equipment, supplies, property or office space, and services, can be easier to acquire than cash, as they generally require a smaller financial commitment from donors (see Figure 6.1). In addition, in-kind resources face far less resource competition internal to the donor organization than does cash.

For example, consider a project that will require the acquisition of 10 computer terminals. For a small organization, it may be difficult or even unrealistic to fundraise from a community whose stakeholders have competing needs for their cash resources to purchase 10 new computers. Even if grants have been awarded for the project, restrictions may limit the uses of the funding provided such that the purchase of computers cannot occur. However, individuals and organizations within the community may have unused computers that they would be willing to lend or donate—a gesture that would likely cost them nothing but give them a tax deduction in return. For the project team, this would provide the same value to the organization—for zero cash outlay—as purchasing new computers with cash.

Volunteer resources are the third program support category. While many people may have little or no money to donate, they often have the time to do so. In addition, when the benefits of the program affect them or their community directly, there is a strong goodwill incentive for people to provide their time and talent on a voluntary basis. Volunteers can be used for almost any aspect of project planning and operation, including graphic design, conducting surveys, community outreach, and even fundraising. People of all age groups volunteer their time. These individuals may be reached through community newspapers, recreation departments, schools, and other sources.

SOURCES OF SUPPORT

Sources of funding come in myriad forms—as donations from individuals, businesses, or foundations, as grants, through events, and from many other sources. In this section, several of these will be described, but keep in mind that this is merely a sample of the many standard and creative options planners may encounter or develop in their own fundraising efforts.

As is true with most business ventures, fundraising programs are most successful when revenue sources are diversified. By drawing from a full range of options, planners can maximize their potential and reduce the likelihood of shortfalls. The following is a generalized listing of the different sources and means by and through which funding is raised:

1. Individual donors
2. Business and corporate donors
3. Foundations and other grant-making agencies
4. Local, state, county, and federal government grants
5. Religious organizations
6. Civic organizations/civic clubs
7. Fee generation
8. Partnerships

Individual Donors

Individual donors account for the vast majority of charitable and other philanthropic assistance that is given each year in the United States. Professional fundraisers expect that, on average, three-quarters of the money they collect will come from individuals, and in total, around 90% of money given outside of federal grants comes from individuals. Individual donations are generally smaller than what is attained through other sources, but such donations tend to be the most spontaneous and unrestricted. Cultivating individual donors tends to require a smaller financial commitment than many other fundraising methods, and the associated outreach helps to promote your project throughout the community (as well as to cultivate additional contacts, partners, and supporters). If your organization is a 501(c)(3) nonprofit organization, any donations are tax deductible for the donor. Finally, individuals who are secured as donors tend to give again when asked in the future (even greater amounts if they are treated well the first time around), which makes subsequent fundraising campaigns easier.

Individuals, like all donors, must be identified and approached. One of the great benefits of working with individual donors is that there is an extensive range of options by which this can be done. A 1996 study that was conducted by the Independent Sector (2008), an association of nonprofit organizations, asked individual donors the question, "How important is each of the following reasons to you for contributing to a charitable organization?" Participants listed the following reasons as either "very important" or "somewhat important":

- 72.1%—Someone I know well asked
- 60.7%—Have volunteered at the organization
- 59.1%—Asked by clergy
- 43.3%—Read or heard a news story
- 38.2%—Asked at work
- 36.2%—Someone came to the door asking me to give
- 29.7%—Asked in a telethon/radiothon
- 28.6%—Received a letter asking me to give
- 17.1%—Read a newspaper or magazine advertisement asking me to give
- 16.9%—Saw a television commercial asking me to give

There are several ways in which you can approach individuals to present your project and to ask for support. They include the following:

1. Direct mail
2. Special events or activities
3. Internet fundraising
4. Telephone solicitation
5. Door-to-door solicitation
6. Planned gifts
7. Workplace appeals
8. Advertising

Depending upon the size of the fundraising goal, the community makeup, and the resources available to the planning team (for instance, a volunteer or member who can design a fundraising Website), organizations will likely employ a strategy that includes several of these categories.

Concluding Remarks about Individual Donors

For most organizations, individual donors are their greatest resource—to neglect them will severely limit potential. Donors become more than givers of money, they become vested in the organization and harbingers of the cause to which they give. It should be mentioned at this point that there are people in the community who can give much more than the average donor. These people, referred to as *major donors*, require special tactics to approach. Major donors deserve special attention because the time invested in educating them about the organization and the project, specifically about how their donation will make a difference, is both wise and worth the effort. Such donors should be approached by the organization's most senior executives and deserve as much professionally formatted information as possible (including a full project proposal, if appropriate). Programs have found their entire goal met by the gift of one major donor.

Business and Corporate Donors

Businesses and corporations are second in terms of charitable contributions provided annually. This category of donors includes multimillion and billion dollar megacorporations whose products and services permeate all levels of society and the corner store on any block in every community. Despite the fact that many large corporations maintain distinct gift-giving foundations, which are the subject of another section, many large companies still provide donations directly through the company itself. The motivation behind each of these business types' giving dictates how they are most effectively approached. The following is a general discussion on business and corporate donors.

The bigger a corporation or business is, naturally, the larger its philanthropic budget will be. However, these larger businesses also typically have more people knocking on their doors for money. Having a personal connection with the company will therefore play a large part in whether a requesting organization receives funds. For instance, if the donor corporation is headquartered or has a satellite office in the target community, has a large sales base there, or even has a board member who happened to have spent his or her childhood there, funding likelihood is much greater. How an organization seeking funds determines which corporations have some connection to its community does require some creativity and research, but this determination is nonetheless a prerequisite to considering corporations for donations.

An organization approaching a business for program support should consider the interaction a business proposition as much as a philanthropic gesture. Planners should determine what they could offer the corporation in return for its goodwill (especially if it is something that others cannot offer). Fundraisers need to sell their organization, their employees, and their proposed project in order to make the decision to donate seem like a wise one. The challenge is determining what can be offered in return.

The number one thing that all businesses seek in return for philanthropic giving is an improvement in their good reputation. If an organization's standing in the community is high, then association with it will help to lift the company's image. A better reputation often translates to more products sold and, in turn, more revenue. Executives and decision-makers need only to be convinced that this positive return is possible. Fundraisers must investigate the company in order to discover how it operates and, more importantly, how it considers requests for donations.

Using resources that are readily available, such as the phone book, the Internet, Chamber of Commerce directories, corporate giving reports, local business directories, and so forth, planners can make a list of companies whose missions parallel their own. Subscriptions to philanthropic services, such as the Foundation Center (www.fdncenter.org), can provide easy access to this kind of information. In small communities, just about any company could be approached because the project, being disaster preparedness based, would be in the interest of all businesses, as it benefits the community as a whole. Moreover, when the community is a large one, because the number of groups seeking donations is also large, organizations should limit themselves to those companies with which they have the greatest likelihood of success. Generally, fundraising teams make a large list from which they focus on between 10 and 20 companies that are initially approached.

Most of the information regarding a company's philanthropic tendencies can be found on its Website and in its annual report (if one is maintained). If it can be determined how much the corporation or business has given to the type of organization planning the public education project in question, this information will be valuable as well. Organizations do not want to be asking for more than the greatest amount ever provided, or less than the least. If the average gift size works well for the program's needs, then the organization would be appropriate.

Small Businesses

Small businesses exist in every community. These entities tend to have a much greater stake in community success and viability because they are much more dependent upon it for their own survival and success. While they share many of the same goals as the larger corporations, such as the need to turn a profit, there are distinct differences between the two and, as such, there are distinct differences in how they are approached for philanthropic giving.

There are almost no reasons why small businesses should be neglected by a fundraising effort. As long as planners understand that donations are likely to be smaller, donor interests are likely to be focused, and the need for personal relationships is great, they will have a big chance of raising funds or acquiring goods from one or more of the millions of small businesses that operate throughout every corner of the nation.

A national survey of small businesses commissioned by the Better Business Bureau (2001) revealed important data about how small businesses contribute to community causes. The summarized findings of this survey are presented in Sidebar 6.2.

SIDEBAR 6.2   SMALL BUSINESS FUNDRAISING SURVEY RESULTS

- Almost all small businesses in the United States participate in charitable giving. In fact, 92% of companies were solicited and 91% donated. For new small businesses, 85% have been approached and 82% have given.
- Contributions are not limited to cash. Sixty-three percent of small businesses provided in-kind contributions of products or services.
- Most (85%) small businesses are willing to participate in fundraising events. The most common event-related support in which small businesses participate includes the purchase of advertisements in charity event programs or publications (60%) and sponsoring youth sports teams or athletic leagues (51%). More than 3 in 10 small businesses also participated in each of the following: charity auctions (37%); fundraising benefits, dinners, or galas (35%); and special fundraising events like walkathons (32%).
- Altruistic concerns matter the most to small businesses when selecting donation recipients. Ninety-two percent stated that helping the community or society is key to their selection, and half claim such concerns are the single most important consideration.
- Second only to altruistic concerns in determining recipients, listed by 82% of respondents, is the small business owner's preference or recommendation.
- Seventy-eight percent of small businesses claim that locally based efforts are preferred, while less than 1% gives to nationally based organizations.

- Small businesses rely heavily on the recipient organizations themselves, rather than on outside sources, for information used to make funding decisions.
- Most (85%) small businesses give less than $5,000 in philanthropic donations each year.
- The top five types of recipient organizations supported by small business are:
  - Police and firefighter (58%)
  - Educational (53%)
  - Religious (50%)
  - Social services (44%)
  - Health (41%)

Foundations

Foundations are nonprofit organizations, either associated with or independent of other private or public organizations, that exist almost exclusively for donating money to worthy causes. Foundations in the United States boast assets of almost $400 billion and give away almost $25 billion each year—approximately 10% of all philanthropic funding. Moreover, the amount that foundations are giving rises each year as the capital upon which their interest-based funding grows (with single-year growth rates of up to 22% experienced in the recent past).

All foundations have a mission and program areas that define what types of projects they fund and what types of nonprofits or other agencies they prefer to work with. Without fail, all emergency preparedness public education efforts qualify in both of these regards for many of the *tens of thousands* of foundations that exist in the United States. However, to acquire these resources, planners will need to have at least the following prepared:

1. Good research
2. A great proposal
3. Time, and lots of it, to wait for the approval process to run its course

The key to winning grants from foundations is a good match between the project's mission and goals and the mission and goals of the foundation. Foundations do not hide their interests and intentions, so with good research planners can increase their funding likelihood considerably. Most foundations require a proposal, and there are often strict guidelines about how those proposals should look and what type of project may be funded.

There are four different categories of foundations, each of which includes members of all sizes and missions. They include (1) community, (2) public, (3) family, and (4) private.

Community Foundations

A community foundation is a philanthropic organization, organized and operated primarily as a permanent collection of endowed funds, the earnings of which are used for the long-term benefit of a geographically defined community. A community foundation is tax exempt, incorporated, not-for-profit, organizationally autonomous, and cannot be controlled directly or indirectly by government at any level, corporations, associations and their members, or individuals.

The primary purpose of community foundations is to provide charitable support to their local communities. They do this by building endowments with contributions from local residents, and administering them for the benefit of their communities. They also administer nonendowment funds. In essence, a community foundation is an organization that gives support, primarily in the form of money, to a specific area—a town, city, county, state, region, or country.

Community foundation funds can be restricted not only to a defined physical area but also to a program area. Oftentimes, however, community foundations have a certain percentage of funds earmarked for specific purposes, while the remaining share is unrestricted and distributed at the discretion of the community foundation management.

Grant application procedures for community foundations can take a long time to process. The foundation's programmatic restrictions, their procedures and deadlines for applying, and any application material should either be on the foundation's Website or obtained from the foundation directly using contact information their Website provides. Grants tend to be made according to award schedules, biannually, quarterly, or at any other interval as they choose.

Public Foundations

Public foundations are foundations that, as defined by the Internal Revenue Service (IRS), receive more than one-third of their funding from the public at large. Many religious, educational, medical, and other population-targeted foundations are considered public foundations if they meet this first criterion. While public foundations often engage in charitable activities (services to the public), grant-giving is a significant part of their collective mission.

Family Foundations

Family foundations (often called either large family foundations or small family foundations) are private foundations whose philanthropic funding base is derived from the gifts of a single family. In addition, family members typically compose at least one seat, if not the majority of the seats, on the foundation's board of directors. Family foundations account for a major portion of foundation giving in the United States, most notably since Bill and Melinda Gates contributed more than $4 billion to the Bill and Melinda Gates Foundation. In the United States, families manage approximately two-thirds of the estimated 40,000 private foundations and make grants totaling more than $7 billion per year ($7 of $22.8 billion total).

Private Foundations

Private foundations are nongovernmental, nonprofit organizations that have collected their funding base from either one source or a few sources. Corporations, families, small businesses, and other entities all have and continue to form grant-giving foundations such as these. Six percent of philanthropic giving in the United States comes from private foundations.

Private foundations often operate with much greater leeway in their giving than the public or community foundations and can move much faster from application to award (see Sidebar 6.3). Private foundations can and do give to the whole range of organizations that exists throughout the nation. These organizations can have self-imposed restrictions, and often do. Whether it is geographic or programmatic, those applying must be aware of any of these restrictions before going through the often lengthy application process.

These foundations differ from regular corporate and business donations in that they come from a separate entity, established by the corporation or business, whose single goal is philanthropy—remember that this is a nonprofit organization. The structure for giving is established, straightforward, and created primarily to guide potential grantees in applying.

SIDEBAR 6.3   THE DIFFERENCES BETWEEN PUBLIC AND PRIVATE SOURCES OF FUNDING

Advantages—Public Sources

- Purpose set by legislation
- Focus on functions usually affecting significant groups in society
- Have the most money and more likely to award large grants or contracts
- More likely to pay all project costs and cover indirect costs

- Easier to find information about and to stay current on project needs or interests
- Application processes and deadlines are public information and very firm
- Use prescribed formats for proposals—many use "common" application forms
- Possibilities of renewal known up front
- Plentiful staff resources—most projects have specific contact person
- More likely to have resources for technical assistance
- Funds available to a wider array of organizations (for-profit and nonprofit)
- Accountable to elected officials if administrative staff do not follow the rules

Advantages—Private Sources

- More likely to focus on emerging issues, new needs, populations not yet recognized as "special interests"
- Often willing to pool resources with other funders
- Wide range in size of available grants—some can make very large awards, others are strictly for small, local projects
- More willing source of start-up or experimental funds
- Full-length, complex proposals not always necessary
- Can be much more flexible in responding to unique needs and circumstances
- Able to avoid bureaucratic requirements for administering grants
- Can often provide alternative forms of assistance, that is, software or hardware donations, materials, expertise, etc.
- Fewer applicants in most cases
- Can generally be much more informal and willing to help with the proposal process

Disadvantages—Public Sources

- Much more bureaucratic
- Lengthy proposal requirements and complex application, administration, and compliance procedures
- Often require institutional cost sharing and matching
- Reviewers tend to favor established applicants
- Sometimes, difficult to sell new ideas and high-risk approaches
- Cost to applicants much higher—expensive application and compliance procedures

- Changing political trends affect security of some programs—availability of funds can change rapidly

Disadvantages—Private Sources

- Average grant size usually much smaller
- Priorities can change rapidly; continuation of support can be difficult to predict
- Applicants have limited influence on the decision-making process
- Information on policies and procedures must be researched and can be time consuming
- Less likely to cover all project costs and most do not cover indirect costs
- Limited staff—fewer opportunities for personal contact and site visits
- May not be clear about reasons for rejection—hard to improve for second attempt

Source: Hall, M., *Getting Funded: A Complete Guide to Proposal Writing*, 3rd ed., Continuing Education Publications, Portland, OR, 1988.

Finding Appropriate Foundations

To find appropriate matches between your organization and foundations with the money sought, planners need to define their organization according to its mission. Then, the same needs to be done for their project. Planners should not limit themselves by getting too specific—it is preferable to make a list beginning with the most specific but expanding to the most general.

For example, imagine a project where volunteers will hold presentations in the local community center to teach senior citizens how to prepare for emergencies. The list might look something like this:

- Senior citizens/the elderly
- Emergency preparedness
- Disaster management
- Public safety
- Public education
- Training
- Homeland security
- Community development

Matches among the various foundations must now be found. As there are over 45,000 foundations operating in the United States alone, it is usually possible to do so. The most appropriate starting point is with community foundations operating in the state in which the project will operate. Then, the search can be expanded beyond local and state borders, with the understanding that competition for resources expands as well.

Several Web-based philanthropic associations assist organizations seeking foundations to suit their needs, although many of these operate through membership fees. A good example is the Foundation Center (www.fdncenter.org), which allows prospective grantees to search through thousands of foundation Websites according to either geographic area served or the sector in which the grant applies (public safety, for example). The following link can take you to the free sector search engine, but other search methods require subscription: http://foundationcenter.org/findfunders/foundfinder/

Local, State, County, and Federal Government Grants

While not all government agencies make grants, there are agencies at all *levels* of government that do make them, for example, the local, state, and federal levels. These grants are a perpetual but unpredictable source of funding for organizations of all types. It is understood that finding government grants can be an incredibly challenging task. An open mind, vigilance (in watching for grant programs as they appear), and persistence are the keys to getting funding through these sources. Having a grasp of the methods by which the federal, state, and local government agencies announce their grants is a great way to stay "in the loop." Unfortunately, this is usually just one part of a multifaceted approach that is required if you are to take advantage of all opportunities for which your organization qualifies.

Like the foundations, government agencies give grants according to specific program areas in line with their stated mission—this is increasingly true as you rise from the local to national level. Though not without exception, very rarely is government funding indiscriminant. For instance, the Department of Health and Human Services is likely to give grants only for health-related programs, while the Department of Homeland Security will focus on public safety, emergency preparedness, terrorism prevention, and immigration issues. If you can think creatively about your project, looking at it from as many programmatic vantage points as possible (as was mentioned earlier in reference to the foundations), you might find that your program is eligible for grants you had not even considered because you did not think of your program in the right context.

Government agencies are strict in awarding and disbursing of funding. They require that applying organizations follow pre-set guidelines and submit applications by pre-set deadlines. These guidelines, however, are well defined and easily accessible from the agencies themselves or through the many online search engines dedicated to government grants. There are even public-oriented publications distributed solely for letting prospective grantees know about the existence of grants as they are announced. Keep in mind that at each successively lower level of government, these processes tend to be more lax, and the turnaround times for grants tend to be much shorter, but the mechanisms for announcing the grants can be less effective.

For NGOs, eligibility requirements will be the greatest obstacle. Many of the federal and state programs, for instance, are limited to state and local governments, with explicit definitions of both listed in the application announcements. Many nonprofits searching for grants do find programs that seem appropriate to their needs in terms of the programmatic details, but see that the eligibility requirements appear to preclude them and they move on. What they are not aware of is that *partnerships* can give them the eligibility they seek (see the "Partnerships" section later in this chapter for more information).

Local Government

Cities and towns control their own budgets and decide where to spend their money. Unfortunately, very few towns have a lot left over to create formalized grant programs. However, special projects that fall outside of any formalized grant programs are much more common at this level of government than any other, and as both a member of the community and an organization whose goal centers upon improving life in the community, organizations may be well placed to get a hold on any resources that exist.

Planners will need to do some firsthand research to find out if there is any funding available through their municipal government. The best and likely only chances come when planners make personal contact with leading local government officials themselves (see Sidebar 6.4). If a town is very small, this might involve setting up a meeting with the mayor or other ranking elected official, while in larger communities you may have to weed through a bureaucratic puzzle to discover which government agency manages the issues your organization or project intends to address.

Once contact has been made, it is up to the fundraisers to accurately explain their organization and project, and how their project will immediately help the community. Each day, people and organizations approach the local government looking for funding, so you must be prepared and able to convince whomever you are speaking with that your project is the worthy one. Having a high-quality proposal will help your case immeasurably, especially if given only a short amount of time to make a case.

Although the local government official first approached may not be able to offer funding, there is a very good chance that he or she will have a handful of ideas to help you find the money you need. By involving the mayor or the local government as a partner in the project, there will be an even greater chance of acquiring funding. The same could be said for the police chief or the fire chief. In the past, organizations have even gone so far as to associate themselves through their title, such as the "Springfield Mayor's Prepared Corps."

SIDEBAR 6.4   DIRECTORIES OF LOCAL GOVERNMENT WEBSITES

- *American hometowns: cities, counties, and towns:* Click on one of the 50 state directories to get to local governments. https://www.usa.gov/local-governments
- *Directory of county, city, and other local government Websites:* Click on your state to find a comprehensive directory of county, city, regional, and other local Websites. http://www.statelocalgov.net/
- *FirstGov gateway for local and state governments:* Information and services for state and local government employees, such as grants, disaster management, and best practices. https://www.usa.gov/state-tribal-governments
- *International city/county management association:* Professional and educational organization for members of the local government community. http://icma.org/en/icma/home
- *Locate in-person service centers in your community:* Find government offices and services such as local motor vehicle offices, post offices, and nursing home facilities. https://www.usa.gov/federal-agencies/a
- *National Association of Countie:* Professional association of county officials that promotes public understanding of U.S. counties. http://www.naco.org/
- *National League of Cities:* Largest national organization of municipal governments, representing 18,000 cities, villages, and towns in the United States. http://www.nlc.org
- *Summary information for U.S. counties:* Information about county officials, county seats, cities in a county, county statistics, and more. http://explorer.naco.org/
- *U.S. conference of mayors:* Official nonpartisan organization of U.S. mayors, representing cities with populations of 30,000 or more. http://usmayors.org/meetmayors/mayorsatglance.asp

State and County Governments

State and county governments are the second option in the search for government funding (see Sidebar 6.5). Oftentimes, the federal government disburses block grants or other formula grants to state governments to distribute to the cities and towns as they see fit. Other times, the state and county governments themselves set aside state-generated funding and create grant programs for which communities and organizations can compete. Either way, planners will need to talk to the appropriate offices to find out if there is any money for which their organization may qualify.

As the projects discussed in this book are emergency- or disaster management-based, it is most appropriate that the first agencies contacted at the state government level be their Office of Homeland Security (which all states now maintain), and the Office of Emergency Management or Public Safety. Then, depending upon the project scope, it may be realistic to talk to representatives in any of the following offices (variations on these names are used in each state and county):

- Office of the Governor
- County Commissioners Office
- Department of Education
- Commission on Aging/Elderly
- Fire Prevention/Control Commission
- Offices of Protection of/Advocacy for Persons with Disabilities
- Office of Emergency Management/Civil Protection/Public Safety
- Office of Homeland Security
- Public Health Department

SIDEBAR 6.5 DIRECTORIES OF STATE OR COUNTY WEBSITES

- *State Offices of Homeland Security:* http://1.usa.gov/210tvnl
- *State Offices of Emergency Management:* http://1.usa.gov/1PSoVwQ
- *State Government Websites:* https://www.usa.gov/agencies
- *County Websites:* http://explorer.naco.org/

The Federal Government

The federal government, naturally, offers the greatest total amount of funding of all the government levels. The key factor in being awarded a federal grant is knowing that it exists. Once aware of the grant, and having determined that their organization type is eligible, planners can begin crafting a proposal that will place their project or program within the restrictions and goal of the grant program. New federal government regulations have been set that require grant announcement and application documents to *all* be posted online, giving you all the tools you will need wherever you are.

Fundraisers can use two primary tools to research federal grants. They are:

1. The Catalog of Federal Domestic Assistance
2. The Grants.gov Website

The Catalog of Federal Domestic Assistance: The online Catalog of Federal Domestic Assistance (CFDA) provides access to a database of all federal programs available to state and local governments (including the District of Columbia); federally recognized Indian tribal governments; territories (and possessions) of the United States; domestic public, quasi-public, and private profit and nonprofit organizations and institutions; specialized groups; and individuals. After finding an appropriate program, applicants can contact the administering office and find out how to apply. The URL for the CFDA is http://www.cfda.gov/.

Grants.gov: The charter of Grants.gov, one of 24 "President's Management Agenda E-Government initiatives," is to provide a simple, unified electronic storefront for interactions between grant applicants and the federal agencies that manage grant funds. There are 26 federal grant-making agencies and more than 900 individual grant programs that award more than $350 billion in grants each year. All grant seekers, which include state, local, and tribal governments; academia and research institutions; and not-for-profits, can visit this Website to access grant funds available across the federal government. The URL for Grants.gov is www.grants.gov.

Grants.gov (see Sidebar 6.6) also sends out emails to prospective grantees as grants become available, minimizing the chance that they miss out on an opportunity. Those interested can register for this service by visiting the grant opportunities email site on the Grants.gov Website at http://www.grants.gov/applicants/email_subscription.jsp. Be sure to see the resources section for links to recommended federal grant programs related to emergency management issues.

SIDEBAR 6.6   GRANTS.GOV

In short, Grants.gov provides:

- A single source for finding grant opportunities
- A standardized manner of locating and learning more about funding opportunities

- A single, secure, and reliable source for applying for federal grants online
- A simplified grant application process with reduction of paperwork
- A unified interface for all agencies to announce their grant opportunities, and for all grant applicants to find and apply for those opportunities

The 900+ grant programs listed on this Website fall into 21 categories defined by the Catalog of Federal Domestic Assistance, including:

- Agriculture
- Arts
- Business and commerce
- Community development
- Consumer protection
- Disaster prevention and relief
- Education
- Employment, labor, and training
- Energy
- Environmental quality
- Food and nutrition
- Health
- Housing
- Humanities
- Information and statistics
- Law, justice, and legal services
- Natural resources
- Regional development
- Science and technology
- Social services and income security
- Transportation

The 26 agencies that post grants on the Website include:

- Agency for International Development (http://www.usaid.gov/)
- Corporation for Community Service (http://www.nationalservice.org/)
- Department of Agriculture (http://www.usda.gov/)
- Department of Commerce (http://www.doc.gov/)
- Department of Defense (http://www.defense.gov/)
- Department of Education (http://www.ed.gov/)
- Department of Energy (http://www.doe.gov/)

- Department of Health and Human Services (http://www.hhs. gov/)
- Department of Housing and Urban Development (http://www. hud.gov/)
- Department of the Interior (http://www.doi.gov/)
- Department of Justice (http://www.usdoj.gov/)
- Department of Labor (http://www.dol.gov/)
- Department of State (http://www.state.gov/)
- Department of Transportation (http://www.dot.gov/)
- Department of the Treasury (http://www.ustreas.gov/)
- Department of Veterans Affairs (http://www.va.gov/)
- Environmental Protection Agency (http://www.epa.gov/)
- Federal Emergency Management Agency (http://www.fema. gov/)
- Institute for Museum and Library Sciences (http://www.imls. gov/)
- National Aeronautics and Space Administration (http://www. nasa.gov/)
- National Archives (http://www.archives.gov/)
- National Endowment for the Arts (http://www.nea.gov/)
- National Endowment for the Humanities (http://www.neh.gov/)
- National Science Foundation (http://www.nsf.gov/)
- Small Business Administration (http://www.sba.gov/)
- Social Security Administration (http://www.ssa.gov/)

Religious Organizations

Every community, no matter how small, is served by one or more religions organizations, each of which likely gives at least a small amount of support back to the community. Every one of these organizations, except in the rarest exceptions, also has a national office that is dedicated to philanthropic activities at the national or international levels. No matter the organization's background, religions organizations are a funding option to be at least considered in any fundraising campaign.

At the national level, many of these religious organizations operate much like the large foundations do—they have a defined competitive process by which applicants submit proposals and grants are awarded. The restrictions imposed by these organizations, however, can be very specific, and, because of these restrictions, the national offices are often an unrealistic source of funding. In addition, some nonprofits themselves have restrictions that limit their access to religiously based grant-giving organizations. Like all the options listed in this guide, planners will need to see for themselves whether these restrictions exist within their own organization.

However, local branches of these religions, though not as well funded, are often great sources of funding and volunteer assistance. If a project plans to work with disadvantaged groups, its chances of garnering support from this group of funders are even greater. Churches can provide the venue planners may need for events, and have the necessary community support they need to bring in prospective individual donors. As has been said throughout this section, creativity is the major limiting factor when it comes to religious groups as donors.

Civic Organizations and Service Clubs

Civic organizations and service clubs such as Kiwanis, the Elks, Rotary, Jaycees, and the Lions are a great contact and funding prospect in local and regional campaigns. These organizations often make grants to organizations in the communities they operate and can be a great source of introduction to other funders in the community.

Civic organizations and social groups are perpetually seeking speakers and guests at their meetings and events. Organizations seeking funding can develop a public relations team that works to get on the agenda of those luncheons and meetings to talk about emergency preparedness and, more importantly, to talk about the project being developed. What is gained in return for speaking is the opportunity to meet local business representatives who are able to assist with donations and in-kind contributions, and who might be interested in helping the organization as a technical assistant or in another capacity. For organizations with a board of directors, this method can be useful for finding new board members who, as individuals, are proven donors—and, as representatives from the organizations where they work, they may even be able to provide equipment, publicity, or a venue for a fundraising event.

Fee Generation

If the organization is permitted to do so, fee generation can be a way to ensure a small but steady income to keep a program running. This is where an organization offers a product to lure donors, and the profits from those sales entirely go to operational expenses. Many organizations have been very creative in this area, selling both products and services to support their programs. Services offered as part of a project, such as tuition fees and equipment, can be accompanied by a suggested donation fee that benefactors can choose to pay depending upon their resources. Planners may find that, with a good fee generation plan and effective marketing, this form of fundraising alone can serve to offer their project the sustainability for which all organizations wish.

However, fee generation requires significant creativity. For instance, people like to advertise their philanthropic support, which can be accomplished by selling T-shirts that are inexpensive to produce and can give 100% in return for the investment. Actual project participants tend to be especially interested in buying such items. Books or other resources related to the project, such as emergency supply kits, first aid kits, or other preparedness materials, can be sold to generate fees, and people may be more inclined to buy these products if they are informed that they are contributing to a program serving their community. An added benefit of this type of fundraising is that it is a form of financial empowerment that can make an organization feel like it is self-supporting and not entirely dependent upon the handouts of others.

Partnerships

Emergency preparedness and response is a concern of all community stakeholders, whether they are a governmental agency, a religious group, a private business, a school, a hospital, a nonprofit organization, or one of the many other groups that are joined in a civil society. While each of these stakeholders possesses unique resources and skills, each also has unique vulnerabilities and needs. By working in partnership with one or more of the various stakeholders in your community, it is possible to pool together skills and resources while addressing each other's needs and vulnerabilities—the result being increased strength and opportunity for all partners involved.

Partnerships may also provide you access to local, county, state, and federal funding to which planners might otherwise not have access. For instance, FEMA's United States Fire Administration (USFA) provides hundreds of millions of dollars in funding through its Assistance to Firefighters Grant program—more than $600 million this year alone. While only recognized fire departments are eligible for the program, a nonprofit working in partnership with a fire department on a special project, such as assisting in home fire safety audits, could benefit from the grant program despite issues with eligibility. Keeping this in mind as they peruse the long list of federal grants available at any given time, planners need to consider what kind of partnership would give them the eligibility they need, and then approach that partner with a plan or proposal. The more legwork planners offer their partners in the project (many of these first-responder agencies, including fire, police, EMS, and emergency management, have very little room for additional responsibilities), the greater their chances are of developing that partnership.

IMPLEMENTING A FUNDRAISING STRATEGY

Planners should always begin with the sources that offer them the greatest chance for success, and move methodically toward those that offer less confidence. Most fundraisers will say that one should always start with family, friends, employees, volunteers, vendors, a board if one exists, and anyone else that they could say that they know. The unfortunate truth is that as one moves farther and farther away from one's organization and circle of contacts, the more time and effort will be needed to convince the donor to give. The good news is that closer does not necessarily mean less money.

If someone who is unfamiliar with the organization is approached, one of his or her first inquiries may be about what other sources of funding already exist. They will probably look to see if those with a stake in the organization have come forward with support. If a board exists, for example, and the board has not supported the project, they will wonder why they should. As for staff, the goal is not to raise a great deal of funds but rather to build a high percentage of participation at any level. This show of support can go a long way in convincing other prospects about the dedication of the organization and its people.

Vendors of an organization—those with whom the organization does business—could also be asked to participate in a fundraising project. While some may have policies against giving to organizations with which they do business, it never hurts to ask. Sometimes, contacting a vendor can lead to a gift from a larger corporate foundation. Other times it may lead to a reduction in price for the services or products you are already receiving from the vendor. Either way, more funds will be available for the organization's mission.

Local business and community leaders have the next closest stake in the project and should be contacted next. Planners should present the value of their work in the community and be prepared to discuss ways in which they can help publicize the generosity of local businesses. While philanthropy is a primary motivation, businesses and politicians are also pleased to have opportunities for good public relations.

Finally, foundations should be approached with grant proposals. Planners can start with local foundations before moving on to the national ones. It is important to pay attention to guidelines and deadlines, provide what is requested, make personal contact when possible, form relationships that can help a funding decision, and be truthful. Substance, commitment, and conviction can actually outweigh a professionally polished proposal.

No matter the fundraising project, planners should always be prepared to prove that they have done all they can with their local resources before they seek additional outside support.

FUNDRAISING STRATEGY FACTORS

The following factors should be considered as planners create their fundraising strategy. Collectively, these factors are the key determinant variables dictating actions.

- *Timing:* What is your total time frame in which you need to raise money? Urgency for requirement of funds should be considered. If cash is not needed immediately, you may have the option of asking for pledges.
- *Amount of funding required:* The size of expected donation should be relative to the size of the project. Ask for a specific dollar amount and be realistic.
- *Available resources:* Number of volunteers, costs involved, and time (work hours) available to conduct a fundraising campaign.
- *Profile of project:* In many cases, your donors must be offered tangible and intangible returns (e.g., public relations or direct individual benefits). Identifying the profile of the project will help to determine geographic boundaries of the campaign.
- *Environment:* Availability of funding from some sources may be conditional on the economy.
- *Sequence:* If more than one source is being considered (e.g., event fundraising used in conjunction with another source), individual contributions may be affected by prior "donations" through special events fundraising. Make sure that your sequence is both logical and set to optimize your chances of being funded.
- *Values:* The organization must be supportive of the method being used to raise funds. Some types of fundraising activities may not meet with the approval of the organization or community (e.g., lotteries, sponsorship by certain companies).
- Legal and regulatory issues (see Sidebar 6.7).

SIDEBAR 6.7   LEGAL AND REGULATORY ISSUES OF FUNDRAISING

There are several factors that organizations need to consider to ensure they are legally covered before you begin asking for contributions for your organization or project. The following information was compiled by Idealist.org, an online forum for nonprofit organizations.

Are my fundraising activities appropriate, allowed, and/or legal? Be sure that the money you are collecting is money that you are allowed to use. Many agencies have legal restrictions that limit certain types of private donations, and many states have laws governing giving. You do not want to appear incompetent later on if you are faced with having to return donated money.

Are there any laws or regulations I need to be sure I follow? Many states have what are called *charitable solicitations laws*. Some cities and counties have similar regulations, and it is often hard to find out exactly how they might apply to your plans. There are requirements for one-time or annual registration, and annual reporting. A group of states has come together through the nonprofit sector and developed a uniform registration form, with about 47 states participating. For annual financial reporting by charities, many states now use the IRS's Form 990, supplemented by their own form for additional questions. Even to obtain the appropriate forms and instructions from all the appropriate state offices is challenging and time consuming. In many states, out-of-state charities soliciting in the state are required to register. In addition, charities often have to file with the secretary of state as corporations doing business in that state. Some jurisdictions flatly forbid raising money for a charitable organization without an agreement signed in advance with the recipient organization.

The state rules are summarized at http://www.multistatefiling.org. This Website was created to help big organizations that ask for donations in many states, but the state-by-state index of regulations will give you a sense of whether you will need to talk with your local charity-oversight officials before starting your campaign. You can find out if your state accepts the common filing forms at http://www.multistatefiling.org/#yes_states.

Are there any taxes that I might have to pay? You will want to be careful not to mix up the funds you raise in your campaign with your own money. You will need to keep careful records. You might want to open a separate bank account that will be used only for this campaign. Since you are raising the money to pass along to someone else, it should not be considered income that you earned, but you will need to be able to document that you kept the funds completely separate if the IRS or your local tax department should ask.

Are the gifts people give to my campaign tax deductible? That depends. First, it depends on the givers' own tax situation. Careful fundraisers never say, "You can take a tax deduction." What they say (when it is true) is "You may be able to deduct this from your personal income taxes. Consult with your tax advisor or review the IRS regulations that apply to your situation to determine whether a deduction is allowed."

However, tax deductions can only be taken for certain kinds of gifts. If you know your campaign is not about raising money for a tax-deductible purpose, you need to be careful to tell people that right up front.

- The recipient organization has to be recognized by the IRS as a 501(c)(3)—or be an established church. (Churches do not have to register with the government, but they do have to meet certain standards about how they operate. If you have any doubts, ask.)
- Gifts to individuals, no matter how urgent the need, are never tax deductible.
- One result of the rule that gifts to individuals are never deductible is that you must be sure you are raising money for a recognized charity before you ask for any donations. You cannot ask people to give you donations that you will later decide how to use (unless you want to go through the process of setting up a new nonprofit organization, with all the complications in that process, before you start your campaign).

What about enlisting other people to help with my campaign? If you do that, you will need to have some sort of internal controls to be sure that everyone sticks to your standards about how the campaign is run and how the money is handled. The usual way of handling one part of this problem is to have receipt books that automatically make duplicates that everyone can turn in with the money he or she has raised.

If you are going to start something that involves several other people, then you might think about setting up a group to help you oversee the project, review progress, and join in publishing reports on your successes. That way the responsibility for making sure the campaign runs right will be shared and you will have help if anything appears to be going off the rails.

If your campaign is going to go on for a while and involve a group of other people, but you do not want to set up a new nonprofit organization, then you might consider approaching an established nonprofit to act as your "fiscal sponsor" or "fiscal agent." Fiscal sponsorship means that the existing organization adopts your work as a "program" under its wing. The sponsor is ultimately responsible for the program, so you would have to follow its rules; usually the sponsor takes a small administrative fee. Donors to your project would be assured a tax deduction, though, if all the requirements of the IRS were met. In addition, you would not have to worry about administrative details like tax forms, bank deposit rules, and accounting packages.

Source: Barber, P., Idealist.org. http://www.idealist.org/if/i/en/faq/404-142/110-77, 2005.

ASKING FOR STUFF

Oftentimes, individuals, businesses, and other organizations who would like to give to an organization or project do not have the finances or ability to do so. However, that does not mean that they have nothing to give. For this reason, fundraising campaigns need to be able to address more than cash gifts, as there are many ways to give. By knowing what resources, supplies, and services are needed in the planning and operation of the project, in-kind and volunteer donations become possible. Examples of items and services commonly donated include:

- Computers
- Printers
- Office supplies
- Books
- Medical equipment
- Office furniture
- Transportation
- Office space
- Uniforms
- Printing
- Advertising

This is but a tiny sample of the thousands of things that could possibly be needed for a public education project. If these items are listed in a proposal or in any literature developed for planning or fundraising purposes, fundraisers can discuss the need with any donor that offers assistance other than cash. However, what is collected need not be limited to the needs of the project, of course. Donated items can be sold for charity or auctioned off. Many local businesses will donate items from their inventory, which they can claim for a tax deduction, and which organizations may be allowed to sell at a significant discount to raise funding for their project. Donated advertising has been mentioned as well. The donation itself will not bring the organization closer to its fundraising goal, but it may bring it the publicity it needs to do so.

Captain Robert Moore (1998) of the Suffolk County Police Department writes,

> When solicited for money and before analyzing the merits of a proposal, potential benefactors make a number of decisions. Questions that instantly run through their minds include:
>
> - Can I afford the amount requested?
> - Do I want to give away that amount?
> - Is the amount requested in line with the scope of the work?
>
> The primary focus of each of these questions is money. The purpose, goal, or task, if considered at all, becomes a secondary issue. And a "no" response to just one of these questions usually ends the discussion. So stop thinking about money. Instead, think about what kinds of "stuff" your organization needs.

If you think about acquiring materials from donors as a separate campaign from the fundraising, you do need to be knowledgeable about what you need before the question is ever asked of you. As for the equipment you need for your project—if it is industry specific, you may want to ask businesses who sell or manufacture that equipment for *either* a cash or an equipment donation. Leave the option up to them. Other equipment is much more common, like desks, chairs, phones, and fax machines, for example, and almost any business is likely to have some of these items lying around that they do not need. You can even place an advertisement in the newspaper asking members of the community and businesses if they would be willing to support your organization by donating anything from the list you provide in the advertisement. Again, remember that office or other space is something that organizations often have donated to them. If your project involves training, you could have classroom space donated. If you need an operations center, an office may be given, complete with paid utilities. You can even agree on certain times or days when you will use them if that is all that you will need. Food and drinks can be donated for events. You will never know what people may give if you do not ask.

Captain Moore offers additional valuable advice in this area (see Sidebar 6.8).

SIDEBAR 6.8   CAPTAIN MOORE'S IN-KIND SOLICITATION ADVICE

Have you ever driven past a home, seen items sitting at the curb awaiting garbage pickup and said to yourself, "Look at all that great stuff!" The same principle can be applied to corporations. Unless you tell them, they won't know that the furniture or equipment they consider obsolete suits your needs just fine. My station acquired desks, chairs, file cabinets, electronic typewriters, and copying machines, at no cost, from a local savings bank. The bank, like most corporations, periodically redecorates its offices and updates machinery. Because I've made them aware of our needs, a bank official always notifies us when they have something available.

A number of organizations, by mandate or corporate charter, or because of good corporate citizenship, distribute informational literature on topics such as driving and pedestrian safety, frauds and schemes, burglary and robbery prevention, preparations for natural disasters, and so on. The brochures are of high quality, informative, and cover virtually every topic imaginable and are often distributed to other organizations free of charge.

If you need meeting space but the rental fee isn't in your budget, call your local library or community college. Both institutions routinely make their facilities available to community groups for training sessions and seminars, and even assist with advertising and registration. They provide audio-visual aids, have adequate parking and bathrooms, and are equipped with just about everything needed to host a successful event. Usually, these benefits are provided at no charge.

Other untapped resources are high schools and colleges. An increasing number of learning institutions are making community service a requirement for graduation. Schools often scramble to find opportunities for young people. It's an excellent way for your organization to help students gain experience while you gain extra personnel. I've heard of many novel programs where community members offer a service in exchange for some action or activity on the part of others. One of my favorites occurred in Contra Costa County, California, where a group of psychologists offered three hours of free therapy to anyone who turned in a handgun. There are no limits to ingenuity.

Major organizations conduct mandatory training. Fire departments, utility companies, police departments, airports, hospitals, and the Army Reserve all conduct large-scale, multiagency drills. There is no finer training available in crisis management, communications, prioritization, systems and procedures, or teamwork than drills. Let these organizations know you want to participate or observe.

A few final suggestions include the following:

- Focus your thinking on what you need or what you intend to accomplish.
- Be specific. Even when stuff is not immediately available, potential benefactors will remember you when it is.

- Benefactors will take your calls and even call you when they know money is not likely to come up in the conversation.

Source: Moore, C.R., *Asking for Stuff. Community Links.* Vol. 3. Winter. http://web.archive.org/web/20060103061515/http://www.communitypolicing.org/publications/comlinks/cl_4/c4_moor.htm, 1998.

A number of nonprofit organizations and associations maintain online and printed resources to help with fundraising. The following is a list of several of these organizations:

- The Foundation Center (www.fdncenter.org)
- Fundraiser.org (http://www.fundraiser.org/)
- Internet Non-profit Center (http://www.nonprofits.org/)
- American Fund Raising Institute (http://www.amfundraising.com/)
- Fundraisingweb.org (http://www.fundraisingweb.org/)
- Minnesota Council on Foundations (http://www.mcf.org/)
- Raise Funds (http://www.raise-funds.com/)
- Chronicle of Philanthropy (http://www.philanthropy.com/)
- Grass Roots Fundraising Online (http://www.grassrootsfundraising.org)
- Fundraising.Com (www.fund-raising.com)
- Contributions Magazine (www.contributionsmagazine.com)
- American Association of Fundraising Counsel (www.aafrc.org)

CONCLUSION

All public education campaigns need funding to survive. When organizations find themselves without the resources to complete, continue, or even to begin their public education efforts, what lies ahead can be daunting. Fortunately, there are countless sources of funding to which appeals may be made, as described in this chapter. The key is that the campaign that is planned and conducted always matches the funding levels that are attainable.

REFERENCES

Barber, Putnam. 2005. Idealist.org. http://www.idealist.org/if/i/en/faq/404-142/110-77. Accessed January 2017.

Better Business Bureau. 2001. Donor Expectations Survey. Wise Giving Alliance. us.bbb.org. Accessed January 2017.

Hall, Mary. 1988. *Getting Funded: A Complete Guide to Proposal Writing.* 3rd ed. Portland, OR: Continuing Education.

Independent Sector Website. http://www.independentsector.org. Accessed December 2008.

Moore, Captain Robert. 1998. Asking for Stuff. Community Links. Vol. 3. Winter.

Poderis, Tony. 1997. *12 Things You Should Know about Setting a Capital Campaign Goal.* Fund Raising Forum. http://bit.ly/1ToavZO. Accessed January 2017.

CHAPTER 7

Emergency Management Public Education Case Studies

CASE: ORGANIZED TRAINING FOR COMMUNITIES

Program Facts

Who: Los Angeles Fire Department (LAFD)
What: Community Emergency Response Team (CERT)
Where: Los Angeles, California
Partners: Los Angeles Fire Department and FEMA Citizen Corps
Mission: To prepare the public to be able to rely on each other in order to meet their immediate lifesaving and life-sustaining needs in the case of an emergency situation in which first responders are unable to meet the demand for these services.

In 1987, the Whittier Narrows earthquake emphasized the threat of a major disaster in California and confirmed the need to train citizens to meet their own immediate needs. As a result, the LAFD created a Disaster Preparedness Division to train citizens.

The program was highly successful, and, in time, FEMA decided that it should be made available to all communities throughout the nation. In 1994, the FEMA Emergency Management Institute and the LAFD expanded the Community Emergency Response Team (CERT) program materials to make them applicable to all hazards and all communities.

Disasters vary greatly from location to location, so training varies based on the probabilities of different types of disasters. CERT team members are taught to assess their own needs and the needs of the immediate environment first (e.g., family, neighbors, and community). The certification process for CERT requires 17.5 hours of training provided over a seven-week period and includes disaster preparedness, light urban search and rescue, fire safety, basic medical principles, teamwork and the incident command system, disaster psychology, and terrorism preparedness, and there is a final exercise. It is provided free to any resident that is at least 18 years old.

Today, there are more than 2600 CERTs registered nationwide. They are sometimes called in to designated staging areas to fill various roles based on needs.

Instructions on how to start a CERT program, how to apply for CERT, a state directory and a map of nearby CERTs, frequently asked questions, all training materials, video materials, supplemental information, and contact information can be found on the FEMA CERT Website at http://bit.ly/29xDaIG. The LA-CERT brochure can be found at http://bit.ly/21XPUCd.

More information about this program can be found at the Citizen Corps CERT Website: http://www.citizencorps.gov/cert/about.shtm.

CASE: VOLUNTEER EMERGENCY PREPAREDNESS PROGRAM

Program Facts

Who: Sunnyvale, California, city government and its citizens
What: SNAP (Sunnyvale Neighborhoods Actively Prepare)
Where: Sunnyvale, California
Partners: City government and citizens of Sunnyvale, California
Mission: To provide Sunnyvale residents with tools to be self-sufficient for a minimum of 72 hours following a disaster and to be able to become an asset to their neighborhoods as well as the city.

SNAP is a volunteer program developed on a neighborhood-by-neighborhood basis to improve the abilities of people in the community to cope with the aftermath of earthquakes. Each self-defined neighborhood composed of 35 to 50 homes is represented by a captain and six disaster task committees. Captains coordinate action-based committees that prepare to use citizens as resources in times of need. Each committee represents one of the key concerns in the event of a disaster:

- Communications
- Damage assessment
- First aid
- Safety and security
- Search and rescue
- Sheltering and special needs

Some captains are also part of a citywide SNAP steering committee that works directly with city staff.

The program offers five different workshops and a full set of informational materials:

1. Basic committee training
2. Topic training
3. Captain training
4. First aid/CPR training
5. Advanced urban search and rescue training

Training provides education and information, and committees provide a joint response of citizens and government. Citizens become part of the decision-making process as well as participate in community improvement.

The program is funded by tax dollars. FEMA is using SNAP as a model for residential emergency preparedness.

More information about the SNAP program can be found at http://bit.ly/1R2hn0u.

CASE: TEACHING EMERGENCY PREPAREDNESS IN SCHOOLS

Program Facts

Who: New England Schools
What: The Student Tools for Emergency Planning (STEP) program
Where: New England
Partners: FEMA and state emergency management agencies with local schools in New England
Mission: To teach basic emergency preparedness skills

In 2008, FEMA and state emergency preparedness agencies teamed up with New England schools to launch a pilot program for New England fourth-grade students to teach basic emergency preparedness skills. The STEP program provides ready-to-teach preparedness lessons for teachers to empower students to encourage their families to make home emergency kits and communication plans. Teachers are required to dedicate one hour of classtime to the base lesson, and have up to ten hours of optional lessons to reinforce the base lesson. The program is free for schools.

In addition to the lesson plan, schools are also provided with ready-to-teach lesson materials (DVDs, handouts, disaster game cards) and items for students to make their own "starter kits," including a water bottle, snack bar, emergency whistle, Mylar blanket, and carrying bag.

The family plan promoted by the program encouraged students to agree with their families on an alternate meeting place outside of the home, designate a person to call in case of an emergency (often in a different state), and for each family member to carry around cards with those important facts as well as work and school numbers.

The entire STEP curriculum for fourth and fifth grade students can be downloaded by accessing the following URL: http://bit.ly/1ptAe8q. The FEMA STEP informational Website is http://1.usa.gov/1ROxqvD.

CASE: EMERGENCY PREPAREDNESS IN PUBLIC TRANSPORTATION

Program Facts

Who: Washington Metropolitan Area Transit Authority
What: Emergency evacuation maps help riders find alternate bus or rail services
Where: Washington, D.C.
Partners: Washington Metrorail stations
Mission: An ongoing initiative to improve communications with customers, particularly during emergencies.

Washington Metro created site-specific emergency evacuation maps that customers can take with them if they have to evacuate a rail station or choose to find an alternate route during a lengthy service disruption. Maps were customized for each of Metrorail's 117 station mezzanines. They list all bus services available near the station and provide walking directions to the closest Metrorail station, along with the distance and estimated walking time. A "You Are Here" icon is provided to assist passengers in situating themselves on the map.

Each mezzanine station initially received 5000 copies of the individualized 8.5- × 11-inch paper maps. Metro staff replenishes the maps periodically or as inventory gets low. The maps were created as part of a larger initiative to improve maps in the Metrorail system in general. Maps are also provided on the Washington Metropolitan Transit Authority Website.

WMATA has created an online instructional course that city residents can access to better understand when and how to evacuate from a metro car or metro station in an emergency or disaster event. The course can be accessed at http://bit.ly/1pa3EIQ. WMATA also offers a number of printed and video resources in addition to this course which can be found at http://bit.ly/1LL6duK.

Contact Information
Website: http://bit.ly/2a4NcDi

CASE: PUBLIC–PRIVATE PARTNERSHIP
FOR DISASTER PREPAREDNESS

Program Facts

Who: Tulsa Citizen Corps Partners and McDonald's
What: McReady Oklahoma
Where: 170 McDonald's restaurants and over 30 other locations,
including city halls, libraries, courthouses, and others through-
out Oklahoma
Partners: Tulsa Partners, the McDonald's Corporation, Oklahoma
Department of Emergency Management, the American Red
Cross, and dozens of others
Mission: To preparing Oklahoma families, businesses, schools,
churches, and other venues and groups regarding the steps that
can be taken to stay safe from tornadoes, severe storms, and
other natural disasters.

In June 2003, Bill LaFortune, mayor of Tulsa; Dwayne Sampson,
president of McDonald's Tulsa Co-op of Restaurant Owners; and
Ronald McDonald held a press conference at a local McDonald's restaurant to kick off "Mayor's Citizen Corps Month." One year later, a new
McReady emergency preparedness campaign was launched statewide.

McReady Oklahoma is a grassroots initiative that provides activities and materials aimed at preparing Oklahoma families, businesses,
schools, churches, and other venues and groups regarding the steps that
can be taken to stay safe from tornadoes, severe storms, and other natural disasters. By distributing and displaying materials at venues popular
with almost all demographics, the program reaches a large and diverse
audience.

The program messages are delivered statewide, primarily within
McDonald's restaurants. Major program elements include: in-store
informational displays with preparedness literature; educational tray
liners and bag stuffers; the opportunity for local emergency managers
to customize the program with weather radio programming and other
local events; a weather safety show presented at schools; a weather
safety DVD provided to schools and local emergency managers; and an
informational Website, www.mcready.org.

McReady displays are located in more than 170 McDonald's restaurants and another 30 city halls, libraries, and county courthouses
(in communities without a McDonald's) as part of a statewide severe
weather preparedness campaign which occurs in the month of April.
The displays contain informational materials focusing on tornado,
flood, and lightning safety. McReady literature includes a Family

Preparedness Guide, a guide titled "Weathering the Storm," and bro-chures that explain how to shelter in place. A weather safety activity book geared toward a younger audience features a word search and pages for coloring (with Crayons available upon request at participat-ing restaurants). Other preparedness materials include McDonald's tray liners and bag stuffers that urge families to prepare for severe weather and provide weather safety tips and an informational map that explains severe weather warnings. A McReady display in the restaurants pro-vides another opportunity for visitors to get program materials and pre-paredness information.

To help reach people who might not be exposed to the prepared-ness message in McDonald's restaurants, the McReady program pro-vides in-school training in the Oklahoma City and Tulsa metropolitan areas. The program includes a show that features Ronald McDonald, Oklahoma Gas & Electric's Lineman Larry, and other corporate mas-cots and spokespersons. More than 12,000 students, teachers, and staff receive the McReady weather safety message via the school programs every year.

And finally, the program promotes the importance of awareness by orchestrating giveaways of NOAA all hazards weather radios. The campaign holds giveaways through weekly drawings for which partici-pants register on the McReady Website. Winners are announced each Wednesday in April on KOCO Channel 5 in Oklahoma City and KRMG Radio in Tulsa following a "Weather Radio Wednesday" drawing con-ducted by the Oklahoma Department of Emergency Management.

More than 5 million individuals are exposed to the McReady cam-paign annually via the McDonald's restaurants alone.

More information about the program can be found at http://bit.ly/1R2mfTk.

CASE: NATIONAL PUBLIC EDUCATION EFFORT

Program Facts

> *Who:* New Zealand Ministry of Civil Defense
> *What:* Nationwide preparedness campaign: "Get Ready Get Thru"
> *Where:* Nationwide, New Zealand
> *Partners:* Television and radio stations, schools, and others
> *Mission:* To boost public awareness and understanding of the need to prepare to face disasters by having a plan, and taking steps to be better prepared.

In June 2006, New Zealand Civil Defense Minister Rick Barker launched a nationwide campaign that urged New Zealanders to "Get Ready Get Thru." The mass media campaign included radio, television, and print ads to encourage New Zealanders to prepare for disasters. The key messages to this campaign were listed on New Zealand's Department of Internal Affairs Webpage as:

> In a disaster, essential services will be disrupted. Emergency services and civil defense staff will be doing their job but help cannot get to everyone as quickly as they may need it. Each and every one of us needs to take responsibility to plan to look after those dependent on us. We need to take steps now to be prepared to look after ourselves for up to three days or more.

In addition to mass media messaging, the Get Ready Get Through program included other methods and initiatives including:

- A school program entitled "What's the Plan Stan?" This initiative was created to support teachers in their efforts to include disaster preparedness training in the classroom. Participating schools are provided with a teacher's guide (including unit plans and activities); a CD-Rom with activities for students and printable worksheets for teachers; posters; an illustrated storybook; and an audio CD of preparedness stories. Program materials are provided to address different age groups.
- The Website www.getthru.govt.nz was created to provide user-friendly information and advice for the public on what they should do to be prepared. This Website offers links to the nearest civil defense council so that people could easily access information specific to their region.
- The ministry also worked closely with the Auckland Council to create the Natural Hazard Risk Communication Toolbox. This guide was produced in order to increase understanding of basic hazard and risk concepts by providing consistent content for communication materials used within council and externally to stakeholders, politicians, and the community. The toolbox contains written and visual materials to describe frequently used natural hazard risk management concepts. Some of the concepts include definitions for resilience, cumulative and cascading hazards, consequence, and hazard versus risk. For each concept, the following information is provided: brief text explanations; more detailed explanations; visual representation; and an Auckland case study.

The program includes an intensive evaluation component that utilizes quantitative benchmark research to understand current national levels of awareness, understanding, and preparedness. The program has also become increasingly involved with the promotion of the annual Disaster Preparedness Week.

A copy of the Get Ready Get Through program guide can be downloaded at http://bit.ly/1pwu47B. The Get Ready Get Through Website is www.getthru.govt.nz. What's the Plan Stan can be found at http://bit.ly/1ptBNTP. The Natural Hazard Risk Communication Toolbox can be found at http://bit.ly/1p6JZc9.

CASE: TECHNOLOGY-BASED LEARNING

Program Facts

> *Who:* American Red Cross
> *What:* Monster Guard: Prepare for Emergencies App
> *Where:* Nationwide
> *Partners:* American Red Cross and Disney
> *Mission:* To help children between the ages of 7 and 11 years learn emergency preparedness

The American Red Cross created the Monster Guard App with sponsorship from Disney to help children between the ages of 7 and 11 years learn emergency preparedness. Children can download the free App which enables them to learn how to prevent emergencies such as home fires and how to stay safe in the event of major disasters while playing as monster characters. The game takes place in the setting of "Monster Guard Academy," and users are able to role-play as different characters that teach them different information about hazards, including tornadoes, floods, and hurricanes. Once a player completes all the episodes, he or she graduates and becomes a member of the "Monster Guard."

The App was created in an effort to make preparedness education more fun for children, and to use a training method they are accustomed to. Examples of activities they encounter in the game include identifying fire hazards, locating safe rooms in a house, and selecting items needed for an emergency supplies kit. Of particular note is that the program allows youth participants to share their accomplishments with their friends or family using social media tools.

The App can be downloaded to either IOS or Android devices at http://apple.co/2a4NkCH.

CASE: LOCAL GOVERNMENT PREPAREDNESS CAMPAIGN

Program Facts

Who: Office of Emergency Management
What: Comprehensive Education and Outreach Program "Get READY! Stay READY!"
Where: City of Henderson, NV
Partners: City Mayor, City Council members, City Clerk, City Attorney, Office of Emergency Management
Mission: To educate city employees and the general public about individual and family disaster preparedness

The City of Henderson, Nevada, is prone to earthquakes, drought, extreme heat, fire, and flash floods. In 2014, the City of Henderson Office of Emergency Management launched a comprehensive education and outreach campaign known as Get READY! Stay READY! to educate city employees and the general public about individual and family disaster preparedness. People working on the Get READY! Stay READY! Campaign set up information booths, produced a series of videos, led interactive sessions, conducted contests, and trained city staff and stakeholders during FEMA's Integrated Emergency Management Course. In total, the campaign reached more than 100,000 people, held more than 55 educational and outreach events, produced 12 videos, and developed a comprehensive brochure and Website.

View the Get READY! Stay READY! brochure at http://bit.ly/1TGLM5e.

CASE: DISASTER PREPAREDNESS CAMP

Program Facts

Who: Serve Alabama, the Alabama Governor's Faith-Based and Volunteer Services
What: Be Ready Camp
Where: Montgomery, Alabama.
Partners: Office of the Governor (AL), U.S. Space and Rocket Center, Alabama Emergency Management, Alabama Law Enforcement Agency
Mission: Promote citizen preparedness and participation

Alabama Be Ready Camp is held at the U.S. Space and Rocket Center located in Huntsville, Alabama. The program provides an opportunity for sixth graders from throughout the state to become youth preparedness delegates. As youth preparedness delegates, they are charged with extending preparedness and safety messages to their schools, communities, and families.

The program, which has won several national awards, is based on the Community Emergency Response Team (CERT) training. The curriculum includes emergency preparedness, introduction to survival and first aid, developing an emergency kit, creating a family disaster plan, water survival, light search and rescue, disaster psychology, triage, career exploration, and terrorism awareness. In each lesson, participants demonstrate their knowledge with hands-on demonstrations in addition to traditional assessments. Participation costs only $75 dollars, which covers the cost of a preparedness backpack, meals, and lodging. The camp concludes with a mock disaster, where the youth perform victim search and rescue alongside professional responders in a realistic setting.

A copy of the camp informational brochure can be found at http:// bit.ly/21Yo0m2.

CASE: COMMUNITY-WIDE DISASTER DRILL

Program Facts

> *Who:* Spartanburg County (SC) Office of Emergency Management
> *What:* Countywide Test of the Emergency Notification System
> *Where:* Spartanburg County
> *Partners:* Spartanburg County Office of Emergency Management, Code Red
> *Mission:* To ensure that residents and businesses are registered to receive emergency alerts, and to verify that they receive them and understand how to act in response.

As a part of the National PrepareAthon initiative (see case study on the PrepareAthon later in this chapter), the Spartanburg County Office of Emergency Management (SCOEM) conducted a city-wide notification drill. To test the Emergency Notification System, SCOEM teamed up with the Emergency Communications Network "CodeRed" program to plan and conduct the drill. The planning team prepared participants by sending out a tornado drill reminder in advance of March 11, 2015, which was the day the county was hosting National PrepareAthon! Day. SCOEM aggressively recruited participants by promoting the drill to local businesses, schools, government, residents, and other stakeholders.

More than 90,000 residents and businesses were called, messages were emailed to nearly 2,000 people, who in turn forwarded those emails or used social media to reach at least 10,000 more people. The county also partnered with a local TV station that provided media coverage leading up to, and on, the day of the drill. The 2015 drill was the largest preparedness event in the county's history, providing an opportunity for the county to conduct a drill that included businesses, schools, hospitals, and the general public for the first time. Over 60,000 people attended.

More information about Spartanburg preparedness efforts can be found at http://www.scoem.org/

CASE: YOUTH PREPAREDNESS

Program Facts

> *Who:* Mississippi State University Extension Service
> *What:* Mississippi Youth Preparedness Initiative (MyPI)
> *Where:* Throughout Mississippi
> *Partners:* Mississippi State University Extension Service, Citizen Corps
> *Mission:* To increase youth and family preparedness throughout Mississippi

The Mississippi State University (MSU) Extension Service created MyPI, a grassroots initiative that provides innovative preparedness training and education to approximately 3,500 teens per year. Teens aged 13 to 19 years enroll in a flexible 5- to 10-week schedule during which time they are given the Homeland Security-certified Teen CERT training as well as CPR and AED certifications. Students must participate at least once per week. The program also includes leadership and teamwork opportunities and technology and career exploration tracks. A comprehensive family and community service project entitled "Prep + 6" in which each participant helps develop emergency supply kits and emergency communication plans for their family and six additional families or households is another component.

MyPI is currently being taught in formal school settings across Mississippi through Allied Health classes, Law and Public Safety classes, and as part of Vocational Tech programs. It is also taught outside of school settings for organized youth programs, community agencies, and others. Instructors include MyPI volunteers, subject matter experts, and guest speakers. Program implementation covers a five-year period ending 2018. During this time, it is expected that the program will reach over 121,000 families throughout Mississippi.

As a coordinating agency of MyPI, the MSU Extension Service coordinates the selection and training of youth preparedness trainers and the youth membership involved in the program and monitors youth progress in emergency preparedness education, training, and service to the community.

In 2014, MyPI received an award from FEMA for Outstanding Youth Preparedness program. It also received an Honorable Mention recognition for the FEMA "Preparing the Whole Community" award. In 2015, MyPI became one of the first entities to be named an official Affirmer of the new National Strategy for Youth Preparedness Education.

For additional information, the MyPI program brochure can be found at http://bit.ly/1ToAh1V.

CASE: MULTI-STAKEHOLDER PREPAREDNESS CAMPAIGN

Program Facts

Who: Do 1 Thing (a nonprofit organization)
What: Participatory Online Training Program with Registration
Where: State of Michigan
Partners: Almost 800 partners drawn from the public, private, and nonprofit sectors
Mission: To move individuals, families, businesses, and communities to prepare for all hazards and become disaster resilient

The Do 1 Thing program was started in Michigan by local emergency managers and nonprofit organizations, with a goal of making emergency preparedness easy and affordable for everyone. Today, the program is organized around a Web-based platform that enables citizens to register and participate. Once registered, participants are provided monthly notifications about preparedness actions they can take which are appropriate for their status as an individual or as a representative of a business. There are 12 actions in all, and participants are expected to complete one for each month across the course of a year. Through their registration, participants are signed up to receive email reminders and can choose to follow the program's Twitter account. The Website itself offers information about different preparedness actions, as well as fact sheets, brochures, and other resources.

The program depends on the participation of partners, who promote the program among their contacts or members. This format is based on the fact that individuals are more likely to take action and do something if the message comes from a trusted source. Partners work with their employees or other stakeholders to influence positive preparedness actions. Do 1 Thing has successfully translated the monthly program into seven languages, as well as into Braille, large print, and audio. Do 1 Thing recently launched the Disaster Resilient Communities for Older Adults and People with Disabilities Project to increase disaster resilience by:

- Working with individuals to plan and participate in their own disaster preparedness initiatives
- Planning and working with public safety, emergency response, community, and neighborhood groups to address the critical needs of older adults and people with disabilities and others with access and functional needs during an event

A brochure describing the program can be found at http://bit. ly/1R2IYIF.

CASE: GOVERNMENT-SPONSORED BUSINESS PREPAREDNESS CERTIFICATION PROGRAM

Program Facts

Who: The U.S. Department of Homeland Security
What: PS-Prep™
Where: United States Nationwide
Partners: U.S. Department of Homeland Security, ANSI-ASQ National Accreditation Board (ANAB)
Mission: To enable businesses and nonprofit organizations to build their disaster awareness and develop the ability to protect themselves against the effects of any type of disruption

The United States Department of Homeland Security established and implemented a voluntary private-sector preparedness accreditation and certification program called PS-Prep™ (Private Sector Preparedness). This program, which began in 2007, is designed to improve the ability of businesses and nonprofit organizations to respond to and recover from disasters. The program works with businesses and nonprofit organizations to develop consensus-based preparedness standards and best practices to which the private-sector entities will voluntarily conform. Through participation in the program, private-sector entities are supported in their efforts to identify and implement different options for instituting and maintaining comprehensive business continuity management system and in addressing overall organizational resilience.

Although participation in the PS-Prep™ program is voluntary, it acts to promote the importance of recovery planning and to encourage businesses to take action prior to disasters. To incentivize participation, the Department of Homeland Security offers certification to businesses that have completed the program successfully, and provides recognition for those entities that certify to the adopted preparedness standards. Certified businesses can claim to be equipped with the necessary plans and resources to quickly resume operations and continue the delivery of products or services in the vital days and hours after a disaster strikes.

Assessment of the program found that businesses may be more likely to participate in pre-disaster recovery planning or preparedness if there is something other than risk reduction to be gained. It was also found that allowing businesses to use branded and professionally marketed logos and materials from standardized government readiness initiatives on their own Websites and materials can increase interest in these programs.

A two-page fact sheet about the PS-Prep™ program can be found at http://bit.ly/1RxSZy5.

CASE: CREATIVE METHODS AND CHANNELS

Program Facts

> *Who:* American College of Emergency Physicians
> *What:* Disaster Hero Game
> *Where:* United States Nationwide
> *Partners:* The game was developed under a cooperative agreement with the U.S. Department of Homeland Security.
> *Mission:* To ensure that children in grades 1 through 8 know what to do before, during, and after a disaster

The American College of Emergency Physicians developed the Disaster Hero game in order to teach children in grades 1 through 8, parents, and teachers and caregivers how to prepare for disasters. The game is hosted online, and there is no cost to play. There is not a requirement to register, although doing so provides additional features.

The goal of the program is to ensure that players know what to do before, during, and after a disaster. The game's content covers four main areas:

1. *Basic preparedness steps*, which include building a disaster kit, making a plan, and getting informed. This is done in order to "protect the participant and family before, during, and immediately following a disaster or large-scale emergency event."
2. *Information about common hazards*, which include earthquakes, floods, hurricanes, and tornadoes. The game describes

for each hazard the associated danger signals, typical effects, common injuries, and appropriate responses.

3. *Basic quick-care tips and techniques* for specific common injuries.
4. *Basic information about geographic-specific disasters.*

In addition to the children who play the game, the program targets parents and teachers with relevant information to ensure that families and school communities become familiar with basic preparedness concepts (namely to make a plan, get a kit, and be informed).

Game players assume the role of one of several "Disaster Heroes," who in the game are contestants in a high-tech game show. The heroes compete against computer opponents to prove their disaster knowledge and preparedness skills for a chance to be named the next "Disaster Hero!" Disaster Hero includes a variety of different gaming genres, tailored to the specific type of educational content to be conveyed such as arcade and puzzles, hidden objects, and quizzes. The game provides additional targeting by applying three different levels of difficulty. The first, "Bronze," is recommended for early readers (grades 1 through 3). "Silver" is recommended for average readers in grades 4 through 6. And finally, "Gold" is recommended for advanced readers which are generally those in grades 7 and 8.

After beating a Disaster Hero opponent, players earn Hero Badges and are able to print out a certificate that shows they have successfully completed a particular disaster scenario.

Disaster Hero can be accessed at http://bit.ly/29ubGFb.

CASE: USING CREATIVE MESSAGING

Program Facts

> *Who:* U.S. Centers for Disease Control and Prevention
> *What:* Zombie Apocalypse Preparedness Campaign
> *Where:* U.S. Nationwide
> *Partners:* CDC Foundation
> *Mission:* To engage new audiences with preparedness messages

The Centers for Disease Control and Prevention (CDC) provides preparedness information on its Website that covers a number of specific actions people can take (http://bit.ly/29ucEBs), actions specific to several different common hazards (http://bit.ly/29ucQ3q), and for specific populations (http://bit.ly/29DWUyS).

In 2011, the CDC created a new page in the emergency preparedness section of its Website that explained to viewers how to prepare for a zombie apocalypse scenario. The site provides a brief history about zombies, tips on what to do in order to prepare for a zombie apocalypse, and finally an explanation of what the CDC would do in response to an actual zombie attack.

While the message itself might seem strange or even ridiculous at first glance, the CDC found that it was highly effective in garnering attention for preparedness actions that are useful in many different disaster scenarios—the zombie theme was simply a means of raising interest. The center's director for communications was concerned that many people fail to see the messages that CDC communicates each year for events like the start of hurricane season, or outbreaks of certain viruses. But the zombie campaign marked a change in public attention given the enticing theme, and the existence of the message quickly went viral. The launch was the first time that the CDC used Twitter and Facebook to launch a campaign that was not tied to an actual disaster or a disaster season, yet the response was so high that the CDC servers became overwhelmed and crashed.

The CDC zombie campaign illustrates how creative messaging can pique interest and provide valuable information to people who might not otherwise visit the CDC site. The items included in a zombie preparedness kit, which are water, food, medications, tools and supplies, sanitation and hygiene supplies, clothing, bedding, important documents, and first aid supplies, are universal. Visitors to the site will also have a chance to view educational videos for other hazards that are prominently featured on the zombie page.

The campaign reportedly cost only $87 to produce, yet remains one of the most wide-reaching of the agency's preparedness efforts.

The CDC zombie apocalypse page can be found at http://bit.ly/29SZW3x.

CASE: CAMPAIGN SUPPORT

Program Facts

> *Who:* Individuals, Businesses, Nonprofit Organizations, Government Agencies, and More
> *What:* America's PrepareAthon!
> *Where:* Nationwide
> *Partners:* U.S. Federal Emergency Management Agency (FEMA), The U.S. Department of Homeland Security (DHS), hundreds of organizations nationwide
> *Mission:* To increase the number of individuals who:

> - Understand which disasters could happen in their community
> - Know what to do to be safe and mitigate damage

- Take action to increase their preparedness
- Participate in community resilience planning

America's PrepareAthon is something of a campaign of campaigns. The FEMA-organized yet grassroots-driven effort exists in order to inspire all community stakeholders, whether they are individuals, government offices, businesses, nongovernmental organizations, or others, to lead or take part in preparedness activities in their community.

The campaign is centered around the America's PrepareAthon Website, which can be accessed at http://bit.ly/29t2wfL. Visitors begin by registering with the program as a 'Supporter,' which adds the individual or organization's name to the Website and enables them to list programs or events. In this manner, the Website becomes a centralized clearinghouse for information on events that are occurring throughout the country. This is valuable both to those who might wish to participate, as well as to others who are planning their own campaigns and are looking for examples or ideas as they do so.

The America's PrepareAthon Website is so valuable because it enables organizations concerned with disaster preparedness to connect with each other, either through the use of several online forums hosted by the site or through direct contact facilitated by the provision of contact information. The site supports preparedness in other ways as well, including access to different campaign planning ideas and preparedness activities that individuals and organizations can take. It centralizes information, including valuable planning resources such as creative materials for different hazards, communications tools, and preparedness research results.

Finally, the program supports campaigns through the provision of marketing materials and contacts. Registered individuals and organizations have free access to logo-branded materials, marketing materials, and other tools. They are also able to promote their programs or events through the list of hundreds of registered contacts.

As of August 2016, the program maintained a roster of over 1,700 supporters.

APPENDIX: WEBSITES AND DOWNLOADABLE GUIDES FOUND ON THE INTERNET

Public Education/Communicating with the Public

CDCynergy: Emergency Risk Communication (http://www.orau.gov/cdcynergy/).

The Website provides a framework for public health communicators to plan for, respond to, and evaluate communication efforts during a terrorist event.

Users are able to download a version of the Centers for Disease Control and Prevention's *Crisis and Emergency Risk Communication: Be First, Be Right, Be Credible*. Both the book and the Website detail the application of emergency risk communication principles.

U.S. Department of Health and Human Services (http://bit.ly/21gjHjX)

Field guide developed by the U.S. Department of Health and Human Services to serve as a guide for media to quickly and clearly communicate terrorism and public health emergency messages to the public.

Social Marketing

Department of Health and Human Services: Centers for Disease Control and Prevention (http://www.cdc.gov/healthcommunication/)

Health marketing Webpage created by the National Center for Health Marketing. In addition to resources focused on both Health Communications and Health Marketing, the Website offers links to resources on the following topics: Audiences, Campaigns, Channels, Health Literacy, Research and Evaluation, Risk Communication, and Tools & Templates.

Institute for Social Marketing (http://bit.ly/1pa7aTC)

The Website for the Institute of Social Marketing, an establishment with over 35 years of experience with the study and dissemination of social marketing theory and practice and eventual creator of the National Social Marketing Centre in England. Links include information on what is social marketing, case studies of social marketing in practice, project descriptions, and links to other social marketing Websites.

National Social Marketing Centre (http://www.thensmc.com/)

Website of a strategic partnership between the Department of Health in England and Consumer Focus (formerly the National Consumer Council). In 2006, the latter launched *It's Our Health*, the first-ever national review of health-related campaigns and social marketing in England. Links from this page include: What Is Social Marketing?; Why Is Social Marketing Important?; Resources, Documents, and Presentations; and Health Literacy and Social Marketing.

Social Marketing: A Resource Guide (http://bit.ly/1TYSRgV)

A basic guide to using social marketing put out by Turning Point, a former network of 23 public health partners started by the Robert Wood Johnson Foundation and the W. K. Kellogg Foundation to transform and strengthen the public health system in the United States by making it more community based and collaborative. The information in the guide was put out to benefit public health program planners, public information and public affairs specialists, health educators, health communicators, and health and wellness promoters.

Weinreich Communications Social Marketing Articles (http://www.social-marketing.com/library.html)

A collection of social marketing Websites compiled by Weinreich Communications, a company founded by Nedra Kline Weinreich, author of the often-cited and widely used *Hands-On Social Marketing: A Step-by-Step Guide*. Links include articles on "What Is Social Marketing?"; "Building Social Marketing into Your Program"; "Getting Your Message Out through the Media"; "Research in the Social Marketing Process"; "Integrating Qualitative and Quantitative in Social Marketing Research"; and "Social Marketers in the Driver's Seat: Motorsport Sponsorship as a Vehicle for Tobacco Prevention, and Strategic Social Marketing for Non-profits."

Index